9/9/14

DILEMMA

A PRIEST'S STRUGGLE
WITH FAITH AND LOVE

FATHER ALBERT CUTIÉ

CENTER POINT PUBLISHING
THORNDIKE, MAINE

This Center Point Large Print edition
is published in the year 2011 by arrangement with
Celebra, a member of Penguin Group (USA) Inc.

All photos courtesy of the author
unless otherwise noted.
The text of this Large Print edition is unabridged.
In other aspects, this book may vary
from the original edition.
Printed in the United States of America
on permanent paper.
Set in 16-point Times New Roman type.

ISBN: 978-1-61173-087-6

Library of Congress Cataloging-in-Publication Data

Cutié, Albert.
  Dilemma : a priest's struggle with faith and love / Albert Cutié. — Center
Point large print ed.
  p. cm.
  Originally published: New York : Celebra, 2011.
  ISBN 978-1-61173-087-6 (library binding : alk. paper)
  1. Cutié, Albert. 2. Celibacy—Catholic Church.
  3. Catholic ex-priests—United States—Biography.
  4. Anglican converts—United States—Biography.
  5. Episcopal Church—Clergy—Biography. 6. Large type books. I. Title.
BX4668.3.C88A3 2011b
282.092—dc22
[B]
                                                                2011001916

I want to dedicate this book to my wife, Ruhama: Thank you for your love and great patience on this journey. I also dedicate this book to the many men and women throughout the world who are often forced to hide their love for one another due to norms imposed by societies and institutions, especially to those required to choose between their love for and service to God and the natural blessing of loving another human being and having a family.

CONTENTS

PREFACE

Today, my wife and I attended her doctor's appointment and discovered that our baby is a girl. In a few short months, I will welcome my daughter into the world. I feel truly blessed.

I imagine every man feels a similar combination of joy, nervousness, and thanksgiving as he awaits the birth of his first child. For me, a former Roman Catholic priest who never imagined this as a real possibility in my own life, it is one spectacular moment on a very complicated journey.

I began writing this book in the midst of great turmoil—after marrying the woman I loved, being chased by the paparazzi for months, and *finally* making the decision to move on from the Roman Catholic Church I grew up in, to serve God in peace as a married Episcopal (Anglican) priest. Ironically, I began writing it at a beautiful retreat house owned by the Episcopal Church in Delray Beach, Florida, just a few minutes down the road from the Roman Catholic seminary and graduate school where I studied theology. I see this as yet more evidence that everything on the road of life is connected. Despite the bumps in the road to get to this point, I am grateful.

There is one particular story that illustrates my own situation well; it's one I told the first time I preached from the pulpit in my new parish, the Church of the Resurrection in Biscayne Park, Florida. It is about a captain who became lost at sea despite having sailed for decades and knowing the sea better than most. Those under his care had great respect for him. Somehow, though, for the first time in his life, he had miscalculated the length of their voyage. Now the freshwater supply for his crew had run out. The men were beginning to dehydrate and the old captain began losing all hope.

Suddenly, in the distance, they saw another ship and immediately began to signal it. As the ship drew closer, the captain and his men made signs that read, "We need water. Please help us!"

The response from the other ship came quickly, but it was completely unexpected: a sign in big letters that read, "Lower your buckets."

The captain was devastated. They were in the open ocean, obviously surrounded by salt water. He asked again for water to drink. Again, the other ship responded by showing the same sign: "Lower your buckets."

Although he had lost all hope, the captain was desperate and feared for the lives of his crew, so he finally gave the order to lower the buckets. When the sailors tasted the water, they were all amazed: It was actually freshwater! It had been there all along. The output and power of the Amazon River were so great that, even that far out to sea, there was still a substantial amount of fresh, drinkable water in the ocean.

This story illustrates how often we forget the importance of learning to expect the unexpected. Or, in the words of the great philosopher Heraclitus, "Unless you expect the unexpected, you will never find truth."

As a man who was once a celibate priest, I never expected to fall in love, much less to become involved in an intimate relationship that dishonored my promises and offended the Church, but that is exactly what happened. Despite the fact that I was in love with the ministry God had called me to, at a deeply personal level I had been struggling for many years with the feeling that I was missing something at the very core of the human experience: love and intimacy with another human being.

During my twenty-two years as a seminarian and Roman Catholic priest, I served several parishes, most recently at St. Francis de Sales on Miami Beach, right in the midst of the noise and nightlife of what is popularly known as South Beach. For years I was called "Father Oprah" by members of the media, because of my work hosting several Spanish-language talk shows and radio programs broadcast worldwide. In addition to parish work, I served as president and general director of Radio Paz and Radio Peace and wrote a syndicated newspaper advice column called

"Padre Alberto: Advice from a Friend," as well as a book called *Real Life, Real Love—7 Paths to a Strong & Lasting Relationship.*

I was fortunate to find good friends everywhere I went, from members of my parish to those of other denominations and religions around the world, as well as with countless celebrities and media personalities. Yet, despite my passion for spreading the love of God throughout the world and the deep satisfaction I found in my work, I often felt an inexplicable void within me.

In my capacity as a talk show host and advice columnist, I heard from many people who felt frustrated because they were having a hard time finding love in their lives. They would often ask, "Father, how do I find someone I can truly love and spend my life with?"

After listening to so many people from a variety of backgrounds and cultures, I knew full well that, even though love is the greatest power in the world, it is also the most misunderstood. Love is not something we can calculate or actively look for, but something that often surprises us. Nobody really plans love. We call it "falling in love" because truly loving someone else requires you to let go and actually *fall* into the embrace of another.

Eventually, like that captain at sea, I lowered my bucket one day and discovered that the love I always thought was beyond my reach had, in fact, come into my life. Love can truly come when you least expect it, and in the most surprising ways.

This book is the story of my struggle to accept that love in my own life. On one level, it is a story about the Roman Catholic Church, the people who serve it, and the dilemmas they face when they try to reconcile their powerful love of God with their very natural desires to love another human being. This dilemma cannot be reduced to the basic fight between good and evil, because it isn't just about breaking a promise to the Church or committing a sin. It is more about the very real emotions and complex struggles experienced by those serving the Church as they try to do what God expects, what the institutional Church expects, and what others expect from them—no matter how unrealistic those expectations may be.

This is an important aspect of the story, because whether you find it sad or offensive, surprising or unsurprising, the fact is that many priests end up leaving their ministry after developing ideological differences with the Church they grew up loving and believing in so strongly. I know, because I was one of them.

In our training for the priesthood, we are led to understand that every decision, attitude, behavior, and word we utter must be connected in some way with this vocation we have received from God. What we don't realize is that we are bound to go through a series of transformations and personal struggles just like anyone else. We mature and grow, our perspectives evolve, and sometimes the very ideas of what we often hold so sacred change. Nobody is ever frozen in time.

This lesson—that each of us must be open enough to embrace our own experiences and give ourselves permission to learn from our own life journeys—is another important aspect of my story. This message applies to every human being, no matter what your religion or your relationship with God. Change—and our acceptance and learning from it—simply means that we are alive.

Regardless of what the future holds for you, when you are truly motivated by love and what is good—no matter what the world may say or think about you—you never really go wrong, even when you are perceived as making a big mistake. It is only by taking risks that we really begin to grow. All changes, no matter how radical, can lead you to the place you were always meant to be. That is where I am now.

I hope you will read this book as a different kind of love story. It is the story of a man who fell in love with life, ministry, and a woman. It is the story of someone who decided to go against the flow, even when the current was pushing strongly in the opposite direction. Most of all, it is the story of a man who has come to understand that God never gives up on anyone, no matter what.

I will always love the Church community I was

born into and served for many years. I have a great deal of gratitude in my heart for the countless people who continue to live and work within it, including those who cannot speak their minds freely because of the positions they hold within the official Church. I am certain many of them would agree with a good number of the controversial opinions I express in this book, but I can only relate my personal experiences, or what I like to call my ideological evolution. I share them with you, opening my heart with the hope of contributing in some small way to the reform that I consider so crucial to one of the world's oldest and most trusted institutions, the Roman Catholic Church.

CHAPTER ONE

RESPONDING TO AN UNPOPULAR CALL

As a child growing up in Miami, Florida, my church was only five minutes from my home, and it played an important role in my family's life, but I never imagined that I would become a priest. My first job after we arrived in Miami, actually, was pulling weeds.

In southern Florida, lawns grow fast—and weeds even faster. My next-door neighbor was my first client. She was a somewhat frugal lady who asked my mother if I could come over and pull what looked to me like an endless field of weeds for just five dollars. Despite the enormity of the task, I took the job, because in those days anything over a dollar was considered a fortune.

It is only once you get down on your hands and knees in the hot sun to pull weeds that you can appreciate the tedious nature of the job and the perseverance it requires. Pulling weeds, like most things in life, requires you to pay close attention to what you're doing. To eradicate weeds successfully, you have to get them out by the roots. You can't yank too quickly, or the weeds will grow back. You must learn to soften the earth around the roots and shake the weeds around a bit before you pull.

I filled big plastic garbage bags with weeds.

Within a few hours, I'd often have two or three heavy bags. Although I did my best, and took satisfaction from seeing how neat the lawn looked once the weeds were pulled, I always knew that the weeds would grow back. Weed pulling is a bit like our constant struggle between good and evil: There appears to be no final victory, but you continue to struggle anyway, hoping to keep the grass from being overpowered by the weeds.

It wasn't until much later that I saw how this menial job was the logical first step on my journey to the ministry. But I did begin to understand, even as a young child, that to make good things grow you need dedication, sacrifice, and patience. I also discovered that whatever you do, whether it is a simple act or an extraordinary one, your actions make an impact on the world.

THE FIRST TIME I EVER felt cold in my life was when the weather changed our first year in Miami. I was one of only five or so Latinos in my class at Olympia Heights Elementary School, and it was the first time in my life I had ever lived in a climate that was less than tropical. I was shocked to see kids actually wearing jackets.

How my family ended up in Miami is a story shared by many, many Cubans. My parents, like so many other Cubans, fled their native land because they didn't want any part of Fidel Castro's dictatorship. My older sister was born in

Cuba, but my father, a mechanical engineer, had already decided to leave the country by then. He had been detained twice as a prisoner—once simply for having blueprints in his hands, because Castro's men thought he must be plotting something against the Revolution.

Castro was determined to prevent professionals from leaving the country, so it was impossible to flee Cuba and come to the United States directly. Instead, my parents flew to Madrid and did what so many immigrants and political exiles are forced to do even today when leaving a repressive regime: They got off the plane with little more than the clothes on their backs, determined to work hard and make a new life for themselves. Eventually my parents moved to Puerto Rico because much of my extended family had settled there; and that's where I was born and called home until I was six years old.

After a few years my father began traveling from San Juan to Miami in search of work and hoping to reunite with the rest of our extended family, which had now settled in South Florida. He worked with a company of engineers that was involved in building the installations for the first U.S. space shuttle, and so eventually it made sense for our family to come to Florida. We settled in a modest neighborhood in southwest Miami made up of mostly Irish and Italian immigrants— this was before the Hispanic boom of the late

1970s, 1980s, and 1990s. Everyone there had tiny houses until they could afford to move to bigger houses in a different neighborhood or expand the houses they had. My mother still lives in that neighborhood.

I spoke very little English, but I attended public school, took the special classes for those who now had English as their second language, and rapidly became bilingual. In fact, my sisters and I started speaking so fluently in English that our parents had to force us to continue speaking Spanish at home so we wouldn't lose our first language.

Outside of school, my life revolved around our parish. When it became time for me to make first Communion, a Franciscan nun, who spoke very little Spanish but understood it because she had worked in Puerto Rico, said, "Alberto, let's see if you know your prayers."

I was a bit shy because I only knew them in Spanish. The nun was very kind, though, and said with a broad smile, "That's fine, Alberto. Say them in Spanish, and you can make first Communion." So that's what I did. What a relief! I always loved the nuns and could never relate to people who told horror stories about nasty nuns who would hit them with rulers. Of course, I grew up mostly in public schools and in the era of the more modern 1970s nuns. I've often thought that attending public school may have been the salvation of my faith, because I had none of those traumatic Roman Catholic school experiences I heard about from so many of my friends.

By the time I was in middle school, I was completely bilingual and at home in our new life. I had moved on from doing yard work. Music was my big love—this was the early 1980s, the disco era, when Madonna and Michael Jackson were the biggest stars—so some friends and I started our own DJ company. We played for *quinceañeras*—those lavish celebrations marking a Latina girl's fifteenth birthday—bat mitzvahs, all kinds of parties, and even a good number of weddings.

I wasn't especially into sports, other than bike riding and some sporadic games around the neighborhood; and I wasn't into my looks. In fact, I had braces and pimples—lots of them! Yet I was a very confident, social boy, perhaps because I was so well loved by my parents and two sisters. I was one of the only teenagers who hosted his own radio program on a local public radio station, and my friends and I did very well with our DJ business, which was booked almost every weekend.

We did so well in the music business, in fact, that one day my parents said, "This kid can't just be all about the music. He needs to learn that there's more to life."

My parents started encouraging me to go to a youth group at our church to help me mature and develop good values. At first I resisted, as any young teenager would, but gradually I began to experience an independent spiritual life. Feeling your own spiritual connection with God is big for a kid, because you start taking God seriously for yourself, not just as an imposition by your parents. I began voluntarily doing more mission work, attending youth retreats, and meeting with other young people from different parishes. I guess you could say I became hooked on church.

I think a lot of people have this strange impression that priests are not real people. Remember on *Star Trek*, when Captain Kirk would say, "Beam 'em down, Scotty"? From some remarks other people make about my vocation, I imagine they must think there is some kind of priest planet where priests come from.

People especially seem to have trouble understanding why a very young person, such as myself, would respond to a radical call from God. Perhaps that's because our society places so much emphasis on immediate sexual gratification and reveres the power of material things. It's true that not many young people are willing to set aside marriage and family, self-fulfillment in the business world, and fantasies about new cars and big houses to pursue the priesthood.

In my case, I think others recognized the priestly vocation in me, even before I did. My mother used to joke that, with my extroverted personality, "Alberto will either become a priest or a politician." A number of people at our parish would say, "Alberto, have you thought about the priesthood?"

And once, while we were on a weekend spiritual retreat with a group of youth leaders, we were expecting one of our parish priests to give us a talk on something spiritual or theological. After we had been waiting an hour and there was still no priest in sight, people around the room began shouting, "Albert will do it!"

At age fifteen, I was taken aback by their enthusiasm, especially because I wasn't accustomed to public speaking. Yet I felt that God was sending me a message through these kids, so I stood up and did it.

Comments and experiences like these made me feel like I was being prepared for a life of service and dedication. I began to have this sense that if I didn't seriously consider the option of joining the priesthood, I wasn't being very responsible. It was like a switch of some sort was turned on in me; I began to open myself up to God and knew that He was asking me to serve Him in some radical way.

Knowing that you are chosen by God is something unique for each person who feels called. The one thing we all have in common is that nobody really chooses the ministry; it chooses you. When God calls you, it's very difficult to argue.

But this was also the 1980s, the height of

Generation Me, a time in my life of dating girls and playing music. Like most of my friends, I was having as much fun as I could in high school, but what made it different for me is that I combined all that fun stuff with a great deal of church activity. It was as if two worlds were coming together, and the noise of parties and loud music was trying to overpower God's voice speaking deep within my heart.

Eventually, I became determined to hear what God was telling me. I began to withdraw from some of my social activities, choosing instead to focus on working at our church, attending spiritual retreats, and spending time with other young people who shared my spiritual searching. My personal relationship with God became more important to me than everything I'd been taught in formal religious instruction or even at home.

By age sixteen, I began seriously thinking about entering the local seminary after high school. I was beginning to realize that it was not only important to live according to what Albert wanted, but according to what God wanted from me. I wanted to give my life to God without counting the costs or worrying about my personal plans for the future.

I first announced my intention to my mother during one of my first times driving. I had just earned my restricted learner's permit and I was excited to be at the wheel. I tried to remember my dad's words as I struggled to master the stick shift: "Clutch in, shift and clutch slowly. Play with the gas in between."

It didn't help that my mother had no idea how to drive a stick shift herself. She just sat next to me, enduring my stop-start-stall driving and occasionally muttering, "You can't drive like this," and, "We're going to be killed!"

Eventually, as I got the hang of driving, my mother and I started talking about my grades and what was going on in school. When I announced that I wanted to become a priest, her immediate response was, "Oh, Alberto, hit the brakes!"

I think my mother probably meant this metaphorically as well as literally, but I did as I was told. We talked some more, and when I had convinced her that I was very serious about the seminary, she eventually said that I should pray and ask God if that's what He truly wanted for me. If the answer was yes, she assured me that I would have her full support. "We just want you to be happy and at peace," she said.

"But what about Dad?" I asked. As the only son in a Latino family, and with a father who was an engineer, I knew that he might not appreciate my chosen path.

"He will understand," she promised.

To my amazement, he did. I went into the living room that night, where I found my dad reading a book, as he did most nights—it was almost always something about mathematics, energy calculations, or physics. When I sat down next to him and announced my intentions, my father said exactly what my mother had: "Pray to God and ask if that's what He wants for you. If it is, then you should follow the call. We only want you to be happy."

In many traditional Roman Catholic countries, the decision to become a priest often results from pressure by the family. Most consider it an honor, even a status symbol, for one of their sons to become a priest. However, I was blessed to feel only support from my family, and never any pressure. I was equally blessed never to feel any horrible family resistance to the idea, either.

Even later, when my father was diagnosed with terminal cancer at age fifty-two during my sixth year at the seminary, my family continued to support my decision. My father's illness and treatments took an enormous toll on our family; as the only son, I felt an enormous sense of responsibility for our home and my family's stability. I offered to quit the seminary, come home, and find work.

My father, despite his illness, refused to even consider this possibility. "Son, you have to follow your heart," he told me. "Continue your preparation for what God has called you to do. We will be fine."

As for my friends, they teased me at first.

"Alberto, is this really what you want? To have to be celibate and give up girls?"

I shot back, "Hey, someday you'll get married, and you'll only have one wife. You'll have to give up girls, too!"

This was mostly good-natured teasing, because we were all from Roman Catholic families that respected the culture of the Roman Catholic Church. It wasn't a foreign idea for one of us to elect to join the priesthood, and my friends generally accepted the idea. For my part, I became more and more convinced that this was my path.

I couldn't enter the seminary for two more years. During that time, I continued getting to know the Roman Catholic Church at the grassroots level. Throughout high school, I spent countless hours working in and around our local parish. I taught Sunday school and led youth ministry programs, answered telephones in the rectory, prepared the physical plant for special activities at Christmas and Easter, and much more.

I was around many priests at that time—both young and old—many of whom were extraordinary leaders. They were well-spoken, knew how to motivate others to do the work of God, were good administrators, and became my mentors and role models.

Were all of these priests perfect? Of course not. Like any family, our church had its share of dysfunctions. I remember, for instance, a very cool priest who drove a sporty car and was the spiritual director of our youth program. He was energetic and charismatic, and someone I truly looked up to; he was also one of the first to ask, "Albert, have you ever thought of becoming a priest?"

Years later, I discovered that this man had come to the United States in large part to hide his sexual orientation and a promiscuous double life from his family. Sadly, he ended up dying of HIV/AIDS. I was heartbroken to see how this gifted and truly caring man had ended up, and to be one of the only people who attended his very hush-hush funeral.

There was also a bodybuilder priest who used to claim that wearing the Roman clerical collar—and the way people looked at him while he was in it—made him feel nauseous. He always seemed angry at something or someone. I will never forget how one Sunday, in the middle of the sermon, he walked up to the fire alarm and literally tore it out of the wall. Another Saturday at around five a.m., about fifty members of my youth group were gathered in the church parking lot getting ready to go to Disney World. This same priest chose that moment to come stumbling back from a long night out in his jeans and T-shirt, wobbling and weaving his way to the back entrance of the rectory as if no one were watching.

Then there was the rookie, the newly ordained

priest who was extremely thin and spent his days fasting, because he believed that was the only way to chase away his sexual desires. As a result, he always looked sickly and weak—yet people called him a saint. Some people in the Church seem to have the strangest notions of saintliness!

After spending ten years in the seminary, our rookie didn't last more than three years as a priest. He just disappeared one day, saying, "I couldn't take it." After all those years, he simply never managed to adjust to priestly life in a healthy way.

Another priest, who occasionally visited our parish and often said Sunday Masses, started an affair with a married woman with five children (and the mother of one of my closest friends), who worked as a church secretary. That was quite a blow for everyone—especially for the young people who had a connection with that family.

This seems like a long litany of dysfunction, especially for just one typical middle-class parish. But I was never judgmental, even as a teenager. I didn't perceive the actions of these troubled priests as betrayals of me or the Church. Quite the contrary: I would defend them, even when the priest who mentored me admitted eventually to sexually abusing minors. He had never done anything inappropriate with me, and I saw him as a serious, committed, hardworking priest. I understood the good, the bad, and the ugly about the Church early on and accepted that every human being has his or her own struggles.

Today, after years of working and living within the Church, I see things with greater clarity. Now I believe that many of these priests acted the way they did because of their lack of adjustment to the celibate state and the loneliness that many of them experienced because of it. At the time, however, those incidents occurred right in the midst of my falling in love with the priesthood and making the decision to serve God, so I didn't think of that. Despite everything I saw at my very own parish, there was a certainty in my heart that my life would be different. I had friends from many denominations, and whether they were Protestant, Jewish, Catholic, or from some New Age church, I always felt that the most important thing was a strong connection with God.

I saw people who were connected to God as mostly happier, more compassionate, and less materialistic; if I could bring the word of God to more people, I reasoned that we would have less war, less hunger, and a better world for all. I truly felt that God was calling me, and that I had to do all in my power to become a good and faithful priest. At times I even thought that if I could do everything right, I could somehow help repair the damage being done by so many others in my own church.

For the last two years before I entered the seminary, I met with my spiritual director once a month. He had entered the seminary when he was just twelve years old, so almost anything to do with sexuality was a big taboo for him—so much so that he sometimes seemed altogether too curious about my personal life and the girls I dated or was attracted to.

When I tried to talk to my spiritual director about my attraction to girls, and my struggle to embrace celibacy as my future path, the only advice he could give me was to say, "Albert, just pray that every girl you ever like finds a good Christian husband, because God is calling you for Himself."

So that is what I started to do: I simply prayed that the girls I liked all found good husbands, because I wasn't available. It seemed so simple at the time, even though it was never easy.

When I look back now at the young man I was then, I see a youthful idealist full of drive and energy. I wanted so much to be one of the priests who could contribute to changing the world, a priest who was above corruption and politics as he gave everything to God and the people he served. I was a rebellious teenager in my own way, I suppose, because I was going against everything society was telling me to do. I wasn't ever going to make much money, or have multiple women, or drive a convertible BMW. My heart was pure. I had no personal desire or ambition to hold power over other people. All I wanted was to be a parish priest and help other people.

And so, at the age of eighteen and right after graduating from Southwest High School in Miami, I entered St. John Vianney College Seminary determined to become the best priest I could be. I was determined to be a model seminarian, one who took every practice and rule of the institutional Church very seriously. And I did.

That spiritual fire inside me burned so brightly that I couldn't see that I was about to enter a sort of spiritual boot camp, much less understand how the priesthood would change every aspect of my life.

CHAPTER TWO

FALLING IN LOVE WITH THE PRIESTHOOD

One hot August afternoon of my nineteenth year, I spent a couple of hours packing and carefully checking things off the list they had sent me from St. John Vianney College Seminary. This was the first time I was leaving home to live on my own, and the seminary had given me a specific list of things that students were allowed to bring—as well as a list of what you were *not* allowed to bring. Headphones were on the approved list, I was happy to see; after six years as a DJ, my most prized possession was my record collection, which I'd managed to compile onto cassettes. I loaded my music, my tiny stereo, my headphones, and my clothes into the backseat of my car, and I was off!

It was amazing that I fit as much as I did into that car, since it was the same 1969 Volkswagen Beetle I'd learned to drive in. I had inherited the car from my father when he finally got a new car after many years of suffering the South Florida heat in a car with no air-conditioning. Now, driving away from home alone with my belongings, I felt a rush of excitement despite the fact that I had left my mother in the kitchen, crying and wiping her tears away with her hands as she mopped the floor.

I think that, like most parents, mine felt that having a child give himself to God meant they were losing that child forever. They knew that, from now on, I would belong to the Church and must go wherever I was sent to serve, while they took second place in my life.

THE PROCESS OF BECOMING A candidate for the priesthood involves countless interviews, psychological exams, spiritual retreats, and a host of other activities designed to help you make your final decision and to prepare you to be accepted by the Church. Much of this process is tedious, and it has become an even more complicated process through the years, as modern psychology has opened up new avenues for deciding who is "healthy" and who is not.

The suitability of a candidate for ministry today has much more to do with the institutional Church and less to do with a person's spirituality or God's divine intervention. I have seen many good people turned away from convents and seminaries because they were not approved by the institution, yet they have gone on to live healthy, spiritual lives.

Despite what I'd already been through to be accepted at the seminary, several weeks before my first day at St. John Vianney, the rector called me into his office. He was a heavy smoker, so stepping into his office felt a bit like climbing into an ashtray. He had a great smile on his face, though, and quickly put me at ease with his cordial manner and heavy Irish brogue.

We chatted for several minutes, and the only awkward moment was when he asked out of the blue, "Albert, do you like girls or do you like boys?"

"Girls, Father," I answered. I was shocked by the question.

"Good, Albert, that's very good," the rector said, smiling even more broadly than before, and then he went right on to the next topic. That was all he needed to know. Later on, I would come to understand why he would ask that question of every new seminarian he interviewed.

This was the only off-key note in what was otherwise a smooth start to my first year as a seminarian, where I was earning a bachelor's degree in philosophy in preparation for theology studies. In many ways, it was much like any college, with classes, hours spent in the library, and friendships forged along the way. It was just a bit more restrictive, with a prayer schedule that started at seven a.m. and a curfew that required you to be in your dormitory by eleven p.m.

At the time I attended seminary, men of all ages were enrolled. Men in their thirties and even men who were older than my father sat next to me in class. They had more problems with the curfew and some of the other rules than I did. At eighteen,

I was a sponge, enjoying the structure and discipline. Anyway, whenever I needed a break, it was easy to slip home to visit friends and family, since my parish was just down the road. If I happened to miss the eleven o'clock curfew by a few minutes, I simply climbed over the seminary gate to get back in. It was a trick to accomplish, but we always found a way in.

My parents continued to show unconditional support for my seminary studies, but that wasn't true for some of my classmates, whose families engaged in what I'd describe as official fights with God, the Church, and anything remotely sacred or holy. When one of my friends entered the seminary, for instance, his mother took every crucifix down in her house, as well as the statue of Mary that had always graced her home, because she took his decision so personally. Without his family's support, my classmate was unable to withstand the rigors of priesthood; he eventually left and married, becoming a gifted theologian and later a religious adviser and diplomat working in the Vatican.

WHEN I FIRST ENTERED THE seminary, I considered myself a below-average student. I had spent most of my adolescence paying more attention to my weekend job as a DJ, attending youth retreats, and socializing than I ever did to studying. Having to read hundreds of pages of homework every night, especially the classic works of Greek philosophers, was something very new for me, but I quickly rose to the challenge. This was largely due to the inspiration and hard work of the faculty, which was excellent.

One of the first people who really encouraged me to take an interest in my own intellectual development was my first-year philosophy professor. A scholarly man who spoke half a dozen languages, he was generous and deeply spiritual, a man who had been an atheist before experiencing a radical conversion to Christianity. He was also brutally honest and often warned us of the problems he perceived in the contemporary Church, especially among those who were pushing progressive agendas and departing from tradition and conservative values.

"Albert, you're a smart young man," he once told me, "but you are an A student who settles for Bs."

From him, and from other dedicated professors, I quickly learned the importance of academic discipline, the value of spending hours reading and researching, as well as the power of prayer and living a more intense spiritual life. Seminary was something very new, but also something that I found fit my burning desire to serve God and humanity.

The rigorous academic discipline wasn't the only new thing for me. This was also the very first time I ever had to share a room with other men. I grew up with two sisters, but since I was the only boy at home, I'd never had to share a room. My first roommate at the seminary was a man twice my age. He had lived with a girlfriend for years before having a conversion experience at a spiritual retreat, which caused him to decide the priesthood was his calling. He often spoke to me like a father giving advice to his inexperienced son, and I learned to appreciate his authentic concern for me.

One morning, my roommate saw me shaving at the sink we shared in our common room. I was wearing my boxers and considered it natural to shave dressed that way. He said, "What are you doing?"

I was startled by the alarm in his voice. "Why, what's the matter?"

"In this room, you can dress like that with no problem, but don't get used to it," my roommate warned. "You have to take care of yourself with the environment around here."

I had no idea what he meant. It was only later in the year that I realized my roommate was referring to the presence of a number of promiscuous gay men in the seminary.

The first time I ever heard any of these young gay seminarians use slang words and expressions of a homosexual nature, I had to ask around to find out what they meant. I really had no clue! I soon discovered that they had nicknames for everything and everyone, including a bishop who was sexually involved with some of his seminarians. Years later, that bishop would be removed and sent to live quietly in a monastery after Church officials couldn't hide his behavior anymore. That was all very awkward to me.

I admit to being shocked by some of this new knowledge, yet I worked hard to ignore it and tried not to let it discourage me. When I entered the seminary, I sincerely thought most of the men who were my classmates and colleagues shared the same struggles I was going through. Eventually I came to see that not everyone shared the same interests or made the same sacrifices.

It isn't difficult for homosexual men in seminaries and religious houses to act out sexually. For one thing, it's easy to hide your relationship in these all-male environments; for another, they have role models in priests who have been getting away with it for a long time, while the institution at all levels turns a blind eye to it.

I used to hear stories about priests and seminarians and their sexual conduct, both homosexual and heterosexual, but I never really believed them—or maybe I just did not want to believe it was possible. It probably would have been too painful for me, an idealistic eighteen-year-old convinced that the institution was all about God, to admit that the Church could ever engage in or protect such dishonesty. At that stage of my life, I had a very romantic concept of the institutional Church. I believed that it was free from sin and very close to immaculate. I did not think any of "that inappropriate stuff" was actually possible and dismissed it all as just more horrible rumors circulated by Church haters.

Yet, as time went on, I began to realize that a lot of what I did not believe possible was actually true. A number of people I had come to know and trust were actually very involved in that inappropriate stuff. For example, it took me years to learn that one of the straight seminarians who on several occasions brought the bread and wine to the altar during our Mass with a girl he'd introduced to the entire seminary community as his "visiting cousin" was actually sleeping with her. She was no relative, just his secret girlfriend.

Among all of the outrageous things I heard in my seminary days, I will never forget the day that our rector looked up from a newspaper article and said to a group of us nearby, "I wonder what cardinal this guy f—ed to get there."

We were standing in front of the community bulletin board right in the main hallway of our seminary building. That board was cluttered with all kinds of information, news, and the usual memos from every department notifying everyone of what was expected. One of the recent postings stood out like a sore thumb: It announced the new position of a former seminarian who had been thrown out a couple of years earlier for sexual misconduct. He had found a way of being accepted to another seminary, in another country, and was now ordained. That young man had become a priest—and a prominent one.

How did this happen? I wondered. Information about seminarians usually follows them from place to place, and the reasons for dismissal from a seminary are usually part of a required report, in case you apply to a new diocese or seminary. In this case, not only did the candidate get ordained, but he was actually tapped for an important job at the highest levels of the Vatican.

The rector seemed upset, but not surprised. He knew, better than the rest of us, how ambitious people within the Church always find a way to get ahead. Was he disappointed? Yes. Shocked? No. He understood the system, and that there are people who know how to work it.

Meanwhile, I was headstrong and convinced that God wanted me to be a priest. I wasn't willing to let anything turn me off. I was there for a specific purpose, because God had called me and needed me. I was sure that nothing could make me stray from my mission to serve Him.

Seeing all of this happen within the ranks of present and future Church leaders was not all bad for me. I decided that God was using this time of eye-opening new knowledge for good: It was sowing the seeds that would later blossom into my greater understanding of humanity. As I began to witness the brokenness and struggles among my fellow classmates and priests, I found that I could feel compassion for them and for others with similar issues. Overall, the years in the seminary served as a sort of reality check for me as an idealistic young man, causing me to experience both heartbreak and a desire to work harder to be the best possible priest I could be.

Even so, a part of me began to struggle with the message that this behavior might send about our attitude toward sexuality to the everyday people in the pews. If priests didn't seem to care to live by the rules of our own institution, how could we expect people in the pews to live by them?

AS A SEMINARIAN, I MADE great friends with all kinds of people from many different backgrounds and cultures. Yet I can honestly say that my focus never wavered: I knew that I was there to learn to be God's instrument for others. I felt motivated by God's love and a desire to spread that love. I wanted to live the Gospel and make it known to all.

Just like those in medical school who must eventually decide on a specialty, seminarians are able to choose between several different means of serving God. There are the diocesan or secular priests, which I had always wanted to be. There are also religious priests who make vows of poverty, chastity, and obedience and go on to become part of a religious order. In either case, many priests become dedicated to serving in specialized ministries; for instance, we might choose to work in education, with young people, in hospital settings, or helping the poor.

As a very young, idealistic seminarian, I wondered if God might be calling me to serve in a more radical way, so I briefly considered joining the Legionaries of Christ, a popular growing congregation of religious priests. I perceived this group as very serious about their mission to serve God; I saw them as almost a Marine Corps sort of group in the Church, so I sent away for information.

The day I received the packet in my seminary mailbox, I gathered with a group of about five or six friends in the seminary to examine the colorful pamphlets and recruiting materials, all of which were expensively done and had a real "wow" effect on us. Part of the attraction was the charismatic founder, Father Marcial Maciel Degollado, a Mexican-born priest and the grandnephew of a Mexican saint.

Despite some rumors that had begun circulating even back then about Father Maciel's drug abuse, financial scandals, and sexual misconduct, he was much admired. Among the seminarians, Father Maciel was always referred to as "Our Father"

(*Nuestro Padre*) and was perceived as having a special aura. His mission in forming his religious order was to inspire lay members of the Catholic Church to take an active role in the Church's mission. What nobody realized back then is that he ran his order like a cult or fanatical sect. Yet the Legion of Christ and the Regnum Christi were responsible for starting many schools and universities, as well as a huge number of charitable institutes that also did a lot of good. They also contributed greatly to promoting vocations to the priesthood in a time when seminaries and religious houses all over the world were closing for lack of enrollment.

"This is great stuff!" exclaimed one of my classmates as we read through the brochures. He and one other man among my group of friends went to visit the order for themselves. One actually joined; to this day he is a priest in that congregation and one of the truly *saintliest* people I know.

I never did visit or join this priestly Marine Corps. As I matured, I realized more and more that living in a religious order was not for me. I longed to be living and working in an ordinary community, much like the priests in my own neighborhood parish, who had been my mentors and the people I admired most. However, I did respect Father Maciel and his followers from a distance for their sense of mission and loyalty to

Christ. Father Maciel had been called to accompany Pope John Paul II on many of his visits to Mexico, and he had been appointed by the pope to the Ordinary General Assembly of the Synod of Bishops—only one of many positions of power Father Maciel held within the Vatican. I had no way of knowing, of course, how many terrible revelations about this man's depraved behavior would become public in just a few short years.

WITH MY MIND INCREASINGLY SET on being the sort of priest who actively works to make a difference in the world, I spent summers and holiday breaks from my seminary studies working at my home parish in the youth programs, teaching vacation Bible school, or working with migrant workers. I still believed that God had given me my personality and way of being to help spread his message of love, particularly to teenagers and young people who were disillusioned with the Roman Catholic Church. As a young seminarian, I was excited whenever I could inspire people to connect with God through me. I felt that I was doing exactly what I was meant to do.

Of course, every summer I also met attractive girls who made me wonder if I had chosen the right path. I found myself playing the "what if?" game occasionally, asking what my life might be like if I didn't continue on at the seminary, but chose another profession instead. The truth was, however, that most of the girls I met picked up on the vibe that I was completely committed to becoming a priest. That came through very clearly.

For instance, I never really danced at a party or even at the weddings of my friends. I didn't want to put myself in situations that might make me feel uncomfortable. A lot of my priest buddies had conversations with women and even danced with them, but I steered clear of these in order to protect myself from temptation.

The deeper I got into my theological studies, the more I began to appreciate the traditions and practices of Roman Catholicism. I wanted to know everything there was to know about the Church. If it came from the Vatican, I read it. I must have devoured hundreds of official Church documents in my eight years in the seminary in my attempts to be current on every development. I was so devout and conservative, in fact, that I was often spoofed at our seminary talent shows as the student who spent the most time reading Church documents and papal encyclicals.

It didn't make a difference. As a young and obedient man at that stage of my life, I was convinced the institution was always right and the people were in error. I remember one priest in our seminary saying, "Albert, you just want to rub your face on the tits of Mother Church." Despite the vulgar image, I knew that he was kind of right. I had an obsessive interest in the Roman Catholic Church as an institution and in the many ideals it promoted. Maybe a lot of this also came from growing up in a culture that was convinced it was the only "true church."

Consequently, I was viewed by many of my professors and some of the priests at the seminary as conservative. Some took issue with me because they were at odds with the direction in which Pope John Paul II was taking the Church in the mid-1980s. They saw that the Church was clearly moving away from the reforms of Vatican II and adopting policies of the past as a way to keep things under control—a movement that a number of conservative theologians called restoration.

For me and many young people of my time, John Paul II's personal charisma and enthusiasm motivated me to fall in love with the mission of the Church. My desire to spread the Gospel message grew daily. I couldn't see then that John Paul's policies weren't realistic, or even remotely practical, for most people. It bothered me that some of my colleagues felt what appeared to me to be some kind of animosity toward the official Church. Despite these negative attitudes around me, however, I remained convinced that my mission came from God and I had to stick to it.

• • •

JESUS SAID, "GO OUT INTO the world and proclaim the Good News." He never said, "Go into your rectory and live a quiet, protected life." I was determined to follow His example. Between the ages of eighteen and twenty-five, I completed my bachelor of arts degree in philosophy at St. John Vianney College Seminary, then went directly on to earn my master of arts in theology and my master of divinity at St. Vincent de Paul Regional Seminary in Boynton Beach, Florida, in 1994 and 1995, respectively.

As part of my education, I became actively involved in every type of ministry as a way of helping myself reaffirm the call to priesthood. I worked with migrant farmworkers and in prison ministry, comforted the sick, and visited the elderly in nursing homes.

I also worked in Miami Children's Hospital under the guidance of a Lutheran pastor, who was the chaplain at the hospital and helped us by supervising our seminary's pastoral summer program. He was a very progressive, open-minded man, and although we disagreed on certain topics, I appreciated his ideas and enjoyed hearing his different perspectives on the world.

One afternoon, I was in the hospital's emergency room when a woman came in with a dead baby in her arms. The baby was black-and-blue, clearly beyond revival. Because the woman was Latina and a Roman Catholic, and because I was not yet ordained and couldn't say last rites for the child, I called a priest from a nearby parish who was responsible for visiting Roman Catholics at that hospital.

I was in the room with them when this priest walked in, then looked this grieving mother in the eyes and said, "You have to accept that this is God's will."

I couldn't believe those words! It was as if I'd taken a blow to the stomach. How could this priest be so thoughtless, to say that this was God's will, rather than offer this poor woman an embrace or words of comfort? I was upset enough that I spoke to the Lutheran chaplain about it afterward. He, too, was devastated, and agreed with me when I said I felt as if what that priest had said and done amounted to spiritual malpractice.

"And what would you have said, Albert?" he wanted to know.

I thought about this and at first thought the best solution was to say nothing and simply listen to that mother's pain. Finally, the chaplain insisted I say something and I told him that I would have said to her: "Life is fragile, a gift that God has given us. Your child was a gift. I can offer you love and compassion, and be with you in your grief, but there are no easy answers."

This stark lesson helped me decide early on that I didn't want my ministry to be black-and-white. I was already moving away from the belief I felt as a younger seminarian that the Church had all the answers—all of the time. I didn't believe that God was sitting up in heaven with some sort of remote control, telling priests what to say to people, as if all of the answers to life's many struggles are in some sort of fix-it manual. I was committed to doing God's will, but I was also committed to trying to understand the full breadth and richness of our human experience. It wasn't easy to find answers to some of life's biggest questions, but I was determined to help people on their individual spiritual journeys do just that.

AFTER I HAD STUDIED PHILOSOPHY and theology for eight years, it was finally time for my internship as a deacon. When the priest in charge of internships asked me what kind I wanted, I answered, "I want to go somewhere different and challenging."

In response, he assigned me to Key West, which is as far as you can send anyone in the Archdiocese of Miami and the southernmost point in the United States of America. As a matter of fact, I was closer to Havana than I was to Miami. It was common for me to drive 440 miles from the seminary to the parish and back almost every weekend. I was the first young man to be assigned to that community in many years.

Although I had spent most of my life in South

Florida, I had never traveled down the entire length of the Florida Keys. In fact, my first and only time driving in that direction with my family, I was about nine years old and my parents, sisters, and I got stuck halfway to Key West when our car broke down near Marathon.

Now, at twenty-five, I was excited to be driving all the way to Key West alone, on this new adventure. I crossed the forty-two bridges that connect more than one hundred little islands, or keys. In Key West, I saw a steeple and pulled right over. Key West is such a small city that I was certain the Roman Catholic parish must be the only church in town.

When I knocked on the door, a smiling woman in her midfifties opened it. "Is the pastor here?" I asked.

"No," she said, "but can I help you? I'm his wife."

I realized that I must not have been at the Roman Catholic church, but I still couldn't believe it. To be sure, I asked, "Isn't this St. Mary's?"

She laughed and responded, "No, this is Grace Lutheran," and kindly pointed the way to the place of my assignment on the other side of the island.

As I got closer and closer to my new church, I drove through Old Town, where the streets get narrower and old black lanterns on the sidewalks give you the sense that you've stepped back in time. St. Mary Star of the Sea, the Roman Catholic parish in Key West, was equally historic—it is the oldest Catholic church in South Florida, and the second-oldest Roman Catholic church in the entire state. Bordered by the Atlantic Ocean and the Gulf of Mexico, St. Mary's was also one of the first Roman Catholic churches in Florida to admit both blacks and whites to its congregation.

When I arrived, I admired the beauty of St. Mary Star of the Sea. It was built in a Victorian Gothic style; the beautiful stone blocks that went into its construction were made from coral rock, which I later learned had actually been dug out of the ground beneath the church. The rectory, on the other hand, was a solid-looking concrete building. This was unusual, because there aren't many concrete buildings in Key West; most are quaint Bahamian wood houses. It was such an impressive, large, and strong rectory that the natives used to call it "the Jesuit Hilton," referring to the religious order that built it.

I took a deep breath to steady my nerves and rang the doorbell. It was 4:55 in the afternoon and I was due in at five p.m.

The pastor opened the door and said, "Welcome! We were waiting for you to go to dinner. I'll show you where your room is and we can go."

The pastor was a stickler for punctuality and I was a relaxed Latino, unaccustomed to having dinner so early in the afternoon. But, as it turned out, this pastor was a great mentor and became a dear friend. He always went out of his way to make my experience so far from the mainland a positive one, and taught me a great deal about parish management, good stewardship, and the inner workings of parish life. While the pastor was indeed sometimes too strict and rigid for my taste, especially to people seeking the sacraments who were not practicing Roman Catholics, he was mostly pretty welcoming and did everything in his power to inspire people about their faith.

The people in that Key West parish were also great. As a deacon-intern, I taught in the parish school, prepared and preached sermons on Sundays, visited the sick, buried the dead, worked with some of the families at the navy base, and helped with almost every daily activity around the church.

Since we were in Key West—popular for its bars and nightlife—I also managed to start a small "bar ministry." We would get together with young adults from the parish and teachers from the school at a local pub to have drinks while we talked about life, spirituality, and every topic under the sun. There was one beautiful teacher in the school to whom I felt strongly attracted, but I kept my distance—sometimes making a great effort to avoid her—to make sure that we would only be friends.

That internship was a special year for me and played a large role in my development as a priest. One aspect of my time there that really made an impact on my heart and soul was my work with Cubans arriving on our shores daily. In 1994, thousands of Cubans were throwing themselves into the Florida Straits in homemade rafts that required a real miracle to stay afloat. The year I spent at St. Mary's, the number of Cubans fleeing toward Florida reached over two thousand people a day—and this wasn't counting the many people who perished in the process of trying to reach freedom.

For me personally, it was a shattering experience to see entire families putting their lives at great risk to escape the Communist regime of Fidel Castro. Naturally, the whole phenomenon was particularly moving to me since my own parents had left Cuba, although it was under very different circumstances, in search of the same freedom from that awful system and a better future for their children.

As a young child, every conversation I heard during family visits between my father and his brothers was about how Castro's regime was going to end sometime soon and we would all go back to Cuba. By now, of course, my father had died without seeing that dream come true, and many of the younger Cuban-Americans I knew didn't have that same longing for the homeland that our parents had. Still, we considered ourselves political exiles, unable to return until the fall of that totalitarian regime.

My parents were among the first exiles from Cuba, the initial wave of those who left the island forty or more years ago. This latest wave of Cuban immigrants was more socioeconomically diverse and included a higher proportion of people who were less motivated by political differences with the regime than by economic circumstance. They were less welcome by the United States, and unfortunately even by my own Cuban-American community. In 1994, American authorities intercepted 36,791 rafters.

It was a fifteen-minute drive from St. Mary's to Stock Island, where I often visited the rafters, or *balseros*, as they were called, in a makeshift trailer set up by volunteer Cuban exiles called *La Casa del Balsero* (Home of the Rafters). My role was to help offer spiritual support to these families after their traumatic odysseys, while other volunteers provided first aid and hot meals. I drove a tiny four-cylinder Honda Civic that could really seat only four people, but I often did everything possible to fit two families—up to nine people— so that they could visit the church, say a prayer, and greet Our Lady of Charity (*La Caridad del Cobre*), the patroness of Cuba.

I will never forget their tears or the expressions on their faces as these rafters, many of them young men like myself, reached their much-desired freedom. It was particularly painful when they realized that while they themselves had made it alive, they still had family that was unaccounted for or had stayed behind in a country where day-to-day life seemed more like a prison camp than the paradise it once was. That whole experience only served to reinforce my love for Cuba, and for the millions of political exiles who have abandoned their homeland and are longing for the day when they can return to a Cuba that is free from Communist dictatorship. It also served to renew in me the conviction that spiritual leaders have to be on the side of those who suffer, whether it is politically correct or not. As a Cuban-American, I had already experienced and heard the stories of political prisoners, people executed without any kind of trial and families divided and destroyed by that terrible regime. My work with the rafters brought many of those ideas full circle for me, and these convictions would continue to be part of me and shape my ministry for years to come.

Another new experience for me at St. Mary's was that of having openly gay couples actively assisting in church activities and attending services. I was not shocked, exactly, but I did have to examine my feelings on what was then—and still is—a very controversial issue in most churches. After a time, I realized that I was glad to welcome them there. These men and women were good, loving human beings, and it troubled me that, in the teachings of the Roman Catholic Church, we were supposed to convey to them that their lifestyles were evil and "intrinsically disordered." I felt strongly that all people should be able to look to their priests to receive forgiveness and guidance, not judgment or a feeling of unworthiness.

I had been in a Church bubble throughout the better part of my seminary years. Slowly, as I started emerging from that bubble, I began to see that there was often a huge gap between people's realities and the rules of the institutional Church. I wondered if perhaps my mission, as a young, extroverted, open-minded priest, could be to serve as a bridge between a Church that didn't always want to hear about the pluralism of society and what was really going on in the world.

AFTER MY EIGHT YEARS IN the seminary and my eventful Key West internship, ordination day finally arrived. Ordination is much more than a graduation. This is the day when you are officially commissioned by God and the Church to take on a spiritual mission and bring the Good News of salvation to the world. It is truly a day that marks your life forever, because this is the moment when you hand over your entire life and promise to spend it serving God.

If that sounds like too much to ask of one human being, perhaps that's because it is. I do believe that there are special people who are called to abandon the world in their dedication to God, disconnecting them from the cares and worries of secular life. However, most priests in the twenty-first century are not called to that "disconnect." I was about to be ordained as a secular or diocesan priest—a priest who isn't supposed to live like a monk, in a cloister removed from the world, but among the people he serves. This is a distinction most Roman Catholics do not understand, because they tend to put all priests in the same category, with little knowledge of what makes us different.

On ordination day, the secular priest makes two promises: the promise of celibacy (on the day of his ordination as a deacon) and the promise of obedience (which is made at both ordinations, as a deacon and as a priest). Moments before my ordination, our bishop called us into a special conference room with our families. It was a photo opportunity and a light moment before a very solemn and sacred celebration. I will never forget the archbishop's words to my mother and to the parents of the two other men to be ordained: "We will take very good care of them." Years later, looking back on that moment, I would often ask myself what "very good care" really meant.

As I mentioned earlier, in my seminary days it

was common to hear of Vatican II bishops versus John Paul II bishops. Those in the Vatican II camp were considered progressive and willing to move forward, while those appointed by John Paul II were considered much more conservative—or were at least willing to play that role to please Rome and keep ascending the hierarchical ladder.

The archbishop who ordained me as a deacon in 1994, Edward A. McCarthy, was definitely a Vatican II bishop. He was known for promoting ecumenical dialogue, women in ministry, greater lay involvement, pastoral programs for people of different cultural groups, media, and evangelical work.

Only five days after I made the promise of celibacy, Archbishop McCarthy appeared on television, where he was asked by an interviewer about possible changes in the Roman Catholic Church. Without hesitation, the first thing he said was, "I believe that priests will be allowed to marry in the near future."

As a twenty-five-year-old man who had just made a lifelong promise of celibacy, I was shocked beyond belief. I simply couldn't understand how the very bishop who had just participated in ordaining me a deacon and received my promise of celibacy could publicly admit that the celibate state was not an essential aspect of priesthood.

"What did I just do?" I thought, torn between

panic and despair. "Even bishops think this celibacy stuff isn't all that important!"

Having decided to give my life to serving the Church and all that it stood for, I was deeply upset. After all, here was this bishop who had me kneel in front of him while I made promises of celibacy and obedience—and then out of the mouth of this very same bishop, a man who had been a priest for fifty years, I heard words to the effect that celibacy might not need to be part of a priest's life and discipline!

All of a sudden, I had to wonder, as some of my reading and studies of Church history suggested, if celibacy was a way of life designed as a convenience for the Church, rather than something the Church really valued. Had I really just made a commitment to an institution that I'd believed in all my life, only to discover that it wasn't as permanent as I'd thought? Whose position was the right one on the issue of celibacy: my archbishop's or the Vatican's?

I was determined to be a good soldier of the Church. Therefore, I chose to believe, with all of my heart, that everything the Vatican said had to be right.

CHAPTER THREE

LIFE AS
A PARISH PRIEST

A few days before ordination, the bishop informed my classmates and me that we would each be assigned to a pastor—someone who would guide us during our first years in the ministry. I was excited by this news, enthusiastically imagining a mentoring program already in place and a guide who could help me adjust to my new life as a parish priest.

A few minutes later, we were handed our assignment letters. The pastors entrusted with our care were standing outside the door; as each new priest received his assignment letter, he got to leave the room and meet his new boss.

Mine was sitting in a wheelchair with a serious-looking middle-aged woman standing behind him. Although my pastor's leg had been amputated as a result of diabetes, he seemed like a happy man. He had rosy cheeks and a marked Irish brogue. He briefly welcomed me and gave me the date of my first day in his parish. This well-respected man had the reputation of being a "priests' priest"—someone who helped priests in trouble—and also had the distinction of dedicating a great deal of his own free time to helping alcoholic priests deal with their addictions.

I couldn't wait to begin. After eight years of

seminary training, evaluations, term papers, and writing a thesis, I was excited to finally put academics aside and begin what I thought would be the "real work" that God wanted me to do.

One of the most challenging aspects of becoming a priest is adjusting to rectory life. A rectory is a place where priests live together. Today, these houses are often independent homes in neighborhoods away from the actual parish, but in those days they were typically huge, impersonal, and institutional-looking houses on church property.

Within the rectory, every priest typically has his own bedroom and, if he's lucky, a sitting room. Other areas—the bathrooms, kitchen, dining room, and living room—are shared among the priests in the house. If the pastor treats you with respect, this life can be pleasant. However, if you live with a dictatorial boss, or with priests who suffer from unpleasant personalities or more serious dysfunctions, you end up living in a type of hell. Many priests have "rectory living" horror stories, mostly due to pastors who treated them as guests living in "their" homes.

Now, at age twenty-six, I found myself living with my pastor, the priest from Ireland, and another priest from India. Both men were in their sixties and spoke with heavy accents. Believe me, those were the only two characteristics they had in common.

At the time, I thought I was very lucky to live with two such experienced priests. Throughout my teen years and seminary days, I had spent a great deal of time learning from older priests. However, this was the first time I had ever found myself caught in the middle between two priests who were so diametrically opposed on almost every aspect of the Church.

My very first dinner at the rectory revealed this clearly, as the Irish pastor began discussing the ordination of women, and maintained that it was time for the pope to open his eyes and allow women to become priests. The Indian priest didn't argue, but I could clearly read the disagreement and disappointment in his eyes. As a matter of fact, I think he may have been experiencing a bit of indigestion due to the nature of the conversation. For I knew even then that the Indian priest was the sort who would never say anything that might be considered to be contrary to the official positions of the Church, no matter what he thought. It was an eventful first dinner at the rectory, to say the least.

As I unpacked my things that night, I found myself feeling a bit put off, even scandalized, by some of the extremely liberal views of my pastor. At that stage of my ministry, I thought it would be impossible for women to be ordained priests; that was clearly the official Church teaching and who was I to go against it? The pope had rejected even discussing it on several occasions. Pope John Paul II had made it pretty clear that he was interested in bringing the Church back to the way it was before Vatican II, and I am now sorry to say that I too had fallen in line with that thinking. Too many contemporary worldviews were "suspicious" to the official Church. In addition, a lot of people, including me, loved the traditions of the Church, especially "the smells and the bells" that many of the more progressive Church leaders wanted to disappear. We wanted to keep things as they were or even return to the days portrayed in the popular 1945 movie *The Bells of St. Mary's*. I couldn't help but wonder what else I would hear my pastor say during my next three years in that rectory.

However, I enjoyed the family atmosphere. We sometimes met for dinner or to watch television together, whenever my pastor wasn't away or too ill. I especially enjoyed eating lunch with the staff and listening to stories about their marriages and children. On my days off, I escaped for family dinners with my mother and sisters.

My first assignment as a parochial vicar was St. Clement's, a church in a predominantly blue-collar, Irish-American neighborhood in Fort Lauderdale, Florida. After I delivered my very first Sunday Mass, the first woman who came up to shake my hand said, "Father, what part of Ireland are you from?"

I laughed. "I come from a different island," I said, meaning Cuba.

"Well, I want to congratulate you," she responded. "You're the first priest to come to this church in years that I can actually hear and understand at the same time!"

At the time, I couldn't be certain if she was making a joking reference to the typically poor sound systems in churches, or to the heavy accents of some of the other priests. With the dire shortage of priests in the United States, the Church had begun importing a good number from foreign countries like India and Africa—a practice that has continued and is radically reshaping the ethnicity of the priest population mostly because so few native-born young people are interested in becoming priests.

I also knew that, on a deeper level, incomprehensible and often *disconnected from reality* sermons may have had something to do with it. The real problem was—and still is—the Church's inability to communicate its messages clearly and effectively.

As I'd witnessed firsthand in so many places, mediocrity prevails when it comes to sermons. Many priests, even if they're native English speakers, struggle to deliver practical, interesting applications of the Gospel message that are accessible to all. Yet preaching is perhaps the most important work of any priest or spiritual leader.

I remember once complaining to a priest friend about this mediocrity and the noticeable indifference to the quality of sermons that I'd seen among so many clergy. He laughed. "Albert, don't knock mediocrity," he said. "For most of us, mediocrity is quite an accomplishment."

I was stunned. This was how standards were lowered instead of raised, I thought, so I made up my mind to work hard on my public speaking, and to spend whatever time it took to prepare sermons that the people in my parish would not only comprehend but might find inspiring as they went about their daily lives.

I was even more confused when the pastor invited me into his office after morning Mass, and the first words out of his mouth were, "Albert, I don't know why they sent you here. This is a dying parish. Besides, you're bilingual, and there are almost no Latinos here."

Imagine my surprise! Here I had been thinking that this older priest would be a mentor I could learn from, someone who would heartily support my efforts to help and inspire people in my parish, and already he was overtly discouraging me. I had arrived at St. Clement's as a young priest ready to change the world. Now my new boss was wondering if I'd have enough to do!

"I'll just have to do my best anyway," I told him.

Afterward, I went back to my room and started praying. As I prepared to kneel and ask God what

His intent was in bringing me here, I happened to glance up. I could see the back of St. Clement's from my window. The church did look a bit neglected; if nothing else, the building certainly needed a paint job. But it was a beautiful structure and it had an active parish school and wonderful parishioners. How could it be dying?

As the weeks went by and I explored the neighborhood and met the people in my parish, I realized that my pastor's statements weren't really meant as a criticism of me, but expressed his own sentiments. He was tired, often ill, and maybe dying himself. He made extraordinary efforts, even just to say Mass, often sitting on a barstool behind the altar. Because of his diabetes, amputated leg, and other illnesses, he suffered from a lack of mobility and was not as able to get out and about as in the past, even though he still worked pretty hard every day. I admired him for his great sacrifice and dedication. Yet even a trip to the local supermarket would have let him see what I witnessed with my own eyes: the changing demographics in South Florida due to growth in the immigrant and minority populations, especially an incredible amount of Latinos. In all honesty, he wasn't alone; very few of the other priests in the area—mostly Irish born—were willing to accept that reality.

At dinner, my pastor often expressed views that led me to understand that he was questioning whether the Church, which he had given his life to, could make any sense to the people in the parish. As one of the more progressive priests who had worked for change within the Church after Vatican II, he was outwardly discouraged by the backward positions the Church held and dismayed by how the younger clergy seemed to be more interested in siding with Rome than in acting as agents of change in the world.

It may sound odd now, but the younger priests—priests like me—tended to be happy to hear that the modern Church was dying. We wanted a return to a more conservative Church. We were, I think, in love with the romantic elements of what appeared to be the "ideal" Roman Catholic Church, especially because it seemed that the pope and the hierarchy at that time were also heavily pushing a backward type of approach to faith. In time, I would begin to understand that many of those ideals and approaches only served to exclude and alienate all kinds of people who wondered why the Church resisted moving forward.

In any case, I quickly threw myself into parish work and tried not to dwell too long on my pastor's personal struggles and disappointments. I was here to serve the people, and I was determined to do that with vision and energy. Regardless of what my own views were at the time, nobody would be turned away from church during my watch.

• • •

WHEN A PRIEST MOVES INTO a new parish, it takes time to become familiar with its unique character, environment, politics, history, and people. Most people are welcoming; some send welcome cards, while others simply smile quietly at you on their way out of church, or shake your hand. A good number also run out of the side door and are in their cars as quickly as possible; so you never really get to know them.

As a parish priest, I soon learned to embrace the emotional roller coaster of ministry. I performed services at weddings and funerals, celebrated daily Masses, heard confessions, visited the sick, taught at the parish school, coordinated special programs, and prepared converts who were new to the Catholic faith. I thoroughly enjoyed every aspect of ministry.

During funerals, I learned how to bring consolation and peace to grieving families and friends, helping them find a sense of closure as together we remembered what was special about the deceased and reminded ourselves that their loved one was still very much a part of our lives. A person may have passed, but spiritual life continues.

One of the most tragic deaths during my early years as a priest at St. Clement's was that of a parishioner in his early forties who had a massive heart attack. His son and daughter were altar servers and I had taught them at the parish school. There was a new baby in the family, too, one whom I had recently baptized. This beautiful, devout family was deeply shaken by the father's death. Despite their strong relationship with God, they asked me the same question that we all ask during times of loss: "Why did God allow this to happen?"

I was struck by that question over and over again in my work as a parish priest. I heard it so often from rich and poor, Latino and Anglo and black alike. No matter what a person's culture or economic situation, I came to realize that we all must suffer. All of us, even the most successful and the strongest among us, become weak and vulnerable when facing the illness or death of a loved one.

I was young to be comforting bereaved families, but I did it with great compassion and understanding because I had already suffered so much loss in my own life: During the eight years of my life as a young seminarian, I had lost eight close relatives, including my own father, a dear twenty-two-year-old cousin who had been diagnosed with a brain tumor at age twelve and another cousin in his twenties who died in a tragic boating accident. After so many premature deaths in my own family, I had already accepted that some people just don't make it to be old and that death is simply part of life.

One thing in my life that affected me most was how a number of my father's friends ran away during his illness. They couldn't deal with the fact that their friend was on his deathbed; they had been with him during parties and good times, but they couldn't deal with the darkness at the end of his life. It was just too painful for them. From witnessing their withdrawal, I learned that the most important thing that anyone can do during times of tragedy—whether you're a priest or not—is to stand alongside those who are suffering, hold their hands, and pray with them, reminding them that God is never far away.

To the wife and children grieving that tragic early death of their beloved husband and father, and to others who have suffered losses during my time as a parish priest, I have tried to convey the message that true peace and joy are definitely born from within. I teach people that God is with you in life during good times and bad. That's an important lesson, because many people in our culture have a tendency to believe that God must be with them only when they're smiling and happy. When you learn that God is with you every day, and that your life is not in your own hands, but in His, there is a great sense of peace and stability that can carry you through the worst times.

Many priests say that they prefer funerals to weddings, mainly because brides can be difficult to deal with, but I've always preferred weddings. In some ways, I guess I saw funerals and weddings as similar: Both involve inviting people to move from old lives into new ones. During weddings, I tried to convey that marriage was a life that demanded sacrifice and communication as people learned to live together.

Even during my earliest days as a parish priest, I was realistic in counseling couples preparing for marriage, especially the great number who were already living together. I would sometimes say, "Look, I know that you're probably sleeping together already, and I want to tell you that if you're having trouble in your sexual relationship or anything else, getting married won't magically fix it." I always felt that if we let couples know that we understood their reality, we would be more effective ministers in helping them seek true and lasting happiness. The least we could do was to encourage them to prepare for marriage and seek counseling if they needed it before they made a lifelong commitment.

While many priests wouldn't have even broached this subject, and while I had no firsthand knowledge of physical intimacy as a celibate priest, I knew from listening to the couples I counseled in my parishes how important sexuality is in a marriage. Often, marriages that flounder and become bitter are those where there are intimacy problems. The fundamental truth is that we are both body and soul. If a couple is connected physically, as well as spiritually, that couple has a better chance of survival.

In confession, many people came to me with struggles about their sexuality. This shouldn't have come as a surprise to me, since the Roman Catholic Church teaches that everything from masturbation to entertaining "impure" thoughts is a mortal, or serious, sin. Even when I disagreed with the Church's teachings and impositions—which happened more and more as time went by—I tried only to listen and say, "I understand how this is a struggle for you. I want you to search within yourself and discover what God is trying to say to you, and what He is asking you to do as an individual." It's unfortunate when people don't credit their own conscience and become overly preoccupied with sexual hang-ups. The guilt associated with sexual sins can be overwhelming. There were people who felt they had to go to confession almost on a daily basis because of some sexual sin. I never denied anyone confession, no matter when they asked for it, because I understood that some people could not live at peace with themselves carrying so much guilt.

Many of the complaints priests hear about sexuality from married couples is that the woman loses interest after having children, the man becomes desperate, and too often infidelity occurs, causing couples to end their marriages in the midst of that transition. In some cultures, as in the case of Latinos, women are given the impression they are to pay more attention to being mothers than they should to being wives. That is a common misconception. The fact is that many marriages could have been saved with the right type of counseling and guidance. Instead, I found that most priests shied away from talking honestly about sexual issues, even within the context of marriage, and the people who ended their marriages went off to marry someone else and suffer through the same issues all over again. I've always thought that if a priest does not feel qualified to talk about these issues, the least he can do is listen to the couple, and then send them to a qualified counselor who can follow up and continue to support them with professional therapy.

One area of great joy for me was working with newly arrived immigrants from every corner of Latin America. These immigrants were arriving in increasing numbers every day, and many struggled to acquire English skills and employment. As a young seminarian, I had spent the summer between my second and third years working with Mexican migrant workers in the camps of central Florida, where they were picking tomatoes. As a Cuban-American, I realized those who came from my parents' homeland had a special status and could easily become residents and American citizens, but that people from other countries throughout the world didn't have this same privilege. I wanted to know more about how they lived, so I went to live and work with them at St. Anne Church in Ruskin, Florida.

Two young nuns from Mexico were dedicated full-time to what was called the Migrant Ministry. Together, we led the rosary and gave catechism to men coming back from the fields at night, and to their families as well. In that type of ministry, you listen to the stories of people who are really struggling financially. I remember one particular night when a family invited us into their home. They had five children and a very small house with a dirt floor. I'll never forget how this family spent some of their hard-earned money on three bottles of Coca-Cola, and how the children were so generous that the minute they saw their guests, the nuns and the priest, they offered us the soda, even though there was so little to go around. What I found amazing is that those kids never complained.

After learning more about the lives of the new immigrants, I made the promise—which I have kept to this day—to always reach out to migrant workers and champion their causes. Wherever I am, I still join in the debate on immigration, making it clear that I believe that immigrants come to this country to work and to contribute to our betterment. If there was a march for immigration rights in a city where I was attending a conference or on a book tour, I made it a point to join that march. Because of my own background, this was a cause I always carried close to my heart.

Another cause that I became deeply involved in from the start of my work as a parish priest was youth ministry. I worked especially hard to build up the youth ministry at St. Clement's. When I arrived, there were just four teenagers in that youth group; by the time I left and with the help of a good number of committed parents, we had over seventy.

Some priests shy away from doing youth ministry because it requires so much energy—you must work not only with youth but with their parents, in coordinating chaperones for retreats and service work. You have to be flexible and open-minded, because kids don't hold back when it comes to questioning why the Church does things the way it does.

One of the first things most youths will tell you is that they're atheists—a statement that causes a lot of priests to scold and say, "It's this way or the highway," a surefire way to turn off any child, especially a teenager. I knew that these statements about atheism were just every teenager's way of opening a dialogue about God and faith, and I thoroughly enjoyed these challenging debates. I believe that in me, children and teens always found someone they could talk to, so they kept coming back. I also recruited a number of adults—well-adjusted men and women—who were my best collaborators at working in this important ministry.

At St. Clement's, there was a beautiful track and field, and other wonderful facilities, including an outdoor stage, a library, and a media center. I couldn't understand why more kids weren't enjoying these resources. Starting with those first few teenagers, we began drawing others into the church. They brought their friends, who found out it was fun and brought more friends. We used music, skits, and games to get the kids to come, but I also got them excited about their faith through prayer, reflection, and meditation. I felt my mission was to motivate young people to pray in creative ways, so I often led meditations and tried to get them to think about their personal relationships to God.

One of the challenges was to encourage the young people of our parishes to work together with other youth groups and learn to respect diverse religious traditions. For example, when a sixteen-year-old in our neighborhood was killed by a drunk driver in Miami Beach, we used this tragedy to bring our youth group together with one from a nearby Jewish synagogue. Together, we held prayer vigils to create awareness about the dangers of drinking and driving and to support our grieving community during this shared tragedy. This helped both Christian and Jewish teens know they can actually pray together.

As challenging as my youth ministry was, I loved having this opportunity to contribute something back to the Church. After all, I had become a priest as a result of good youth ministry, and that's why I was here: to inspire others to know and spread God's love.

A FEW WEEKS INTO MY assignment at St. Clement's, I was thrown a couple of curveballs. The first was when the Irish pastor who was supposedly my three-year mentor was abruptly moved when the Church asked him to replace a pastor in another parish who was being investigated for embezzling money from parishioners and the elderly.

In addition, I discovered that there was a ghost priest at St. Clement's. I called him that because he showed up only to celebrate Mass on certain occasions. Like me, this priest had a room at the rectory and received his mail there, yet we rarely saw him.

If anyone ever asked about the empty room upstairs, the one where the door always stood wide-open, people would say, "Oh, that's Father So-and-So's room." I peeked inside and saw that there were indeed a few books on the shelves and the bed was properly made up, as if someone would eventually come back to sleep in it.

Everyone talked about this priest as if he lived with us, but in the three years I spent at the rectory, he never once slept there. What was the big deal? I wondered. Why did we all have to tiptoe around the facts and pretend that the ghost priest was among us, when he clearly resided somewhere else? Priests often had apartments. There was no actual requirement for us to live in a rectory.

Eventually, however, I heard whispered rumors that the ghost priest actually lived with another man in an apartment several miles away. The other man was supposedly his lover and life partner.

I dismissed this gossip at first. At age twenty-six, with my zeal for the Church and the priesthood, I simply couldn't believe that these rumors were true.

Then, one sad day, the ghost priest came to lunch with us and informed the rectory staff that he had HIV/AIDS. He was well liked and the staff was clearly devastated. Everyone at the rectory offered him our friendship, prayers, and support. Nobody on the staff ever speculated or spoke about how he contracted the disease; that was never an issue that any of us discussed.

I couldn't help but wonder if his life might have been spared if he could have talked openly about his sexuality. From my experiences in Key West and other parishes with openly homosexual couples, I had come to accept the idea that homosexuality was not necessarily a "disordered state," as the Church so vehemently taught, but one where people could give and receive love. If people like this ghost priest didn't have to keep their lives such a secret, perhaps they wouldn't be putting themselves at such risk for disease or opening themselves up to a life of promiscuity. Why couldn't the institutional Church allow well-adjusted homosexuals to be clergy, when they were well aware that so many clergy were indeed gay and often promiscuous?

IN 1996, DURING MY FIRST summer vacation from my work as a priest at St. Clement's, I finally had the opportunity to meet the icon I had revered all of my life: Pope John Paul II. As a young seminarian and priest, I had revered this man as a spiritual giant, to the point where I had pictures of him hanging everywhere in my room. Mother Teresa and John Paul II were like two great beacons of hope for me.

I was invited to Rome by a priest from a neighboring parish. It was spectacular and amazing to walk the streets of ancient Rome and see the Vatican, the very center of Church operations. I spent most of my time there listening and soaking it all in. St. Peter's Basilica, the gardens, multiple beautiful churches on almost every block, and the museums were breathtaking!

When it was time for our private audience, I shook the pope's hand. He had been secretly diagnosed with Parkinson's disease by then, but nobody knew about it. It was speculated that he suffered from some neurological disease, but it was not confirmed by the Vatican until years later. At that time, his walk was still remarkably upright and steady. I could barely speak, I was so much in awe of his presence—he was my hero, after all— yet I still had the audacity to say to him, "Pray for the freedom of Cuba."

The pope briefly stopped and turned to really look into my eyes, and said, "I pray for Cuba every day." That was a moment I will remember forever. Later, on my second visit to Rome and after knowing all I did about the scandals in the Church, I would come with a more skeptical eye, and I would see that the pope was very much a functionary of the Church, a spiritual leader, yet very human indeed—and part of a flawed institution. At that juncture in my life, however, I still felt goodness and spiritual authority radiate from the pope's presence.

AS A MAN OF FAITH, I have always tried to see the hand of God in my life. This applied to the good, the bad, and the ugly events. I truly believed then—and even more so now—that God always has a purpose in putting certain obstacles in your path. We just might not readily understand the purpose of them at the time.

As I gradually became more comfortable in my various roles as a parish priest, I developed my own style of ministry. It wasn't long before I became known as a "yes" priest because I was more flexible, and perhaps more welcoming, than a good number of my colleagues. Too many priests spend a lot of time repeating a list of man-made rules and impositions to their congregations, as if they were biblical. Besides, most priests do not even listen to laity, especially in matters of church governance. I have often thought that many of the problems we see in today's Church could be solved, if laypeople were more active in decision making, including choosing their own pastors and bishops as they did in early Christianity.

You don't find a lot of flexibility within the Church—in fact, you might say that the Church has a control issue—and this tends to create a negative attitude. With time many priests become arrogant, irritable, and unapproachable because they live like what they eventually become: elderly bachelors. People, especially the young, do not find priests accessible.

Instead of bringing people into the fold, too many priests drive people away, because these priests live within the confinement of Church rules that are far removed from the rules that ordinary people could possibly live by. On TV or radio when I asked people why they left the Roman Catholic Church for another denomination, or simply stopped going altogether, I would most often hear, "The priest was nasty," or "Father mistreated me."

Too many priests today are seen as aloof or unavailable. Many are sticklers for only holding weddings on certain dates and times, for instance, and many even require people to make appointments for confession. If there is a dying person to comfort or a funeral to attend, often a priest's first question is likely to be, "Was he or she a registered or contributing member of this parish?"

Young couples, too, are given a hard time by many priests when they call about a wedding. Instead of a heartfelt welcome, these young people hear endless rules, requirements, and restrictions. The sad consequence is that many more people are turned away from the Church than are welcomed to come as they are. In a world as pluralistic and diverse as ours, this legalistic attitude is perhaps the one thing that turns most people away from organized religion.

I couldn't stand to be perceived as this sort of grumpy, unavailable priest, so I tried hard to be more lenient in meeting the needs of the people I served and to respond to those needs whenever I could. I loved all of the liturgies and customs of the Church, but I also felt that it was essential to be flexible with some of the nonessential norms wherever possible.

One day, an electrician was installing exterior lights in my parish and he was visibly upset. When I asked him what was wrong, he told me that his grandmother was dying in a hospital located right next to the parish assigned to it, about forty miles away from my own.

"Father," he said, "we called the priest there for three days and no one has come to see her." When he told me the name of the parish, I knew exactly which priest he was referring to; I also knew that this particular priest often ignored hospital calls, despite the fact that he was the only one responsible for that hospital and was in charge of a very small parish.

In order to defend my brother priest, I told the worried electrician, "It must be a mistake. Let's call again. If they don't answer or send a priest, I will go."

I asked my office to call three times that day, but the priest never went. When I finished my work at ten thirty that night, I drove for forty minutes to give the electrician's grandmother her last rites. She died later that night.

I was determined to spread God's love to all and make my ministry a church of open doors.

CHAPTER FOUR

ABANDONED BY THE CHURCH
TO SINK OR SWIM

Shortly after arriving at St. Clement's, I received a "welcome to our area" note from a brother priest working in a parish about five miles south of mine. He invited me out to lunch, and we immediately struck up a friendship.

"Rob" was an energetic pastor and he offered me unconditional friendship. I was profoundly grateful to him for reaching out to me, because as a priest you really do need to interact with others who share your life and ministry. We both had the same vision and worked to create a more welcoming and youthful church in our parishes. Besides, he was the only pastor under the age of sixty-five within a ten-mile radius, and I was blessed by Rob's friendship immensely.

In 1998, however, I was deeply saddened when I discovered that Rob was charged with a sexual misconduct incident that was heartbreaking and painful for his parish, his family, and those of us who were among his closest friends. When Rob called to tell me the news, I went to him immediately to help him say morning Mass. He was shaking so badly that he couldn't even lift his hand to his forehead to make the sign of the cross.

I celebrated Mass for Rob the next few days and camped out in his rectory to keep the media from hounding him. It was a zoo, yet nobody "official" from the Church appeared to help Rob in those first few days. It was as if he was out there on his own, and nobody ever bothered to call me and ask, "How is he doing?" Not a word. On the contrary, they seemed to stay as far away as they could. This infuriated me and pained me on my friend's behalf, while at the same time, it also made me wonder what kind of church I had given my life to. Yes, Rob had committed a grave mistake. But shouldn't this have been the most important time that the Church—this institution that he had devoted his life to—reached out to him?

Apparently the Church thought otherwise. That became increasingly apparent as the sex abuse scandals involving Roman Catholic priests, which I had been dimly aware of as the earliest stories began surfacing while I was still in seminary, inflamed public disappointment toward the Roman Catholic Church and caused many to question the institution they had trusted since childhood. Rob's was the first such situation that I'd witnessed firsthand in my first years as a priest, and it clearly demonstrated that priests were truly out there on their own. The institution and its leaders really cared very little if you swam or sank.

This lesson was repeated over and over again in the next few years as I continued my priestly work in various areas. In fact, it is still ongoing today. In 1998, the year my friend Rob was removed from his parish, sexual abuse victims of Father Rudy Kos in Dallas agreed to a reduced settlement of $23.4 million with the Dioceses of Dallas after a jury awarded them over $100 million. The following year, a Boston-area priest, Father John Geoghan, was indicted on child rape charges; in 2002, Cardinal Bernard Law acknowledged that he had moved Geoghan from parish to parish despite evidence that the priest had molested children.

Cardinal Law apologized to Geoghan's victims and promised to bar any abuser from ministry in the future. He also claimed that he would never step down as archbishop, saying, "When there are problems in the family, you don't walk away." I am sure he firmly believed that, but he would eventually be forced to resign.

Later that same year, an eight-hundred-page personnel file of Father Paul Shanley was released. The file outlined claims that Shanley had abused children and publicly advocated sex between men and boys, yet continued to receive the archdiocese's support, leading Pope John Paul II to arrange an emergency summit with U.S. cardinals and other Church leaders in Rome on the sex abuse crisis. By the end of 2002, thousands of personnel files made public by a court order revealed that many priests in the Archdiocese of

Boston had been accused of abuse. Law finally turned in his "symbolic" resignation as Boston's archbishop. To this day, I have always believed that Cardinal Law was only a scapegoat, or a way for the Church to respond to the public relations nightmare and appear to be truly contrite. The fact is that Cardinal Law did not do anything so different from the rest of the bishops in the United States and in so many other countries, yet none of them was forced to resign at that time. I believe his resignation was symbolic and in time it was clear that it had nothing to do with a real commitment by the Church to change anything in the way abuse cases were being handled.

Along with the rest of the public, as these stories came out, I was infuriated that, for far too many years, the Church had moved priests from place to place after these allegations, trying to hide the misconduct among their own and never dealing with it head-on. I was equally irritated that the Church often removed dedicated priests without due process, which meant that the hierarchy never seriously examined the charges or took responsibility for the well-being of possibly innocent priests. Oftentimes, it was easier to settle cases with lawyers out of court rather than sort out the truth or falsehoods involved in many cases. I am convinced that many priests have been thrown under the bus by their own bishops, in order to protect the Church's image.

While I became a "media priest," it didn't take me long to realize that the Church was truly terrified of the media, and that it was ill equipped to deal with crises, both internal and external. For instance, a couple of years after Rob was dismissed, another very prominent pastor and friend of mine was removed without hearing anything from his bishop in over two months. I believe he was literally heartbroken, and a few months later, on Christmas Eve, he was found dead. That night I was on the phone for hours with the priest who found his body; he had also been removed at the time. Immediately after that, I was preaching and presiding at my first Christmas Midnight Mass. What a transition! During the entire Mass, all I could see in my mind was the image of that priest's face. I was sure that priest died of real heartbreak, because chancery officials were sent to tell him that he had to leave his parish and vacate his home in a matter of hours—after he had served the Church for almost thirty years in several high-profile capacities. Again, he may or may not have been guilty of the charges, but I still felt that his Church shepherds were all too busy wrangling with lawyers and lawsuits while the sheep on both sides of the altar were hurting.

In addition, the group I had once dreamed of joining as a young seminary student, the Legionaries of Christ, was once again commanding the spotlight. Since the 1970s, rumors had abounded about Father Maciel working his connections in the Vatican and using money received from the wealthy benefactors of his various movements to buy his way into top Church circles. The Legionaries had become known as "the Millionaires of Christ" even by their own colleagues and supporters in the Vatican. Many clergy criticized them for having fancy air-conditioned buses and for wearing immaculate double-breasted suits, which probably made them the best-dressed religious order on the planet.

Unfortunately, their leader, Father Maciel, wasn't just money hungry and ambitious. It was discovered that he was also a very sick man who abused drugs, sexually abused and tormented dozens of young seminarians, had secret affairs with women, and fathered several children out of wedlock—some of whom he also sexually abused.

Many of these stories were denied for decades by leaders in both the Vatican and the Legionaries, despite the fact that several credible sources, including former seminarians and Legionary priests, tried to bring this misconduct to the Vatican's attention. In 1997, however, a group of these men was fed up enough with the apathy and indifference they encountered within Church circles to organize and present real documentation of their specific accusations. While the institution still ignored them, they caught the media's attention.

The immediate reaction of Church officials, as always, was to deny these rumors as false and malicious. The accusers, who were concerned for the well-being of their Church as well as for possible new victims, were told to go away and be silent "for the good of the Church." Officials repeatedly said that nothing could be done because "the pope holds Father Maciel in high esteem."

Why didn't the institution step up to help not only the many victims of Father Maciel but also the laypeople, seminarians, and priests of this order who wished to move on and continue doing good works despite the stigma of their sick founder? Why didn't anyone within the institution approach Father Maciel about his known addictions and other problems, and try to help him come to terms with all those issues in a healthier and more transparent way?

I was beginning to learn that, when it came to the Church, silence was the default coping strategy. Besides, the Legionaries were known for fund-raising and promoting the priesthood, and the Vatican always needed more money and more priests. It seemed like a winning combination!

I was as horrified as everyone else when the truth came out about Father Maciel. I trembled when I remembered how close I had come to joining his group, and I still knew some of the Legionaries, whom I continue to admire greatly. Many of these men maintained a strong sense of mission and loyalty to Christ. Yet, from my point of view, they had become victims of an institution that froze when it should have acted, a system that was broken but couldn't admit it.

After the accusations about Father Maciel came to light, I encouraged any Legionary priests I met to hold their heads high. I felt great compassion for them; I knew that many had been brainwashed by the Church for years to believe that accusations against their founder were "attacks by the enemies of the Church" and by "the evil media." It must have been a struggle for these young men to maintain their love of God after finding out that the teachings of a man they had once admired were actually the teachings of a twisted mind. But for the grace of God, I might have been among them.

AS THE PUBLIC'S KNOWLEDGE OF clergy sex abuse scandals widened, I sometimes wondered what people thought of me as I walked down the street wearing my clerical collar. I had heard horror stories from priest friends who were insulted in stores and malls; they were now afraid to wear a clerical uniform in public. But as a very public priest I thought it was my obligation to continue wearing my collar and to show the world that despite all the bad news, I was still proud to be a priest and represent the Church in public. It was no time for fear!

I also thought it was important for people to know priests as human beings, and as proud of the vocation they had chosen. I cringed whenever some devout woman in my parish would say, "Oh, Father, how I wish my son would become a priest just like you," only to immediately and thoughtlessly add, "But he likes girls too much!" I always considered that a kind of insult. Besides, it was a way of radically separating the priest from the rest of humanity, as if a priest does not like the things "the rest of us" like. Almost as if there was a great abyss between "common people" and priests. Maybe that abyss has been created and projected by the Church, but it is certainly not real. Priests are human.

Over and over again, I reminded myself that serving God as a priest was not something I chose, but part of God's plan for my life. Whatever I could do to be a good priest—no matter how difficult—was worth the effort. I was certain that the priesthood needed to be portrayed as a healthy and happy life and as a good choice for those who were truly called. I therefore decided to wear my collar everywhere and with pride. For me, the priesthood was about God and the spiritual mission I had received to reach out to all. How could I do that by hiding? Perhaps this was my greatest motivation in choosing to accept the call to work in mainstream media. I always believed the Church should be more visible and that religious people or spiritual leaders should not limit themselves to a pulpit on Sunday mornings.

In fact, I found that wearing the collar even during those tumultuous years always served to open doors for those who had fallen away from the Church and were just waiting for someone to invite them back. It helped to put my parishes on the map, because people would come up to me on the street or even in the supermarket to ask, "Father, where is your church?" Without a collar, that connection rarely happened.

Surely, I thought, I could continue doing God's good work despite the flawed institution I served. I was convinced that the negative attitudes of so many toward the Church wouldn't affect me. It took me many, many years to eventually acknowledge that it did. I now allow myself to recognize that I was deeply hurt by the level of dysfunction and lack of responsibility of those who had the power to do things differently and chose not to. I guess it would be fair to say that the best way to describe myself at that time—and many in the institution I had grown to love so much—can be found in the words of an old Spanish proverb: *No hay peor ciego, que el que no quiere ver.* . . . (The worst type of blind man is the kind that does not want to see).

CHAPTER FIVE

THE MEDIA AND FATHER OPRAH

In May of 1998, I was assigned to a new parish, St. Patrick's Catholic Church in Miami Beach. In June, after I had just finished offering my second Sunday service and was chatting with various people out on the front steps, a woman caught my eye. She was beautiful, with a shapely figure, long dark hair, and deep brown eyes, but the attraction was more than just physical. When our eyes met, it was magnetic. Something clicked and connected between us, and I had trouble looking away from her. I was sure I was looking at the woman of my dreams!

All of my life, I had been attracted to women, but never like this. People had often confided in me about falling in love at first sight, and romantic movies and novels were stuffed with tales of frustrated lovers who had trouble staying away from one another, but I had always discounted those stories as nonsense.

My own parents and grandparents were deeply in love and had solid marriages. I knew—or thought I did—that two people could only truly love one another if they spent enough time together to develop a solid connection, one strong enough to survive the ups and downs that are a normal part of any couple's relationship. I tried to convey this to the young couples I married in church.

Now, however, I was shaken to my very core. During my time as a seminarian, and even when I was a young priest, people would occasionally ask me, "What happens if you fall in love after becoming a priest? What do you do then?"

"I don't think that will happen to me," I always responded. "But, if it did, I'd just have to deal with it."

Now I felt a bit like doubting Thomas, who missed seeing Jesus after the Resurrection and said, "I won't believe it until I see it!" For here I was experiencing love at first sight as something very real.

I knew nothing about her, not even her name. I only knew that this lovely woman came to services with a young boy, whom I at first took to be her brother, for the woman looked like she was scarcely into her twenties and almost always attended church with two older women.

I watched for her every Sunday after that first glance, and every time, the same thing happened: This woman's brown-eyed gaze drove me wild. Even while I was preaching and very much focused on my message and mission, I couldn't help but sneak looks at her. It was impossible to keep my eyes away from hers for more than a few minutes at a time, no matter how hard I tried.

At times, it was almost a comical tug-of-war:

When I looked at her, she looked down, and then she would look back up at me and I'd have to look away again. The more I told myself to look somewhere else, anywhere else, the more I found myself wanting to look at her. Then I'd give in, and the whole eye dance would repeat itself. There was so much attraction and energy in the air that I half expected to see sparks flying from the pulpit across the pews.

Gradually, I learned more about her. The little boy, who was just five or six years old at the time, was always friendly. He would approach me after most Sunday services to say hello. Through those conversations, I discovered that the young woman was his mother, and that the older women were his grandmother and great-aunt. His mother avoided me, disappearing out a side door while I greeted everyone after Mass.

At last, I could stand it no longer. "Why doesn't your mom come over with you to say hello?" I asked the little boy, and so he brought her to me.

She introduced herself and we talked for just a few minutes. Her name was Ruhama, and she was extremely shy. She was also even more attractive now that she was standing in front of me. Immediately I felt there was a very strong mutual attraction between us. Everything about her was beautiful, and I had never desired anyone more.

I had also never felt so guilty. I never expected to be in this situation. I had always had a great deal of control, never allowing myself to be tempted this way. As a young seminarian and priest, I had been pretty well trained to ignore my own desires and pray to make them all go away. I had lived the celibate life for a long time. I didn't want to blow it now.

"It's okay, Albert," I told myself, taking a deep breath. "This, too, shall pass."

Still, I looked for her every Sunday after that, and our brief conversations after services were the only way I had of getting to know her. Our contact was made easier by Ruhama's own natural reserve and—as I found out later—her devout nature and determination not to be the sort of woman who might tempt a priest. Whereas most of the other women at the church freely kissed me on the cheek in greeting, which is a very common Latino custom, Ruhama would only shake my hand. This was just as well, because even her touch made me a bit weak in the knees.

Our first real conversation happened only after Ruhama wrote a letter to me saying that she wanted us to be better friends. I struggled with this idea for a while before responding. Could we really develop a friendship despite our intense attraction? For I had little doubt that she felt the same spark I did.

Eventually, I decided that I ought to be able to handle this. Perhaps I could defuse my desire by seeing more of her.

"Let's get together and talk," I said finally.

We began talking, simply as friends, typically during church events or spiritual retreats. I found out that Ruhama supported herself by working at several jobs, one of which was as a photographer for tourists around Miami Beach. She was half Greek and half Guatemalan, which explained her unique, exotic appearance. I can honestly say that I had never seen anyone quite as beautiful.

I later learned that Ruhama lived on her own with her son, Christian. She had divorced when she was in her early twenties and her son was just six months old; now she struggled to support herself as a single mother and make a home for her son. Yet she was extremely charitable, and always made time to be active in church affairs, such as a weekly prayer group she and some friends put together for people of various denominations. I saw a deep spirituality in her, and I think that's a big part of why we connected: We were both committed to being servants to God and doing His work. Our friendship steadily deepened, as did my desire for her.

Then, after years at St. Patrick's, I was reassigned to another church to replace an abruptly removed priest. Although inwardly I was disappointed to be far from her, I knew it was the best thing for both of us. Since the very first moment I had felt called to be a priest, I was sure it was for life. God was making sure that I wouldn't have to remain in a situation that would endanger the promise I had made to be celibate.

IN OCTOBER OF 1998, as my friendship was slowly developing with Ruhama, I received a phone call from a talent director at Telemundo, an American television network that produces Spanish-language shows. Someone in the Archdiocese of Miami had given her the names of several priests in our area. This network was the second-largest Spanish-language producer in the world, behind Univision, reaching into the homes of over a million viewers every week, but I knew nothing about television at that time. I was twenty-nine years old, ordained just over three years. The network offices were in Hialeah, a popular Latino suburb of Miami, and the talent director asked that I come there to discuss appearing on a talk show. That's all the information I had, when someone from the archdiocese informed me that they had given my name and I should go do it.

"You've got to be kidding," I said. "Who is going to do my parish work?"

On the way there, I thought once again about how I'd always felt, as a young priest, like my mission was to create a bridge between the traditional Church and a fast-paced, ever-evolving global society. I still harbored my original intention to change the world and make it a better place. Despite the fact that I was saying a bunch of Masses at the church every week in English and Spanish, running the parish youth group, teaching theology at a local high school and at the parochial school, officiating at weddings, funerals, and baptisms, I knew that I was reaching only a fraction of the people I could reach through television—especially through a show broadcast by an international network that would be seen not only in the United States but all over Latin America.

I didn't know exactly what to expect at the network offices, but I was under the impression somehow that it would be a small meeting, where we would talk about doing a program or two. Instead, when I arrived I found rooms crammed with actors from different agencies, and I was thrown into a full-blown television audition, being asked all kinds of questions on camera. It was all very new to me.

As I learned later, Nely Galan, Telemundo's president of entertainment, was searching for a priest to host a different type of talk show. She wanted this priest to be young and current, so that the show would draw an audience of young Latinos looking for spiritual and practical guidance. She spent a year auditioning some five hundred Latin American priests for the job. I always think that since she ended up with me, she did not look well enough!

In the middle of the audition, a woman in a business suit walked up to me and said, "Father, you're the one who's going to do this."

Nely, who was a feisty, aggressive, and business-smart Latina, shook her head in doubt at this pronouncement. "I don't know, Father. You look way too white, and you have blue eyes. How many Latinos have blue eyes? Besides, you're young and you have no gray hair yet. This is going to be a show about all kinds of dilemmas and problems that ordinary people face."

I wondered what had just hit me; later I learned that the *New York Times* had nicknamed Nely Galan a "Tropical Tycoon"—that's exactly what it felt like. Frankly, part of me was relieved by her apparent disapproval.

"That's fine if you don't want me," I told her. "I'm very happy to be a parish priest and I have plenty of work to do. I'm really not that interested in this. But you should know that Latinos come in every color."

She looked at me once more and said, "All right. We'll call you when we've decided."

"Well, I'll need to pray about it first," I said. "If God wants it, I want it. But if He doesn't, I want it even less. . . ." She looked at me as if she thought I was crazy; people were dying to get the opportunity to host shows on television, and here I was telling her I needed to talk to God about it. In any case, a couple of months went by and I was happily minding my own business with my parish and busy ministry, never thinking of the possibility of a television gig.

The call came in January 1999: I had been chosen for the show after all. I had no clue that television producers had been secretly sitting in on my Sunday sermons and taking information back to the executives at the network. I really didn't have a clue as to what I was getting myself into. Neither did the Church. Nonetheless, I was soon sitting at a table of television executives and going over a thick legal contract the likes of which the lawyers of the archdiocese had never seen, since they mostly dealt with issues like elderly ladies falling down on a slippery floor at church.

The archbishop, however, gave me his blessing. "If Jesus were here today, He would probably need a television program to reach people," he declared.

A few weeks before the show aired for the first time, I was flown to four of the most important cities to do publicity events for the network. In Los Angeles, I stayed at the Hollywood Roosevelt Hotel, a historic Spanish-style hotel that served as the site of the first Academy Awards ceremony in 1929. The hotel was right on Hollywood Boulevard and could claim such luminaries as Marilyn Monroe, who took up residence there for two years after her modeling career took off, as past guests. Other notable stars who had stayed here included Judy Garland, Cary Grant, Courtney Love, Will Smith, Gloria Swanson, Elizabeth Taylor, Shirley Temple, Bruce Willis, and many more.

When I got to my room, the Shirley Temple Suite, I opened the curtains on one side and saw the famous white "Hollywood" letters on top of the hill. "What am I doing here?" I asked aloud.

When I opened the curtains covering the window on the other side, I spotted a church steeple. "Albert," I said to myself, "this is a lovely hotel, but what you really need to do is pray."

I studied the church steeple to determine how far it might be from the hotel. Thirty seconds later, I was back down in the hotel lobby, asking the concierge to point me toward it.

He directed me just one block over to Sunset Boulevard, which is not as glamorous as people would think. Actually, Sunset Boulevard looked a bit deserted for three in the afternoon. But I continued walking until I arrived at the entrance of the Blessed Sacrament, a beautiful, traditional-looking Jesuit church in the midst of Hollywood's gritty glamour.

To my surprise, the church was locked up tight and there wasn't a soul in sight. I had to walk around the building in search of the office, where I begged the secretary to let me into the chapel to pray. She hesitated, even though I was wearing my black priest suit and Roman collar, but I kept insisting until she eventually let me in.

Once inside that cool, peaceful sanctuary, I knelt and spoke to God. "I don't want to be famous," I began, "and this show is not about preaching. Please, tell me what You want me to do and I will do it."

God made it clear to me at that very moment that my mission was to bring a nonsectarian, uplifting message to all, regardless of their faith traditions or religious convictions. There was no doubt in my mind that it would be an uphill battle. Television networks certainly weren't all about lifting people up, and many conservative Latinos wouldn't expect a priest to be on a talk show at all. But now I knew what I had to do.

PADRE ALBERTO **BEGAN AIRING ON** weekday afternoons at four p.m.—the prime-time slot for afternoon talk shows. I fully expected that this innovative show would be canceled within a few weeks, especially because I was airing opposite a woman who was already a very popular Spanish-language talk show host.

Instead, *Padre Alberto* was an instant hit and brought the network many new viewers and a lot of recognition. An article in *Newsweek* summed up our goal as offering a self-help show for the international Spanish-speaking world, and that was fairly accurate. I was far less comfortable with *Newsweek*'s description of me as "more like a character out of Central Casting than out of the Archdiocese of Southern Florida. He is six feet tall, athletic and handsome. That his last name is Cutié only adds to the superb package." Often, those descriptions were a conflict for me, especially in my role as a spiritual leader and priest.

The show was truly a unique concept, and it quickly caught the attention of Latinos living in the United States and all over Latin America. What's more, *Padre Alberto* soon began drawing more advertising revenue than any other show on that network. We received many national and international awards; *Padre Alberto* was the first Spanish-language show to receive the Christopher Award for excellence, in the year 2000.

Because this was the first time a priest was hosting a daily talk show on secular television, many viewers wrote into the network asking, "Is he a real priest, or an actor dressed as a priest?"

As annoying as it was for me to hear, it was a reasonable question. Most Latino *telenovelas* (soap operas) have priest characters. Once people discovered that I was for real, I went from a parish priest to a celebrity priest in what felt like an instant. Yet I never felt like a celebrity and I deliberately shied away from acting like one. Nevertheless, almost immediately, I was dubbed "Padre Oprah" by the media because of the show's format, which was designed to have me engage in conversations with ordinary people and celebrities about every issue under the sun, from youth and drugs to divorce, marital affairs, lying, money problems, and homosexuality. Many of the topics on my show were still very taboo for Latino audiences, raising the eyebrows of conservative viewers and some Church leaders.

I wasn't making much money from doing the show, but I was satisfied to be making a positive impact in the Latino world. I was reaching out to many, many people. I felt my presence in the media was a way of opening doors for people searching for a way to be spiritual without making them feel that religion was being forced upon them.

I was often criticized because I was seen as too conservative by some and too liberal by others—especially by many in the Church itself—including Latino priests who would say evil things behind my back without ever bothering to meet me. Even certain media people found fault with the way I tried to offer balanced, compassionate conversation.

For instance, I'll never forget the time I happened to be in the makeup room at the network with an experienced news anchor. We were watching the TV monitors hanging from the ceiling, one of which was broadcasting the Spanish equivalent of *The Jerry Springer Show*. A female host was screaming at her guests, highlighting their misery despite the fact that many of them were from the poorest sectors of Latin America.

The female anchor then pointed her finger at the TV monitor and said, "Father, you should wag your finger like she does and tell people that they're all sinners. That would be a hit!"

I laughed, but then I said, "No, I couldn't ever do that. It's not my style, and I'm not about to judge anyone else's behavior."

Truly, I was disgusted by shows like these and often voiced my opinion of that type of program. How could an educated and apparently intelligent TV host exploit poor people to that degree and get away with it? Eventually, after years on the air, the show was removed from the network when journalists and others began to complain about the way children and the poor were treated and exploited, and especially the way that the host's own country was being portrayed.

The network executives never did take well to my dissent, even though I never spoke negatively about her or her program to any of them. It was clear that they saw that particular TV hostess as a cash cow and one of the few programs that regularly beat the competition, even though the quality and content were so poor. It was also a very cheap show to buy. Her ratings were out of this world, and that's all that really mattered to the executives. They were thrilled when she became so successful that her direct competitor, the longtime daily talk show host on the top-ranked Spanish network, was reduced to a weekly show and moved to another time slot due to the fierce competition. She gained so much power within the network that she pushed to have some of her colleagues fired.

On my program, regardless of how long it ran or what the ratings may have been, I was determined to create a program that could make a positive impact on people's lives. There were times when this seemed impossible among all of the controversy and politics around me. Sometimes I'd have to sit by myself in the studio and stare at those blank brick walls between shows, thinking, "Albert, what are you doing here? You have enough trouble dealing with the politics of the Church. Now you're dealing with network politics." I have to say that I often did not know which was worse!

But I knew that God had put me there for a reason: to connect with people of different backgrounds, religious traditions, and ideologies. I wasn't there just to host a show. I had a mission, and media was my mission territory—one that typically wasn't friendly to organized religion or any of its representatives. Millions of people were tuning in to see what the *padrecito*— literally, "little priest," an expression Latinos use

119

to describe a young priest or seminarian—was going to talk about today.

As much as I tried to present a balanced version of certain hot-button issues on TV—like birth control and homosexuality, for instance—this being the real world, controversial topics were bound to surface over and over again. I believed it was always best to let my guests speak for themselves while I listened without passing judgment, though I did offer my final thoughts at the end of the debate or controversy. In those comments I often tried to bridge the very evident gap between today's realities and the Church's official positions. It was never easy.

For instance, if I was interviewing a celebrity, and she said, "Father, I take care of myself," a phrase often used in Spanish referring to the fact that she used artificial contraception, I knew that if I made any comment about that whatsoever, I'd be in deep trouble. Instead, I would often move on by asking, "Have you taught your kids the value of abstinence?"

I would say this, knowing in my heart that internally I was beginning to question the Church's increasingly rigid position on that topic, as well as on so many other things. How could I tell anyone, especially a married woman who was already caring for several children and working outside the home, that using contraception was a mortal sin? I believed in my heart that many people had no choice but to use contraception, and I didn't for a minute believe that God would condemn them for that. What's more, how could the Roman Catholic Church continue to condemn the use of condoms to fight AIDS, when condom use would prevent so many deaths around the world, especially in poor countries?

What century was the Church living in, anyway? I found myself asking this question over and over again, as I continued to listen to people in counseling and on my show struggle with their problems. I had been led by the Church to believe that the world was an atheistic place in need of salvation. Instead, what I was slowly letting myself see was that the world, in fact, was full of good people in trouble looking to God and spiritual advisers for answers to their problems. How could I turn any of them away?

I was beginning to think that perhaps I was a better priest for lost sheep, the people disconnected from the Church or fallen through its cracks, than for those who were devout followers of its doctrines.

AFTER I HAD BEEN IN television for several months, one of the unconventional things I did was visit my direct competitor in her own home. In the Latino world, competition is very strong and you never see people from one network on the other—no matter what. It never made any sense to me, but that's just how it works. From the very first time my show was put on the air, the Spanish tabloids had tried to pit us against one another.

I was determined not to take this personally. I really didn't know my competitor, and I had never had a chance to really pay attention to her programs, though I was well aware of her notoriety. I wanted to talk to her face-to-face, mostly because I really didn't want any of the animosity and tension the tabloids were trying to create between us. So I picked up the phone and called a dear friend who knows almost everyone in the entertainment industry.

"I want to meet with my competitor," I told him.

He hesitated. "Are you sure that's okay with your network?"

"I really don't care. God has put this idea in my heart, and I'm going to follow through." He immediately got me the number.

A few days later, we met in her beautiful waterfront home. "I am not here as your competition, or even as a priest," I told her as soon as we'd had time to make ourselves comfortable. "I'm here as a human being who wants you to know that you can always count on my friendship."

We became friends almost immediately. Eventually, we stopped being on at the same time and she was moved to a successful evening show, where she had me on as a guest several times. Our friendship continued to develop, and eventually I was the one who blessed her studios, buried her parents, and baptized her grandson.

Once I completed my contract with the secular TV network, I continued my work in television, radio, and the press, reaching people everywhere and through a variety of media. I also attracted criticism from all quarters. When I was compassionate, I was attacked by some conservative groups as being too liberal and not tough enough. If I was stern and stood my ground, I was immediately attacked for being the typical judgmental priest who easily condemns people. When it comes to priests, people prefer to categorize you according to their predetermined stereotypes and rarely consider you a human being with your own ideas and personal criteria.

Many people were bothered by the idea that I refused to use my television platform to moralize or preach, since that's what most people expect from men of the cloth. However, as the months and years went by and I became ever more a media presence, I continued to feel strongly that I had a broader mission. My role was to help everyone through their struggles. I would not allow my show to become a series of sermons or theology classes; that's what I felt my work at the parish was for. My open approach allowed me to reach people of all denominations and even very diverse religious traditions.

My goal from the start with this media ministry was to create opportunities for open conversation and a new way to help all people live a better life, offering practical advice regarding current, complex issues. This is what made my work different, even groundbreaking—and my show one that was loved and understood by many, while at the same time feared and despised by others.

When my talk show guests said something totally contrary to my belief system, many viewers were shocked when I did not scream or berate them. But I was convinced that I wasn't put in the public eye to judge other people. On the contrary: I was a regular human being who happened to be a priest willing to listen openly to other people's dilemmas, without worrying whether the ideas I was hearing were contrary to official Church doctrine. My ideological evolution was well under way; I just didn't comprehend yet how extensive it would be.

FOLLOWING MY DAILY PROGRAM, the network asked me to host a live weekly talk show called *America en Vivo*. It was a relief for me to stop the daily program, because it gave me more time to enjoy parish work and to begin to focus on the radio ministry I had been assigned by the Archdiocese of Miami, a job that required a great deal of fund-raising. At the same time, I was writing advice columns for *El Nuevo Herald* in

Miami, which were syndicated to other newspapers in the United States and Latin America.

In 2001, I began hosting radio programs, such as *Al Dia* and *Linea Directa* and I was also assigned to take over as general director of Radio Paz and Radio Peace Catholic, a twenty-four-hour radio station. I was later promoted to president and general director, in charge of the direction and daily operations of Pax Catholic Communications, Inc., a multimedia ministry in the Archdiocese of Miami, until 2009.

When I look back on my schedule now, I have no idea how I managed it, except to say that I was fully committed to each and every one of my roles and had a great deal of help from God. I never taped a program without praying first; typically, I started every day by praying privately and then saying Mass. The parish was a spiritual oasis for me and prayer was a very important part of my day.

After prayer, I would drive across the bridge from Miami Beach into the city of Miami to cohost a radio program with other anchors. Along with laymen and laywomen, I'd talk about the day's news, offering a faith perspective on events. We offered programs in English, Spanish, and Haitian through various radio stations. We also transmitted internationally in Spanish by satellite radio, as well as operating youth and music programs online. As president and general director of Miami's Catholic radio station, I began with a budget of $2.5 million, but raised that to almost $5 million during my time there, always striving to operate in the black—and we did. Most priests don't usually find themselves presiding over downsizings, but I did, because the radio ministry could not afford the number of employees they had employed before I arrived.

I would be on the air with a cup of coffee in one hand and a newspaper in the other, commenting on the day's news. Afterward, I'd sit and have breakfast for perhaps fifteen minutes before dealing with whatever budget and administrative issues were on the table that day. Around noon, I'd cross the bridge back to Miami Beach to work at the parish, where I kept appointments with people seeking spiritual direction, dealt with employee issues, and made wedding and funeral arrangements. Afterward, I'd try to take time to exercise and clear my mind.

About three times a week, I crossed that bridge into Miami to host the taped talk show on television. Later on, I would host a weekly prime-time international show with a newsier format. At any given program, I might find myself in conversation with a mother whose daughter didn't want to leave her delinquent boyfriend, a psychologist talking about domestic violence, or a medical doctor offering the latest heart disease research.

One of my most memorable guests was Bishop Leo Frade, the Episcopal bishop of Southeast Florida—who today is my bishop. He and I had already struck up a friendship; when I'd had him on some years before on a television show discussing celibacy, he had handed me his business card afterward.

"Call me when you're ready to get married," he joked.

Years later, I asked him on my radio show when the Episcopal Church allowed Eugene Robinson to become the first gay, partnered bishop to be ordained, in 2003. "I want you to explain what this controversial move means for the Episcopal Church," I told him.

I had met Bishop Robinson shortly after his consecration. We were both walking quickly through the Ronald Reagan Airport in Washington, D.C., and I was in my official clergy suit. When I saw him, I approached and said, "Congratulations, Bishop. In our Church, men in your situation are closeted and cannot say or do what you have said and done. I congratulate you for that! All of this controversy will die down eventually."

He then smiled and looked at me as if he were really not so convinced that the storms would soon disappear, but he appeared at peace and thanked me before he went on.

While on my show, Bishop Frade outlined his

views on human sexuality, which were admittedly much broader than most Roman Catholics typically hear. After the show, I received many calls and e-mails from viewers protesting his appearance, saying that he was far too progressive. However, I also received a lot of compassionate and understanding feedback.

I was beginning to learn that I wasn't the only one entertaining certain progressive views. I was just one of the few willing to express them. In any case, I was becoming more determined than ever to create a positive Catholic presence in the media, particularly after the sex abuse scandals broke and it became so clear to me that the institutional Church was backward and incompetent in media affairs.

In both the United States and Latin America, religious media was mostly an activity limited to fundamentalist groups; there seemed to be a total absence of mainstream churches with preachers on television. With so many people—especially young people—claiming to be turned off by organized religion, I knew that the presence of a priest or priests—not just me—was important. Yet I never sensed that the official Church ever really valued that presence.

Sadly, often those who appear on television from the megachurches that attract thousands of people each week and are watched by millions more at home have no formal theological training or background. Yet they're the ones who seem to have mastered the electronic pulpit. I took them on as a personal challenge, convinced that most people could better relate to spiritual leaders with a broader perspective.

The only downside of this media mission of mine—and it was a big one—was the hectic schedule. Juggling media work with my commitment to parish work meant that I was always accessible to anyone who showed up at church—frequently with a tape recorder or camera rolling—as well as to those who sent emergency e-mails seeking my guidance in the midst of family crises.

Plus, people seemed increasingly convinced that, because I was on television, I was the priest with the answers, so more and more of them sought me out. At the same time, I was dealing with celebrities, media personalities, politicians, community leaders, and others who started showing up at my Sunday services because they'd seen me on television. Coupled with listening to people from all over the world who called into my show, I began to feel that there was no real sanctuary for myself.

While most priests could change into a polo shirt on their days off and go out on the streets unnoticed, I was always recognizable and had to be ready to have my picture taken or listen to a person in need—on the spot—no matter where I was. I "heard confessions" at airports, on city sidewalks, in shopping malls, and in other unconventional places. On my off-hours, I tried hard to relax by reading books or going to the movies, or occasionally getting together with priest friends, but that was becoming more and more difficult.

At times it was a blessing and at other times a great cross, but for the most part I was fine with the direction my life had taken because I saw it as God's mission—not mine. After all, hadn't I made it my mission in life to offer comfort and provide a listening ear to all who needed it? Besides, many times all of this activity was a welcome distraction from thoughts of Ruhama. And she knew it. She would often ask me, "Why do you work so much?"

CHAPTER SIX

CHURCH SCANDALS, POLITICS, AND DISAPPOINTMENT

Between 2001 and 2002, the Roman Catholic community in the United States saw many of its most talented and dynamic priests thrown out and removed with almost no due process. I was directly affected by the sex abuse scandals because I was assigned to replace priests who had been accused.

Some of the accused were men I had come to respect and even considered among my mentors, including my pastor at the Key West church and the pastor of the parish where I grew up. Besides that, my work with the media put me squarely in the spotlight, as I was asked to give interviews on both Latino and mainstream television shows covering the issue of sex abuse. I did my best to make the official Church look good in the midst of very ugly accusations. However, many times my only possible response to interviewers' questions had to be, "We must pray."

In the midst of this chaos, I was assigned to replace a man I considered to be one of the most talented priests in America. Ordained by a pope, after studying for years in Rome, this man was gifted and well connected. He had friends among the cardinals, kept in close contact with several of the pope's closest collaborators and assistants, and was totally dedicated to his work. His evangelical work on behalf of the Catholic Church had made an incredible international impact—almost like a Catholic Billy Graham. His parish, San Isidro Catholic Church in Pompano Beach, Florida, was a booming megachurch that also served as a makeshift television studio, so that he could broadcast his Masses on international Spanish television every Sunday as well as his popular English and Spanish preaching shows.

As an eighteen-year-old seminarian, I had heard other priests openly and often hostilely criticize this man's San Isidro megachurch and media ministries.

"Who is going to replace him when he retires or dies?" they demanded. "Nobody is going to be able to continue that."

What had this priest done to raise their ire? He had become the CEO of an international television ministry, turning what was once a poor little run-down mission into a megachurch and a parish with more than one hundred ministries—all of them extremely well run and hugely successful.

On May 7, 2002, I was attending a conference on religious media in Santo Domingo, when this San Isidro priest's scandal hit the front page of the newspapers. I called the radio station I was in charge of that very morning. The employees were all crying and devastated, since most were well aware of the ministry of this talented priest. Not only that, his program played every day on our radio station. Some of the station employees had been married before him, and he had baptized many of their children. They felt understandably hurt, confused, and betrayed. While other priests were also removed that day, this man was by far the most popular.

I had no choice but to call the archbishop to find out what to do with this priest's program, which was set to air in the next couple of hours. When I called the bishop's office, nobody was around—not the communications director, not the chancellor, nobody.

Finally, a secretary came on the phone and said, "Oh, Father Cutié, we're so glad that you called. The archbishop is looking for you."

I was very surprised, because my bishop had never called me for anything in all my years of ministry for any reason, good or bad. When he came on the phone that Tuesday morning, I could feel the tension in his voice.

"Your life is going to change today," he announced.

First, the archbishop informed me that I couldn't air the accused priest's programs anymore. Then he added, "Now I have something else to say to you: I have named you the administrator of San Isidro Catholic Church, effective immediately. I need you to be moved in to Pompano Beach by Friday."

Looking back on this event, I suppose that, from the archbishop's point of view, his decision made sense: I was already known internationally as a priest who was comfortable working with the media. At the time, however, I was so shocked that I had to get down on my knees right then. I prayed to God with my eyes closed while the archbishop continued speaking.

"Albert," he was saying, "with these scandals we'll all have to double up on our work from now on. It won't be easy for any of us." He informed me that I would be continuing my work directing the radio stations, while at the same time assuming the additional responsibilities of heading up the media ministry in San Isidro for the priest I was replacing.

In an instant, my workload tripled. Never mind the hundred-plus-mile drive between the radio station and San Isidro, which alone would consume two hours each day with no traffic. However, I could say nothing in response. I had made a promise of obedience. I wasn't about to argue with the archbishop.

The bishop's final words to me were stern, strict instructions: "Please, Albert. Do not tell anyone about this matter until we've sent out the press release on Thursday."

I followed the bishop's instructions to the letter and told no one of my new position. However, by the time I flew back from Santo Domingo to

Miami International Airport that evening, the television cameras were already waiting for me as I walked down the concourse. The word was out: I was the one being sent to replace the accused and hugely popular charismatic pastor.

It was only then that I discovered that the archdiocese had already sent out a press release—a day earlier than they'd told me it would appear! Many priests called to ask if I was crazy to take on so much more responsibility. Most asked, "Why didn't you refuse?"

I simply responded, "I was never asked what I thought about the assignment. I was told that I had to take it on. Besides, he's the archbishop, not me."

One sensible priest friend pointed out that I was already working overtime. "You're going to burn out," he warned. "They're going to kill you with this."

I knew that he might be right. I was already exhausted and overwhelmed. On the other hand, I was not yet in the habit of questioning authority. I reminded myself that whatever the bishop asked me to do must have been part of God's plan for me. That was what I had been taught, and even after all I'd seen, I still firmly believed this. It was that simple.

Four months into my job as administrator at San Isidro, I finally went to see my bishop to find out how much longer I would have to stay at the megachurch. He assured me that I would only be there a few more months. Instead, I remained assigned there for nearly two full years, working fifteen hours a day.

What was most disappointing to me is that never again in those two years did the bishop speak to me. Not once! He never visited the parish, called, or asked how the San Isidro church was doing or how the parishioners felt. There was no discussion about what the game plan should be for the future of this important international parish, either.

Finally, after a few more months had gone by, I called his priest secretary—a young monsignor—to ask when we could expect the archbishop to visit; I still thought that he might be planning to speak to the hurting flock and to listen to their pain regarding their ousted pastor. The secretary's response was curt: "I'm sure the archbishop will visit San Isidro the next time that he is scheduled for Confirmation."

I couldn't believe it. Church officials were acting as if nothing special at all had happened in that parish, despite the blaze of bad press and the obvious knowledge that the people this pastor had served were feeling shattered. Never mind the fact that I had been thrown into this situation to face the press and the parish with zero support. I knew that I'd get through everything with a lot of prayer and help from the people in the parish, many of whom were wonderfully understanding. What bothered me more was that Church officials obviously felt no real need to face the people of this parish, who were hungry for answers and wanted to know about the future of their spiritual home. These people had invested a lot of their time and resources into this megachurch, yet the officials of the archdiocese ran from them like the plague.

Again, I had to observe that this removed, rigid, and dysfunctional way of conducting business was all too common for the Church. It appeared as if those in positions of authority seemed determined to keep their distance from anything— or anyone—that might contaminate them or hurt their chances of continuing to climb the Church ladder. Until the time these incidents occurred, I was convinced that bishops were shepherds with a spiritual and pastoral role to fulfill. Unfortunately, what I saw was Church leaders who ran and hid from difficult situations, including those which needed them most.

There was—and still is—no doubt in my mind that many of the priests accused of horrible crimes, such as molestation and rape, were guilty as charged. Yet I also knew that a good number of priests were victims of unethical lawyers and weak bishops who were too concerned about their own images to trust even some of their most trustworthy priests. Lawsuits were being speedily settled right and left, with priests being removed long before the allegations against them could have possibly been fully explored and supported—or tossed out. Nobody knew what the truth really was in many of these cases.

Those who were supposedly our spiritual fathers were clearly disconnecting themselves from their own "sons" in order to avoid conflicts and financial problems that came with the allegations—founded or unfounded. It was now abundantly clear to me that I belonged to a Church that was disconnected from the very people it was meant to serve, and incompetent in dealing with crises. The way they dealt with their fallen soldiers was complete insanity. In the case of the pastors I had replaced, yes, they were accused of abusing teenage boys, many years earlier. On the other hand, those priests also gave decades of their lives to the Church, and I often felt that the officials totally separated themselves from them—as if they were lepers.

On the other hand, matters got even more complicated, because in 2002 the Church made a promise to keep track of priests charged with sex abuse. Instead, once they stopped moving many of these priests from parish to parish, the Church just let them go, cutting them loose following various plea bargains—to do what? To retire and sail off into the sunset? To abuse other victims in shopping centers or public bathrooms? To live in a car with no money or health insurance, as one priest friend of mine did, claiming that he was innocent of the charges and refusing to take the Church's offers to practically disappear him?

Roman Catholics sitting in the pews have no clue what so many priests are going through. Meanwhile, I found myself feeling more and more disconnected from an institution that I increasingly perceived as inhumane.

WHEN I FIRST BEGAN TO work in media, one of my greatest satisfactions came from knowing that I was able to connect with almost every corner of Latin America. Shortly after the first season of my daily talk show, I was invited to attend NATPE (the National Association of Television and Programming Executives), one of the most important conferences in the television world. People came from around the world to attend this conference; often they were executives who were interested in purchasing new programming for their particular television stations, both great and small.

At NATPE, I engaged in fascinating conversations with Jerry Springer, a number of TV judges, several actors, and many television executives. In the midst of the hubbub, one man in particular stood out in the crowd. From his mismatched clothes, I suspected that he must be a priest; since most priests are unaccustomed to wearing everyday clothes, we're prone to make enormous fashion errors, like wearing socks with our sandals.

The priest in the mismatched clothing turned out to be the director of the Catholic television channel in a very poor Latin American country. After that first meeting, we began exchanging e-mails, and after a few years, we were good friends. We both became priests around the same time, we were almost the same age, and we were both working in the media, so we had many things in common. I was very pleased to have him as my friend. For now, I'll call him "Father J."

At the time we met, I was juggling all that I have described here: directing the radio stations of the Catholic Church in Miami, writing newspaper advice columns, serving as a parish priest, and hosting a weekly TV show.

Only a week after I had conducted what I surely thought would be my last television program, I received a visit from a prominent cardinal in Latin America who had a television channel that was not doing well. He visited me in my office at the radio stations with a former chancery official—a priest—who assured me that my archbishop was aware of this request and had given his approval. The cardinal went on to explain his vision of creating an international television network for all of the Americas. He was just starting to meet with people around the world to get this project off the ground, and he asked me to serve on the board for this lofty project.

I was happy to do so, since this project was designed to spread a good message and to reach out especially to the poorest countries in our hemisphere. The project never really took off, but I did spend a little more than a year trying to help out by producing a program in that country, which earned positive feedback.

By 2002, EWTN (Eternal Word Television Network), the network founded by the dynamo cloistered nun Mother Angelica, was transmitting Spanish-language programs around the world. To this day, it is one of the largest cable religious networks in the world and a testament to this incredible woman's courage. This is where my priest friend who dressed funny comes back into the picture: He created an alliance with EWTN to begin producing a talk show program called *Hablando Claro con el Padre Alberto* on the channel he directed. Supporting that program would help his channel receive the funding it needed to operate. At the same time, the program would create more Spanish content for EWTN at a minimal cost.

It was a brilliant plan. Even if it meant more work and travel for me, I considered the program and this nonprofit Catholic network a very worthy cause and devoted myself to it from 2003 to 2009 as a volunteer. Finding the time to fit the program into my already jammed schedule was an enormous challenge, but I knew that I could do it if I worked on my only day off and added additional hours to my other workdays. I taped the shows every seven to eight weeks.

The archbishop who founded that channel was an extraordinary leader. He had always been supportive of my work in the media and encouraged me to continue producing television programs, especially in order to reach Latin America, where large numbers of people were abandoning the Roman Catholic Church. In Brazil alone—one of the most Roman Catholic countries on the planet—the statistics are staggering, with over half a million people abandoning the Church each year. The exodus around Latin America was so great that countries that were 95 percent Roman Catholic until the 1970s were now barely 65 percent Roman Catholic. Many were leaving Roman Catholicism simply because there was a shortage of priests, and other growing religious groups didn't need ordained leaders to bring together congregations for worship.

On several occasions, the archbishop and I met to converse about everything happening in the Catholic world. This particular archbishop was very close to Pope John Paul II and eventually became a cardinal.

The cardinal had a nephew—I'll call him "Father P."—who was a priest recognized by everyone in the clergy as a dreadfully ambitious man. Father P. made it widely known that he longed to become a bishop and acquire greater status in the institution. He worked the system better than most to achieve his goal. He became friends with the nuncio, the diplomatic papal representative before the government, who is often the person consulted by the Vatican in the appointment of future bishops. Father P. also bad-mouthed every priest on the list to be bishop as a means of raising his own name higher on the list.

The clergy knew what he was up to and did not like him. He officially worked in a nearby country, but only spent a few days a week there because he chose instead to "help his uncle," the cardinal, by serving as his uncle's personal secretary. Few people in the country he was assigned to even knew who he was.

My friend Father J. also did a great deal to help the cardinal, including writing a number of his sermons and newspaper columns. Consequently, he was asked to leave the rectory in the church where he had been working as an assistant and move into the cardinal's personal residence, where he was expected to continue working with the media.

On the other hand, Father P. was so successful in working the system that he was soon promoted to bishop. This move was a shock to some clergy, and to some of the laity as well. To those of us who knew how Rome chooses its leaders, where decisions come down from the top and the laity are rarely consulted about anything, even their own local pastors, this was just business as usual. I was not surprised.

After a few months in the cardinal's residence, Father J. began noticing that Father P.—now Bishop P.—was bringing a male "friend" into the residence regularly to sleep in one of the guest rooms. Eventually, a room was added to the cardinal's residence, a car was purchased for him, and now the unidentified man was also living there. The cardinal's house and cleaning staff were confused by the arrangement, naturally, and Father J. was put in a very awkward position, as he was the only other priest in the house.

Father J. spoke to Bishop P., who blatantly denied that any such arrangement existed. Father J. then went to the cardinal, who didn't want to believe this was happening beneath the roof of his own residence. Finally, Father J. went to the nuncio, the papal representative.

Even after all of these confrontations, nothing changed. This caused great heartache for Father J., a young priest who had every right to expect Church authorities to do the right thing once they were made aware of the situation. The situation caused the young priest to feel sick to his stomach; he could no longer live in that house and feel at peace.

When Father J. finally confided in me about the situation, I told him to get out. "You don't have to live there," I said. "Just leave."

In response, he explained that he couldn't do any such thing, because it might offend the cardinal, who had been so good to him. I encouraged Father J. to try writing to the cardinal, who traveled a great deal. He did so, explaining his position and opening his heart to him. Father J. spoke the truth about what he saw and what several others were witnesses to, yet still nothing changed.

Finally, Father J. resigned his position as director of TV, radio, and press for his diocese and asked for a leave of absence. He never came back. After a year or so, he married and left active ministry.

Was Father J. a bad and unfaithful priest? No. Was he unhappy, disillusioned, and hurt? Yes, absolutely. What's more, those among us who knew of Father J.'s great humanity, competence, and pastoral expertise were also hurt. Ultimately, Father J. was just one more priest who couldn't live within such a broken, dishonest, and hypocritical system.

Over time, I saw how more and more priests grew so disillusioned every day that they were forced, like Father J., to simply move on. I couldn't help but fear for the future of my Church—and for my place within it.

• • •

ON JULY 12, 2003, I was at the rectory of St. Mary Star of the Sea in Key West, Florida, where I had served as a deacon-intern from 1994 to 1995. For once, I wasn't working, but taking a few days off—within my scheduled vacation time—to recuperate from all the running around I was doing between San Isidro and the radio station. The parish had hundreds of ministries and dozens of daily activities, and while I had three priest associates, none of them was a priest of my diocese. What's more, they were all from other countries and had very little knowledge of life in the United States. I was also still managing the finances at the radio stations of the Archdiocese of Miami.

While in Key West, I learned of the imminent death of Celia Cruz, a Cuban-born singer who had been dubbed the Queen of Salsa by everyone who appreciated her work with the legendary Afro-Cuban group La Sonora Matancera and with stars like Johnny Ventura, Gloria Estefan, Johnny Pacheco, Tito Puente, and David Byrne. Cruz even had a star on Hollywood's Walk of Fame. In Miami, the main drag through the Cuban community was called Celia Cruz Way. The Smithsonian Institution granted Cruz a Lifetime Achievement Award in 1994, and President Clinton honored her work with the National Medal of Arts. The year before, Celia had won a

Grammy Award for best salsa album, the second Grammy of her life.

Celia's manager and longtime collaborator, Omer Pardillo-Cid, was grief-stricken when he called me from New Jersey to say that Celia, only seventy-seven years old, was near death after surgery.

"Celia always said that if she couldn't return to Cuba, she wanted to go to Miami," Omer said. He asked if I could possibly travel to Celia's home in New Jersey to offer last rites.

After a few conversations, we came to the conclusion that the priest at her nearby church would anoint her. Meanwhile, a group of community leaders from various government and nonprofit entities, led by Jorge Plasencia (the CEO of Republica), took on the responsibility of preparing two public wakes and Masses for her: One would take place in Miami, where she would lie in state, and the other in New York, where she would be buried. This way, her many fans in both parts of the country could honor her in person.

County, city, and community leaders quickly convened a conference call to begin preparation for the largest funeral that South Florida had ever seen. My job was to organize the church portion, and as you can imagine, it wasn't easy. While I was asked to coordinate, celebrate, and preach at the Mass, I wanted to also include a number of other priests as a way of demonstrating the

Church's presence, since this funeral would be followed closely not only in the United States but throughout Latin America.

I considered organizing Celia's funeral a great honor, mostly because of my personal affection toward her as a great human being and artist. She had defected from Cuba when Castro took power, as my parents had, and all Latinos, myself included, loved her music. Celia Cruz was not just an icon for the music world; she was an icon for immigrants who fled their countries for a variety of reasons and started at the bottom, making their way to the top—as she did so well. I was certain that her funeral would be a great opportunity to bring people closer to God and to the Church.

I should have known better. Church officials—what I had come to think of as the "antiseptic Church"—wanted nothing to do with this funeral. This celebrity, like so many others, did not fit in the box of the official Church and had too many germs. Yet I had gone through the same type of thing with unknown common folks many times before. Luckily, I didn't absorb the whole impact of this gap between the Church and the funeral ceremonies for Celia until after the ceremonies had concluded.

Organizing anything with priests is usually quite a project, as many are not very flexible and don't typically deal with the "unchurched" (those who do not attend church regularly) very well. It's common for priests to get all caught up in who can receive Communion and who cannot. Many priests categorized Celia as a "lapsed" Roman Catholic, so I would imagine that many of her colleagues in the music world—at least in their eyes—would also fall into that category. The few priests who did attend this great woman's funeral did so because they understood the importance of their presence among the people. However, with the exception of two or three, the priests in attendance were mostly Cubans in their late seventies—those who had grown up knowing Celia's musical legacy.

The wake service in Miami took place in one of the city's most popular buildings, the historic Freedom Tower—a kind of Ellis Island for Miami Cubans. This was the place where, between 1959 and 1972, many Cuban exiles were processed, received government assistance, and made their first official entry into the United States after fleeing the Castro regime.

We chose the historic Gesu Church, the oldest Roman Catholic church in Miami, for the funeral Mass because of its location only blocks from the Freedom Tower. I had been asked to call the Jesuit pastor there and make arrangements. This proved to be an ordeal, since the pastor had absolutely no idea who Celia Cruz was and was a particularly difficult character. After a lot of persuasion on my part, he finally agreed.

The pastor at Gesu was quickly overwhelmed by all of the community leaders, people from the county, the police, and other personnel visiting his church and doing the necessary logistical and security work. Because of this Jesuit priest's lack of contact with the community outside the church walls, he must have thought this would be a typical funeral with family and friends. He had no idea that this would be the largest funeral to ever take place in Miami—or that everyone else would also be watching it around the world.

To be fair, I'm sure nobody imagined the kind of turnout we had for Celia's funeral. According to some estimates, more than 100,000 people attended the wake that day. You could see lines of people for blocks and blocks in the streets of downtown Miami, many of them waving flags from Nicaragua, Puerto Rico, Panama, and Venezuela. The Queen's salsa music played and people sang outside as they made their way into the building, where they found the coffin adorned with a Cuban flag made of flowers. Some cried as they sang, while others danced. We were all there to demonstrate an unmistakable heartfelt reverence for the woman who had shared her unique style of Latino music with the world. It was truly an inspiring sight.

Nobody really knew where to put all of the people. Huge television screens were installed around the perimeter of the church so that those who wanted to be part of it all could follow the funeral Mass from the streets. And they did, with noticeable respect.

The celebrities in attendance—actors, musicians, TV personalities, and entertainment executives—were transported from Emilio and Gloria Estefan's restaurant in downtown Miami to the church, while a small group of priests and a huge crowd of people walked on the street in procession near the funeral car. The procession was surprisingly orderly and respectful, given that we were in downtown Miami, where people are usually shopping, parking to go to school, attending basketball games, or on their way to big rock concerts. The mood was solemn—many were grieving the loss of this great musical talent—while festive at the same time, because Celia was such a beloved entertainer and outstanding human being who had made an incredibly positive international impact.

That funeral Mass caused something that rarely happens in the Latino entertainment world: Both of the major Spanish-language U.S. networks and CNN en Español broadcast the event simultaneously, with no evident concerns about competition. It was watched by millions upon millions of people, including those who saw it live on the big screen in Times Square.

Even *Sabado Gigante*, one of the longest-running shows in television history, was replaced with the funeral Mass for Celia Cruz; the host of this show, the charismatic yet formal Mario Kreutzberger (known as Don Francisco), was actually present at Celia's funeral. In the U.S. Latino world and in Latin America, you know something special is going on if *Sabado Gigante* isn't on TV, since this show is seen in almost every Latino home on Saturday night and is actually the longest-running prime-time variety show, according to the *Guinness Book of World Records*. The world had paused to say good-bye to the Queen of Salsa.

I had arranged a traditional Mass with incense, altar servers, and a choir. I also asked the group Coral Cubana, a popular chorale that combined classical melodies with Caribbean rhythms, to accompany the Mass and chant during the appropriate parts. For many years, they had played the music at High Masses and cultural events in the community whenever Latinos were involved.

The Mass was celebrated with reverence and respect, but with joy as well. Because of our belief in eternal life, Christian funerals are as much about the hope and joy of the resurrection, not just about the sadness of a temporary death. As I saw it, that incredible woman, though her remains lay in the coffin, was bringing together people from all walks of life that rarely bumped into each other: fans, fellow artists, executives from competing networks, ministers of various denominations, and so on. The same way that Cruz brought all kinds of people together around her music, she was bringing them to pray.

With the sermon, my intent was to express sentiments unique to Celia's life that might also appeal to a broad audience. On a light note, I said I believed the choirs of angels in heaven would receive Celia singing, "Quimbara quimbara quma quimbambá"—the most famous line from her song "Quimbara." I wanted to offer the kind of personal sermon that I would give at a family funeral, where I'm trying to share the hope of eternal life with those who are grieved by the death of a close relative. I was a bit nervous, because in all honesty I had very little time to prepare, since my job was to accompany family and friends, while also assigning readings and other obligations to those participating in the Mass. Nonetheless, the response to the sermon was extremely positive. Both those who regularly attended church and those who never participated in any formal religious ceremony reported that I'd said the right things and taken the correct approach.

Throughout the following week, I received thousands of messages from people congratulating me. Many said that they were motivated to "go back to church" and "return to the sacraments." I was pleased by this. Nothing makes a priest happier than bringing people to a greater awareness of their faith —and that's how I had always perceived the mission God gave me as a priest.

After all was said and done that very long day, Celia's remains were to be transported to New York the following morning for another wake, Mass at St. Patrick's Cathedral, and finally her burial near the Bronx. I hadn't really been planning to go to New York; I had several Masses that Sunday and too many obligations to leave behind. On the other hand, I still had several vacation days left and the family insisted on me joining them, so I did.

In New York, as in Miami, thousands of people attended Celia's funeral. They crammed the quiet blocks along East 81st Street, waving flags and white roses—Celia's favorite flower—and lined up outside the funeral home in the Upper East Side of Manhattan to take a brief peek at the legendary woman they had come to love. When the doors to the funeral home finally opened, fans streamed past Celia's solid bronze coffin, where she lay with her hands crossed around a golden crucifix under a Cuban flag.

Some say up to forty thousand people attended the wake and Mass in New York. You could tell the crowd was diverse, yet mostly were simple working people—Dominicans and Cubans, Venezuelans and Puerto Ricans, and all else. A great number brought their children to pay respect to this magnificent woman whom they had admired and considered family. I was extremely moved, and once again I felt honored to share the homage to this great artist's life.

These good feelings were marred, however, when I received a very strange phone call that afternoon from the former auxiliary bishop of Miami. He had already been assigned to another diocese, but he was still in town. When he heard my voice, the bishop exploded in anger, calling me a "bad priest" and saying that the Mass I had said for Celia Cruz in Miami was "scandalous." The main source of his fury was that I had "given" Communion to someone who was not permitted to receive it.

I knew at once that the bishop was referring to the Reverend Martin Añorga, a well-respected Presbyterian minister and icon in the Cuban-American community, who had been invited to stand behind me at the altar by a group of elderly priests—some of them ordained fifty years or more. Obviously, none of those older priests present thought it was a problem for a minister from another Christian denomination to stand by us. Before I could give any explanation or share my side of the sequence of events, the bishop went on to warn me that a priest in Europe had been recently excommunicated by the pope for doing what I had just done. He insisted that I explain my actions, because they were bad for the Church's image.

As I listened to this ranting monologue, I was in a state of shock! I also was aware of a building fury: I was working two full-time jobs, running the radio stations and the San Isidro megachurch that I had inherited, and trying my best every minute to make the Church look good. Because obedience is one of the promises we make, I had no choice but to bow my head and take the blows as they came—but that didn't mean that the blows were painless. I was deeply hurt by the bishop and never received any type of apology for the angry phone call.

I was certain that Celia's funeral Mass had created a positive impact in the minds and hearts of Latinos all over the world—especially among those nominal Catholics who never step foot in a church. How could this be a problem?

Once again, this incident illustrated the great disconnect between the hierarchy and the people. Almost nobody outside the Church had perceived the revered and respected Presbyterian pastor's own initiative to receive Communion; I had not given it to him, but I was not about to take it out of his hand if he chose to freely receive it. Those on the outside of the controversy wouldn't have known, either, that this action was something that Reverend Añorga later apologized for, since it went against Roman Catholic protocol and he had always made it a point to respect the particular practices and rules of all religious traditions. It was simply a spontaneous choice he had made.

Ironically, what most people watching the Mass saw was a reverent, tasteful celebration. Only the officials of the institutional Church insisted on putting out a statement describing every detail they perceived as "wrong" with the Mass, and even wrote that it was "tasteless."

As I could have predicted, after the release of that statement the entire Latino community was appalled, not by Reverend Añorga taking Communion but by the official Church's insistence on excluding a man of God from receiving it, and by the many negative expressions the Church used to describe a celebration that had been so positive and meaningful for so many. The result of this statement was that the Church hierarchy appeared to be castigating me for celebrating a meaningful, respectful, and joyful liturgy and looked bad for doing so. What started out as something very good was turned into a missed opportunity, with this inane insistence on protecting the Church's immaculate and antiseptic image. All the while, on the inside, I was dealing with a good deal of the dirt and growing accusations involving the sexual abuse of minors.

Incredibly, this event mushroomed into a problem at the highest levels of the Church, to such an extreme that even the Apostolic Nuncio of the United States inquired about my "orthodoxy" through the local bishop. To someone like me, who had publicly defended the official Church and its many archaic positions for such a long time, this felt like a slap in the face.

Once more, I was thrown into such a tailspin of sadness and anger that I had to ask myself, "Albert, what are you doing in this inflexible, dictatorial, and merciless institution?" My notion of what I always thought "church" was supposed to be—a loving, caring, forgiving, and understanding community—was quite the opposite of what I was experiencing.

IN 2003, MY SCHEDULE FINALLY calmed down a little. I left the unwieldy, exhausting San Isidro megachurch at last and returned to my role as a parochial vicar at St. Patrick's Catholic Church in Miami Beach. I continued to work crazy hours, but I could finally relax a bit and take more joy in ministering to the people I served at the parish and through my media ministry. Certain conservative people in the hierarchy of the Church still complained about me; many in the clergy think that if you work in the media and hang out with celebrities, as I did on occasion, then you must be a frivolous person. However, I was just as seriously committed to my spiritual growth and life as ever.

There was just one problem: My ideological

evolution had reached a point where I was in serious disagreement with many Church teachings and practices that I considered outdated and in need of revisiting. In fact, when I occasionally got together with Episcopal friends, they would listen to me speak about topics like contraception, divorce, or church governance, and exclaim, "You think more like an Anglican than we do!"

I understood, of course, that I was going through some pretty deep ideological changes from my somewhat conservative past. On the other hand, I also knew that many, many Roman Catholic priests felt the same way I did—they just wouldn't talk about it because they didn't want to be ostracized or isolated within the Church.

For example, I was aware of a great number of gay priests and bishops who appeared to be pretty open about it—and had partners—some even living promiscuous lives. How, I wondered, was it possible for them to remain Roman Catholic, when the Church considered them intrinsically disordered, and at the same time to follow Church practice and exclude parishioners who lived just like them from participating in the sacraments? I felt that the official teaching of the Church on homosexuality was wrong, especially in excluding people from Communion. Who can judge another human being worthy of receiving Communion? Only God knows who is worthy.

What's more, how was a Roman Catholic priest

supposed to rationally tell a man who already has five or six children that he should have sex with the possibility of procreation every time he had intimate relations with his wife? That stance might have been all right for our grandparents, but not in today's world. So many people suffer because of these and other issues, and they are told they are in mortal sin if they use any form of artificial family planning; those couples are also excluded from Communion.

I sometimes couldn't help but wonder why my Episcopal friends and colleagues of other denominations were so free to be priests and have their own families. They took great pleasure in spreading God's word, but also had the sanctuary and joy of life with a wife and children. Love between two people—physical as well as emotional—is the most human of all experiences. What else defines us as truly human and unique in creation, if not love?

Yet many Roman Catholics still accept the idea that a priest should be celibate without giving the issue much real thought. Ironically, many of those who publicly agree with celibacy will also tell you they wouldn't want their sons to be priests. They want priests, but they also want to have grandchildren of their own. So celibacy is okay for other folks, but not for people in their own family.

By now, I knew with great certainty that there

was a big difference between the external image of the Church and the reality of what happens on the inside among the clergy. However, I was still passionate about serving my God and my Church. I was struggling and asking questions; I was even sharing my opinions and disagreements with Roman Catholicism more openly with friends. Meanwhile, I kept reminding myself that I had been called, I had made a choice, and I had a duty to remain on this path.

Little did I suspect that I, too, was soon destined to make headlines as a "fallen" priest.

CHAPTER SEVEN

THE SECRET LIFE OF
A VERY PUBLIC PRIEST

Returning to St. Patrick's meant seeing Ruhama with more frequency again. We'd had less communication during my time in the faraway parish. I was convinced that our friendship could resume, especially now that I'd had so many new experiences, some of them not so pleasant. I remained determined to be a good priest, and I knew that she wanted that for me as well. Somehow I thought that maybe now I was a stronger priest and I could keep her away forever.

As soon as I saw her, I knew that I was wrong: I desired her no less than before. If anything, the attraction was stronger. I struggled not to feel what I felt and tried to keep distance between us, remaining so aloof at times that I later found out Ruhama often wondered why I was so cold toward her, when we had been friends before.

It was a struggle not to touch her or kiss her, but I was determined to conquer this foolish desire and to love her in every other way, and be a supportive part of her life. Despite this determination, Ruhama occupied my mind whenever I let thoughts of her creep in—which seemed to happen no matter how busy I was.

According to Roman Catholic moral theology, a man sins even if he has no physical contact with a woman but thinks about making love to her. The idea behind this is that rather than act on your "impure" or sexual feelings, you learn how to manage them before you become involved in an intimate relationship. Yet even entertaining those thoughts can be sinful.

I certainly had sinned by that definition. I made my periodic confession, explaining my emotional and physical desires to my confessor, and he was usually understanding and compassionate.

I will never forget the first time I confessed falling in love. You have to understand that my confessor lived very much in what I like to call "the box"—the Roman Catholic box. That box is very comfortable for most people, because everything in it is black-and-white—there are no grays, or even the suggestion that there *could* be grays.

Most priests live in that box. The Church hierarchy loves it, because it's the best way to control people. The reward for priests is that if you live in the box all your life, you usually go places, even though people will never really know what you think about anything personally. On the other hand, if you openly express dissenting opinions about persons, places, and things within the institution, you are out of the box and a threat to all.

My confessor lived in the box and was 100 percent faithful to it. The first time I told him that

I wanted to have an intimate relationship with Ruhama, he said, "Remember, Alberto, you will probably be asked to be a bishop one day, and you cannot be discovered in a situation like this."

That response was incredible and horrible. Here I was, dealing with this difficult struggle between my love for God and my love for a woman, and his only concern was that I keep my situation secret! His advice had nothing to do with my personal dilemma; it was all about whether my actions could make the institution look good or bad. I had no interest in Church politics or in climbing the Vatican's ladder of power. I became a priest because I wanted to evangelize and spread the Good News—that was my mission.

Confessing had become an ongoing frustration. I needed a different approach. After I had been back in the area for a few months, I decided that my chilly behavior toward Ruhama was useless. It wasn't doing either one of us any good. My feelings for this woman were going to be there regardless of how I tried to turn them off. That didn't mean I had to curb our friendship.

I worked up the courage to ask Ruhama to have dinner with me. She and I understood each other and the impossible situation we were in; I thought we should be able to sit down like two adults and have dinner, enjoying each other's company as friends. So I asked her to join me one night at a quiet restaurant where I knew the food was good and we would be unlikely to run into anyone we knew, because it was a particularly isolated place.

Even as I drove the car to the restaurant, I was extremely nervous. Ruhama and I had rarely been alone together, and I knew that putting myself in such close proximity to a woman I was so attracted to wasn't a sensible thing to do for a priest. I should have been throwing cold water on this relationship, not prolonging it. I knew all the right things, but my mind was in a real conflict with my emotions.

Not surprisingly, we were both a bit tense during dinner. We sat in a little corner as we shared a meal, and I was highly aware that this was the first time I had ever been with Ruhama without wearing my clerical collar. Other priests routinely donned street clothes to go out and about, but I was nearly always in uniform, mostly because I was always working.

We talked, but I had trouble paying attention to the conversation or even to the food we were eating. Despite the fact that we were at a restaurant outside of Miami Beach and it was unlikely that anyone would recognize us, I was almost consumed by the possibility that someone could see us. I worried, even though we weren't really doing anything wrong.

I kept reminding myself that lots of priests had women friends, and that there was nothing wrong with going out to have some fun. I'd been overworked for a long time and I needed to give myself permission to enjoy myself. At the same time, I still felt incredibly guilty for allowing myself to continue desiring this woman and acting freer than I was free to be. I was also very scared of my own emotions and reaching that point of no return.

As I drove Ruhama home, I couldn't help but say to myself, "Oh, my God, I'm alone with this woman I have dreamed about kissing for so long." I parked in front of her house and turned to her to say good night.

And then, just as it had always happened in my dreams, I leaned over to kiss her. That kiss was very strong, just the way she and I had both dreamed it would feel, confirming our special connection.

That was the moment my dilemma really began.

MY DESIRE FOR RUHAMA INTENSIFIED with that first passionate kiss. So did my dilemma. No matter what I did or thought to keep from desiring that fiery kiss to be repeated, and more, I had to ask myself this question: "Albert, how can you live without this woman, knowing that love has reached your life?"

Despite all I had been taught by the Church that these feelings were sinful for a priest to have, I knew that this love was so good that it must have come from God—the very same God I had been

171

serving all of my life. With that knowledge came a surprising sense of peace, even with the daily torment of trying to put distance between us.

"I love this woman." I longed to say these words aloud. To shout them out on the streets, even! The rules of the institution I had committed my life to prevented me from feeling this love, but how could I be a slave to such an institution, when this love was clearly so good and so pure?

Week after week, month after month, these questions roiled around in my mind. In the midst of all of the craziness of my life, despite my fifteen-hour workdays and my ongoing ideological evolution away from the Church, I was often deeply happy just thinking about Ruhama and our feelings for one another.

I had no desire to hurt the Church or to be a hypocrite by leading a double life. I knew of priests who lived that way and often wondered how they could live in peace. Yet I struggled: How was it possible that my Church was telling me that belonging to a woman and loving her in this wholehearted way meant that I loved the Church less? Many clergy in other denominations were married and raised families. Why couldn't I?

Because I was a Roman Catholic priest. And so Ruhama and I talked again about the impossibility of our situation and struggled to keep apart. I often told her, "This is an impossible relationship." We knew that what felt right according to our feelings was not considered right by the Church we'd both loved our whole lives, though in different ways.

Keeping away from each other was not easy. We managed only as much distance as we did, I think, because of the craziness of our lives—hers, as a single working mother with a son in elementary school, and mine as a priest who worked long days and nights to manage his parish and media ministries.

I kept my emotions in check with the usual priestly maneuvers: prayer, confession, exercise, parish work, and focusing on new ways to spread the word of God. I took comfort in times of deep personal prayer and silence. Yet I wanted Ruhama next to me every day, and to lie with me at night as my wife, but I knew that was impossible.

And so we saw each other in this way for a long time, sporadically pulling away and coming together again when we could stand our separations no longer. Ruhama wasn't the one with the impediment to our relationship; she had been married, but she had been divorced for many years. I was the impediment: My celibacy commitment was the only thing that stood in the way of us really being together.

More than once, I said to her, "You should find someone who is free to love you. This is impossible, no matter how much we love each other."

Ruhama would respond that it wasn't her choice to fall in love with a priest, but she couldn't help it, either. Sometimes I thought of us as this pair of magnets: When you put them together a certain way, you can make magnets slide apart. Turn them just a little bit toward each other, though, and the powerful attraction forces them to slide together again.

That's how it was with us. What was in our hearts was stronger than our willpower to face away from one another.

WHEN WE WERE TOGETHER, I did everything possible to love Ruhama while serving God. I saw her only once or twice a week, often for just a few minutes, but however I could, I tried to be a positive part of her life. She lived alone with her son, so we most often met at her home after he was in bed or when he was elsewhere. We would talk about whatever struggles she was having with friends, work, and parenting, and I'd try to give her the emotional support she needed.

Whenever we did venture out together, we would choose quiet restaurants, go to the movies, or take walks, generally meeting after dark and avoiding places where we might be seen. Even then, we acted as just friends when we were in public. We wanted to avoid the rumors that would surely spread through the parish if we were seen together.

Our lives were very different, of course—Ruhama was a shy, almost self-effacing single mother, while I was a relatively well-known Roman Catholic priest often in the public eye. From the outside it would have looked as though we lived in radically different worlds. As our love deepened, and our intimacy grew both emotionally and physically, however, our worlds began to come together as one.

Anytime I said to Ruhama, "I can't handle this anymore," she wouldn't hear of it.

"I know that you want to keep being a priest," she would say. "Ministry is your calling. This is what you were meant to do."

And so I kept on, leading the sort of double life I had seen so many priests live. I worried and often felt guilty, but I felt joyful, too. The relationship with Ruhama had rapidly become an oasis for me. She was right: I did love the Church and serving God. My spirit was good, my ministry and professional life were successful, and I still took great pleasure in preaching and guiding people through their struggles.

At the same time, I was acutely aware now that the one area of my life that had really been stifled was my emotional life. People relate to their priests and try to be supportive, but most of them do it only superficially. For most, a priest is a kind of "sacramental machine," almost like a spiritual ATM; once you dispense what they wanted, you're done. Parishioners feel free to stop by the filling station and get what they need, but then they go home and you go home.

As one experienced pastor told me, "Albert, ten percent of the people love you, ten percent of them hate you, and eighty percent don't really care who you are!" That is not far from the truth. After a couple of years, people can't even recall the name of the priest who had served them at one time or another. They will say, "Father . . . Honey, you remember that priest's name?" Often, priests can be in a parish for several years and deal with hundreds and hundreds of families, yet they get invited home for dinner by only two or three families a year.

Now I was learning that there is something wonderfully basic, even primal, in a man and a woman sharing a life together. I was slowly becoming a better human being, not just a better priest, by loving this woman and being loved by her.

IN MY HEART, I KNEW what choice I wanted to make in my life with Ruhama: I wanted to make this woman my wife! Why, then, did I struggle so? Why didn't I just leave the Roman Catholic Church to follow my heart's desire?

I have asked myself many times why I didn't move on sooner—though possibly not as many times as the media did later. Whenever I try to make sense of why things happened the way they did, I realize that the events unfolded in this way largely due to my desire to avoid disappointing so many people who counted on me to affirm the teachings of that black-and-white world they were so faithful to. I had represented the Church publicly for a very long time, and it's always difficult to leave your comfort zone and move on into unknown territory—even when you are convinced that it is the right thing for you to do.

There were days when I would actually kiss Ruhama and then almost immediately push her away, saying, "This is not right! I can't do this, no matter how much I want to!"

At the same time, I couldn't help but wonder if turning away true love was the real sin, since I felt so incomplete without her. I knew this emotional roller coaster hurt her as well, especially during all of those times when we couldn't see one another or celebrate birthdays and holidays together as a couple. Part of me wanted to be able to bring her everywhere I went and introduce her to everyone I knew, including all my very Roman Catholic friends, but I was too afraid. I knew that people would immediately notice our strong connection and mutual attraction. I wanted to protect Ruhama as much as I wanted to guard my own secret feelings, because I knew that, especially among Latinos, it is usually the woman who is blamed for distracting the priest from his calling.

Many times in my ministry, I had seen the destruction brought about to individuals and within families by infidelity. I knew what it did to marriages and the pain it caused those involved. I knew that if I left the Church for this woman, I would shake the faith and trust of many, many people. I couldn't make myself do that yet.

The longer Ruhama and I saw each other in secret, the larger and more powerful my dilemma became, feeding off of my secrecy. My mind and heart were by now completely disconnected. I tossed and turned at night and often felt as though my mind was spinning. There was no biblical or doctrinal foundation for this situation. At the same time, the Bible and Church doctrines loomed over me, making me feel guilty and causing me to mutter aloud, "I have to end this relationship right now."

All along, my mind continued to believe and transmit the "right" things I had learned growing up with the Church rules. As I had since boyhood, I still longed to be that exemplary priest who changes the world, but now my heart wasn't so sure that I was that priest. The most incomprehensible part of my conflicted internal struggle was that I was so strong and determined in my convictions about the Church and the disciplines I had accepted as a young man choosing a life of celibacy, yet I couldn't figure out how to make this forbidden relationship go away no matter how much I tried.

After I had spent many years listening to people with similar dilemmas regarding their love lives, now it was me—the priest—who had to come to grips with falling in love, even if that love was considered a mortal sin by my Church. Ironically, I didn't feel that I was sinning at all, because my love still felt like such a gift from God.

Words from the Book of Genesis—"It is not good for the man to be alone. I will make him a helpmate"—became all too real for me. On Saturday afternoons, as I stood before the altar celebrating weddings and hearing those couples repeat the words "In good times and in bad, in sickness and in health, for richer or poorer, all the days of our lives," I often fantasized about standing on the other side of the altar with Ruhama and what that would feel like.

"Why can't we do that?" I thought quietly to myself. "What is it about the priesthood that won't allow me to give my life to another human being, in an exclusive relationship and in the most loving and committed way?"

Again, I ran up against that easy, black-and-white answer: the rules of the Church. That was it. That was all that stood between me and my love.

AS A MEANS OF CONTROLLING my growing frustration, I threw myself into my work.

This was made easier when I was given a new parish in June 2005, a struggling small church called St. Francis de Sales. I would be this church's sole administrator, and there was much work to be done.

Once again, I was putting in fifteen hours a day between my work in the media and my new parish. I was convinced that this is what good priests did: Do God's work until you drop. Now, of course, I see that I was hiding from my own emotions in my three full-time jobs, not to mention all of the executive boards and advisory councils I had joined. I led an organized life, but it was often an inhumane one.

Many of my family members and friends complained. "Albert, we hardly get to see you anymore!" they said, but I claimed not to know what they were talking about.

I was running as fast as I could away from my dilemma, from Ruhama, and even from myself—while at the same time I was becoming increasingly entangled. It's not easy to make peace between your own desires and the call you are sure has come from God. I somehow lacked the ability to simply come out and say, "I need to move on." I was too afraid of the consequences—for us, for the people who believed in me, and for my Church. And fear always has a way of paralyzing us.

What was I afraid of? Besides worrying about

how I might hurt the people who knew me, I didn't want to contribute to the many scandals already plaguing the clergy. How could I allow myself to be the next one? For many Catholics, a scandal is a scandal, regardless of what's involved. Every violation of celibacy is somehow lumped into the same category of sin, with little regard for the circumstances involved.

Of course, it didn't help that I was this ultrapublic priest in the Latino community in the United States and throughout Latin America. We Latinos are very traditional. I felt real pressure not to go against those who expected "their" priest to be free of the normal earthly needs and wants experienced by other human beings.

Many priests I knew had hidden, long-term relationships. This path wasn't acceptable to me, despite the fact that I was already on that path. With varying degrees of guilt, I allowed this duplicity to continue in my own life without having the courage to say aloud what my heart was saying with every beat: "I'm in love with a woman, and I must therefore abandon my ministry as a celibate priest in the Roman Catholic Church."

The stress of hiding my secret took its toll. Several weeks before my relationship with Ruhama was discovered by the media, I was sitting in my office at the radio station. I had celebrated the morning Mass at my parish earlier that morning, as always, and I had just finished the morning news commentary.

As I sat there, mulling over the endless list of tasks I had to complete that day, one of the cohosts came into my office and said, "Father Albert, I must tell you something."

This was the most senior member of my team, and I knew him well. I understood from the solemn expression on his face that whatever he wanted to tell me was serious. I suddenly felt nervous on his behalf. What was this man going through that I didn't know?

"Yes?" I asked. "What is it?"

He took a deep breath, then plunged right in. "I have been listening to you on this program for a long time, Father," he said, "and I can tell that you are dissatisfied with your life right now. As someone much older than you are, I recommend that you make whatever difficult decision you need to make and move on. Don't look back. You are young, and you still have time. Do whatever it is you have to do and be happy."

"Thank you for being so honest," I said, and acknowledged that I was indeed going through a deep personal struggle that I was in the process of resolving. He nodded, wished me well, and left.

I sat for a few more minutes at my desk, absorbing his words. I was shocked by this man's clarity and wisdom. He had been able to read my heart and soul as easily as if I had confessed my dilemma to him.

For the first time, I realized that the secret I thought was so safely hidden inside me was beginning to surface whether I wanted it to or not.

ONE OF THE FINAL OUTWARD signs of my inner struggle occurred during the annual celebration of Holy Week about a month before the scandal became public. There are several important services associated with Holy Week, since these are Christian High Holy Days. One has to do directly with the priesthood and the renewal of priestly promises. We call it "the Chrism Eucharist," because chrism is one of the sacramental oils blessed by the bishop to be used throughout the year in celebrating the sacraments.

I had already been in conversation with one bishop and several priests in the Episcopal Church about my ideological struggles without confessing the details of my situation. This Holy Week, I received a number of invitations to the Chrism Mass at Trinity Episcopal Cathedral in Miami. I was immediately conflicted, because this Mass was being held on the same day at precisely the same time as the Chrism Mass at St. Mary's Roman Catholic Cathedral, just a few minutes' drive from Trinity.

As a Roman Catholic priest, naturally I was expected to be at the Chrism Mass for this yearly celebration with all of the other priests. This time, however, I deliberately chose to attend the Episcopal version of that same Mass, which included a clergy conference with priests *and* their spouses.

You can imagine how different that was for me. I found it refreshing to see; in fact, even though this was the first time in twenty-two years that I did not attend Chrism Mass at the Roman Catholic cathedral, I felt right at home with the Episcopal liturgy, the beautiful organ music, and the atmosphere; it felt as if I'd belonged there for a long time.

When Bishop Leo Frade saw me walk into Trinity Cathedral that day dressed in my black clergy suit, he didn't look surprised. Besides the fact that we had always shared a good relationship as members of the ecumenical community and in our common work in the media, I knew that Bishop Frade understood some of my ideological struggles; even if he didn't know of my exact personal dilemma, he had always shown a great deal of compassion toward me. Also, a bishop and a priest in our diocese had already told him that I was pretty close to making the transition. I am sure he was aware of my dilemma.

The bishop introduced me to several of his priests, especially some of those who had formerly served as Roman Catholic clergy; one of them had even attended the same seminary I had graduated from. As I heard their stories, I felt a stab of recognition; it was like listening to myself and what I was going through, over and over again.

It wasn't easy to admit, even after all I'd been through to this point, but I felt more comfortable ideologically with them than with many of my colleagues. I also felt at home within the walls of Trinity Cathedral and with the Mass itself, since the basic worship and sacramental rites of the Episcopal (Anglican) Church are actually very close to those of the Roman Catholic Church I had served for most of my life.

The next step had to be mine. I had to change my direction and finally make the decision to move on as a man and a priest who would be free to serve God, while at the same time having a wife and family. Why, then, did I still feel so afraid to make that move?

Ironically, none of my brother priests from the Roman Catholic Church ever called to ask why I was not at their Chrism Mass. While that saddened me, I was also relieved. I had no idea what I would have told them if they'd asked where I had been. I still didn't feel ready to talk about my ideological struggles with anyone in the Roman Church, and only my confessor and a few friends in the clergy were aware of my inclinations toward Anglicanism. I used to say to my staff at the parish and at the radio station,

"Don't be surprised when I become Episcopal!" But they were convinced I was joking.

You would think that being in such a restrictive situation would eventually have ended or frustrated the great love that Ruhama and I felt for one another. Try to imagine what it's like to be in a situation where even your own family and closest friends cannot know that you are in love, when all you want to do is tell the whole world!

Yet our love never diminished. On the contrary, our love continued to grow. Ruhama and I both suffered. We both hurt one another with all the secrecy. Yet we never allowed the difficulties of our impossible relationship to get in the way of the deep love we felt for each other. Being in this situation and having to hide it for so long required a great deal of patience and resignation. But, in my heart, I had always felt sure that the future was totally in God's hands.

As time passed, once again this proved to be true.

CHAPTER EIGHT

A SUNNY DAY AT THE BEACH: THE DAY MY SECRET WAS DISCOVERED

Ruhama and I always chose quiet, isolated places to be together. One sunny morning, we decided to go to a quiet beach to celebrate a belated Valentine's Day. We had both been working hard, and we were looking forward to having a quiet morning to ourselves just to read and relax in the sun. This wasn't the first time Ruhama and I had ever been to the beach, but it was the first time we had ever chosen one less than five miles from my parish. Neither of us was particularly worried about being discovered, however, since this beach wasn't easily accessible from the street. Besides, it was February in Miami, and Florida natives think anything below seventy degrees is too cold for the beach. When it gets down to the sixties, as it was this morning, almost everyone puts on sweaters, as if snow is going to start falling any second. As a matter of fact, whenever it gets a little cold, someone is bound to say, "Remember when it snowed in Miami?" They are referring to the only time anyone remembers that happening, in the winter of 1977.

In any case, it was wonderful to be alone. It happened so rarely; even when I visited Ruhama at her home, we were always worried that

Christian, now a young teenager, might discover our secret. As far as he and everyone else were concerned, his mother and I were just good friends.

We loved feeling free to do what all people in love do when they go to the beach: We walked, we talked, we kissed, we caressed. Most of all, we felt the blessing of the warm sun on our skin and thoroughly enjoyed that moment of being together.

Suddenly, however, Ruhama went rigid against me. "Alberto," she whispered, "I think that woman over there is photographing us."

Startled, we quickly separated and pretended that we were just there to read our books, though we had been cuddling and holding each other just moments before.

After a few seconds, I glanced over my shoulder and was shocked to see that there was, indeed, a woman videotaping us from about a hundred feet away. She had hidden her large video camera under a towel while pointing the lens at us and looking the other way.

A thousand thoughts went through my mind at that moment. There was only a handful of people on the beach, all of them a good distance away from us. Yet now it seemed as if a thousand pairs of eyes were on us.

Even though I had worked in media for so long, my first reaction was to wonder who would be doing this, and for what reason. I was rarely the object of any paparazzi, even though I was familiar with some of them.

"Go over there," Ruhama insisted. "Take the camera away from her!"

I wasn't about to do any such thing. I knew that if this woman really was here to film us, it would only make things worse if she caught a confrontation on camera. After avoiding violence on television all those years, I wasn't about to create some of it now.

After a few minutes, I glanced over my shoulder again and saw that the woman was still videotaping us, while pretending to look the other way. After the initial shock and feelings of violation, fear was starting to settle in the pit of my stomach.

I picked up my cell phone and called Emilio Estefan. If this person was part of the Miami paparazzi, he would know. Emilio and Gloria had been my friends for years, yet knew nothing about Ruhama. I had no choice now but to tell him.

"I'm here at the beach with a female friend," I told him in a low voice, "and someone is taping us." I cleared my throat and added, "This woman is someone I love. She is my girlfriend."

Emilio, bless him, seemed not at all scandalized. "Don't worry, Father. I'm glad you're in love. There is nothing wrong with that. Everything will be fine. Describe that camera person and let's see if I can figure out who it is."

I took another glance at the woman with the camera and described her. "That's not anyone I know," Emilio reassured me. "Maybe she's there taping the beach for publicity or a tourism brochure. Try not to worry too much about it. It may be nothing. Meanwhile, I'll see if I can find out who she is."

Ruhama and I gathered our things and left the beach. I wanted to believe my friend's words, but I suspected that something was up. Earlier that week, I had noticed mysterious cars parked near my parish here and there; had someone been following me?

Now I was really feeling paranoid. "Why was that woman taping us?" I kept wondering.

For the first time, I was aware that my secret relationship with Ruhama might become public before I could admit it to my family, friends, and community, as I had been planning, even longing, to do. What if my internal dilemma was going to be revealed before I was ready?

I wanted very much, still, to be a priest. I knew that. I wanted to serve God with all of my heart and soul, though I was having a lot of ideological issues with the Church. But I also very much felt called to be a married man, even a family man. I was a priest in love and contemplating marriage; I no longer believed the two things to be incompatible as I had been taught. Now I worried that I might not have any control over how the world found out about my intense personal struggle. Had God grown impatient, waiting for me to make the right decision and come clean? Was He about to take matters out of my hands? At that moment, my mind was filled with all kinds of conflicting thoughts and I knew my internal dilemma was soon to become public.

Throughout the following hours and days, the stress was immense. But I continued to bottle it inside, thinking that I still had so many things to take care of before making an official and final break from the Church I was born into. The only person who really knew the entire situation I was struggling with was my priest confessor, who like all confessors had a sacramental seal and a sacred promise that could not be broken under any circumstances until death.

My greatest worry was how this would hurt the people I loved and had served for so many years. My family, my parishioners, and the members of my community had absolutely no idea that I was in love with a woman. How would they all react?

Day after day, nothing happened. Finally I began to relax a little bit. I remembered Emilio's words to me that day: "Don't worry about it, Father," Emilio had said. "Nobody ever publishes celebrity photos without calling the celebrity up first to tell him that the images will be published."

Almost three months went by before the images finally appeared. Hindsight is twenty-twenty; now I think with regret of all of the missed opportunities I had during that time to announce my desire to marry and move on as an Episcopal priest. I could have said something from the pulpit, on air at the radio station, on television at the live TV Mass, or even by calling a press conference. For so long, I had thought hard about all of the ways I might take that critical step of letting the world know that I was no longer able to live within the many ideological constraints of the Roman Catholic Church—especially those that had so much to do with Church policies or disciplines and so little to do with biblical principles.

I was in agony, knowing that I should do the right thing and be honest, but the words seemed to stick in my throat. I was still too afraid of the effect such a move would have on everyone who relied on me or looked up to me. I didn't want to quit the Roman Catholic Church without preparing my family and my parish community. I was at peace with God, but not with my Church. Emotionally speaking, I was still deeply attached, despite the e-mails and correspondence I had been sending to priest friends complaining about Church politics and practices for the past four years or so (mostly former Roman Catholic priests in Latin America and others locally who had previously made a similar move and were now Episcopal priests). Once again, I felt frozen in place, hoping that the photographer wouldn't find anywhere to publish those pictures; in fact, I still wanted to believe she was not really there taking pictures of me, but of the scenery of the sand and ocean.

As the weeks went by, I slowly began to put the photographer out of my mind. Maybe I could do things my own way after all. But what was the right time?

ABOUT THREE MONTHS AFTER the incident on the beach, I noticed a bunch of photographers outside of St. Francis de Sales, where I had just finished celebrating the Sunday Mass. I didn't think much of it at the time; I was accustomed to entertainment people showing up at my church. With them came the obligatory paparazzi to camp out near the church steps to photograph celebrities. I was usually very cordial to them, because I maintained an open-door policy at my church and welcomed everyone.

The only unusual thing about this particular Sunday was the sheer volume of photographers; I had never seen so many. That and the fact that one of them actually came into the church with the camera. He said only that he was a visiting photographer from a Chilean media outlet as he asked me some questions in my office before disappearing again. I didn't give him a second thought.

It wasn't until Tuesday evening, as I was in St. Augustine visiting a priest friend, that I got the phone call I had been dreading. The call was from a reporter, saying that compromising photographs of me with a woman on a beach were about to be published in a Mexican tabloid.

My heart dropped to my feet. "Good Lord," I thought. I was shocked!

The reporter proceeded to inform me that this would be a big story and asked if I had anything to say. I immediately told her that I was in love and that I was in the process of making a transition in my life and ministry. I told her that I was thinking of moving on from the Roman Catholic Church for a variety of reasons, one of them marriage.

It wasn't until after hanging up the phone that I wondered if I'd said too much. Many other questions were racing through my mind as well: *How can I keep Ruhama's identity a secret? How will I tell my family? How will the community react—a community that I have tried to love, serve, and set a good example for over many years?*

Officials from the magazine confirmed by telephone that night that the magazine was already being published in Mexico and that it would reach the United States later in the week. This prompted me to start making phone calls immediately. I had to act fast, especially to try to protect the people I loved.

I first called Ruhama and told her the news. I could hear in her voice that she was scared. "What will happen now?" she asked.

For her sake, I put on a tone of tranquillity. "Everything will be fine," I said. "Just pray for us."

I was sure that she really had no idea how much fuss and controversy this would cause. I prayed—foolishly, knowing how the media works—that nobody would discover Ruhama's identity or address. Ruhama was a shy, very private person. She had never dealt with the media and the effects of being recognized in public. I hated knowing that because of my own fearful hesitation, she would now fall under great scrutiny and possibly get hurt. Some people would go out of their way to be cruel and vicious. Unfortunately, I was right.

What could I do to support her? I wondered. How do you prepare someone you love to be constantly followed and harassed by paparazzi? How would she deal with becoming a public figure after being so utterly private all of her life? I was also very concerned for her son, Christian. I didn't want him to have to face public scrutiny and possible harassment of any type.

The second person I called was my older sister, because I was concerned about my mother hearing about me on the news. I asked her to go and speak to our mother in person.

As I was to learn over and over again, even in the midst of shock and crisis, there can be rays of light. When I explained my dilemma, my sister said, "Albert, don't worry. I'm sure everything will be fine. Everyone deserves to love and to be loved."

You can't imagine how much comfort those words brought me, as my big sister conveyed love for her kid brother in the midst of an extremely painful situation. Both my sisters and my mother were understanding and supportive.

That same night, I received a phone call from my station manager at the Church's radio stations, where I served as president and director. He notified me that the pictures were already circulating on the Internet and that the staff at the radio station was praying for me. I thanked him and told him to take care of the station.

At that moment I realized that the phone call from the reporter wasn't actually a heads-up at all but a call to let me know that the pictures were already out. I got online and looked at them immediately. There were only a couple of teaser photos—the rest would be revealed in the magazine—but they were clear enough to see that it was me on that beach with a woman.

It was time for me to face up to contacting Church officials. The first person I reached was the communications director and spokesperson for the archbishop. Thankfully, her immediate reaction was one of complete understanding. She didn't appear to be shocked at all, and she went out of her way to be compassionate.

"Albert," she said, "I'm going to speak as your friend, and not as the Church spokesperson for a moment. If you are in love, that is a good thing. Not too many people find real love in their lives."

The communications director suggested that I telephone the archbishop early the following morning, but I wanted to see him in person. I was given an appointment later in the afternoon the following day—several hours after the archbishop had already composed his official statement, speaking of the terrible "scandal" I had caused. It read as follows:

STATEMENT FROM MIAMI ARCHBISHOP JOHN C. FAVALORA

May 5th, 2009

I am deeply saddened by the news surrounding Father Alberto Cutié. I apologize on behalf of the Church in Miami to the parishioners of Saint Francis de Sales Parish, where he serves as administrator, to the listeners and supporters of Radio Paz and Radio Peace, and to the entire Archdiocese.

Father Cutié made a promise of celibacy and all priests are expected to fulfill that promise with the help of God.

Father Cutié's actions cannot be condoned despite the good works he has done as a priest. I ask for everyone's prayers at this time. Scandals such as this offer an occasion for the Church on all levels to examine our consciences regarding the integrity of our commitments to the Lord and to His Church.

Seeing this, I couldn't help but compare the words and tone in his statement with other statements written about priests involved in various forms of criminal sexual activity. There was no difference! I worked in media and paid attention to the contents of press releases and official statements; I'd never heard him "apologize on behalf of the Church of Miami" for the truly criminal, outrageous, and blatantly immoral behavior of so many priests in the past. At first I felt hurt and angry, especially because the archbishop had written this statement even before taking the time to speak with me in person.

I met with him the next afternoon after his statement had been released to the media.

"The woman in these pictures is the woman I love," I stated clearly.

The archbishop made absolutely no response to this. Instead, he asked, "What are you going to do now? Will anybody want to take you after this?" He meant he thought no other bishop, diocese, or local pastor would want me to work in the Roman Catholic Church again, because of the "seriousness" of this scandal.

In the midst of the shock I was personally experiencing that day, I was doubly shocked at the archbishop's cold and totally rigid approach to the very difficult situation at hand. Yet I remained calm. I lowered my head and apologized several times for the way my actions might have hurt him and the Church community at large. I really had no chance to express what I was thinking, feeling, or planning to do next.

"I will give you the same advice that I have always given to priests and married men who have had trouble with women," the archbishop said. "Cut off this situation and honor your public commitment."

The archbishop never asked if I was contemplating marriage or if there was anything the Church could do to help. Nor did he voice any personal concern for me or my family.

Needless to say, the archbishop's advice was simply not an option for me. How was I supposed to "cut off" the woman I loved?

"I want to request a leave of absence," I said, "so I can think about things for a few days."

"You can request that in writing," the archbishop said.

The entire conversation lasted a total of nineteen minutes.

AS I LEFT THE OFFICE that afternoon, it was very clear to me that my former boss—the person who had ordained me to the priesthood—didn't want to deal with me or with the issue at hand. When I wondered why, one priest friend told me that the reason was obvious: "Your actions embarrassed him too much."

Possibly. Yet when a priest in the middle of a crisis goes to see his bishop, shouldn't he be able to expect a certain degree of personal concern and compassion, no matter how awkward the situation may be?

I knew other priests who had committed actual crimes, or were accused of truly outrageous behavior involving minors, who had claimed that the archbishop treated them well and embraced them. Some of these priests had been involved with several minors years ago and continued ministering until the day their lawsuits were presented to the Church. Ironically, those priests perceived him as "paternal," a term often used in the Church to describe a bishop who actually carries out his role as spiritual father.

This wasn't my experience at all and I couldn't understand it. Even today, I don't know if the archbishop's harsh attitude toward me was due to the fame and recognition of my media work or to something else that I'll never understand for as long as I live. While I had seen so many other priests mistreated and undermined, I had thought things would somehow be different in my case.

I had worked hard on behalf of the Church and made them look good for so long, and in many ugly situations. The least I expected from the archbishop was a forgiving word and some degree of compassion or understanding. I was saddened and disappointed by our encounter. I have known priests, bishops, cardinals, and many people who work closely with the pope, yet I had never met anyone in the Church hierarchy who appeared as disconnected and uninterested in my life as my own bishop; this was just one more confirmation of the personal impression I'd had for so long.

Years earlier, I'd composed a letter in which I described some of my many disappointments with the Church. I never ended up sending this letter to the archbishop; what would be the point? He was never going to change or even respond.

Here is part of what I wrote to express my disappointment:

The spiritual fatherhood of a bishop, which is so often presented in the Church's documents, was something I experienced through other bishops, but not from you personally. I saw this "spiritual paternity" in action in Latin America and, in some very limited cases, in the United States. I was blessed to know cardinals and bishops all over Latin America, and several I admire for their dedication to Christ in very difficult situations. I saw them affirm their priests, support their efforts to evangelize, and personally care for them when problems arose. In the case of my bishop—you—I never once received any indication that you understood the complex nature of my work or even noticed that I carried it out with fidelity and great dedication to the Church.

I was the first priest you ordained as archbishop of Miami and you sent me to my first parish. You sent me to a sick pastor. He was a great man, but nevertheless, he needed taking care of, and I did that. I tried to make him look good on every occasion. When he could not get up or make a meeting, I stood in. He was my brother priest, and a great human being; how could I do anything else? Yet you never received a complaint from me, or a request for a change of assignments, which is so common among young priests. I was there for three years (the maximum time for a first assignment in your tenure) and always faithful to my work.

I went to my second parish, where the pastor was a member of your Curia. He would leave the parish every morning and say, "I am going to work." He thought he was not working while he was in his parish; he was only really "working" in the office at the Chancery, where he handled money matters very effectively. As a matter of fact, he was such an aggressive fund-raiser that I had to meet with parishioners on several occasions to reassure them he really did love God more than money. In his heart he knew he was not pastoral and that pastoral things did not interest him. When I was named pastor of the parish down the road, which he knew was in terrible shape, he never offered me a dime to paint a wall or fix a broken pew. The former pastor of that same parish, which you removed, had several dozen ministries and services going strong when he was abruptly reassigned. The pastor you appointed managed to destroy almost every ministry in a matter of months. When I arrived, I worked hard to start youth programs; I also taught adult classes in addition to teaching at the elementary school and at a local inner-city high school you asked me to teach at. Even that "teaching project for young priests" disappeared after a few years, because young priests were "exhausted" from saying one or two Masses a day in their parishes. The work ethic among priests in your diocese is deplorable. How many put in even forty hours a week? Not many.

I never had the luxury of sitting around. While I was at St. Patrick's, I was asked to host a television program on international Spanish television. One of your auxiliary bishops gave the names of several priests as possible hosts for the program. They called me and I did not call back, not because I was being rude, but because I was very involved in parish work, teaching, and happy being a parish priest. I did not want to involve myself in anything else. But one day the auxiliary bishop saw me and said, "Albert, call them back. I gave them your name." As a result of that conversation, I decided to call. I was chosen to host the program by a group of television executives who had absolutely no understanding of the inner workings of the Church. I told them three things:

1. I have to pray and talk to God about it.

2. I have to see my spiritual director and a couple of priests whom I consider mentors.

3. I have to ask permission and get approval from my archbishop.

Immediately, these executives looked at each other and said to me, "Father, we have interviewed hundreds of priests in several states, and even in Mexico, and nobody has told us that." They were shocked that a priest had to ask for permission or even consult with his spiritual director. That is the type of priest I have always been.

I went to see my pastor, who was one of your close collaborators in the Curia at the time, and he said, "You have to make sure you see him when he is in a good mood." And he added, "Albert, this will change your path in the Church."

I naively asked, "Monsignor, what path?"

He was speaking about possibly studying in Rome or pursuing higher studies in order to later pursue other positions in the Church. I told him, "Monsignor, I became a priest to evangelize and evangelization is the only position I seek in the Church."

He nodded with a smirk on his face and asked me to send a letter to you. I then wrote a letter explaining everything—in detail—and you granted me an appointment. The archdiocesan lawyers reviewed the contract and you asked that I not work more than two to three days a week in television, so that I could continue parish work—which I was happy to accept, since I always wanted to be a parish priest. You gave me your blessing, which I appreciated, and I began working in the media.

When I started in television, I tried calling your personal priest secretary weeks in advance to ask you to come for a five-minute blessing of the studios where the first talk show conducted by a Roman Catholic priest on the entire continent was to be taped. The studios were only a ten-minute ride from your office. Yet your secretary informed me that one of the auxiliary bishops would be sent. Several priests who attended that day asked, "Why isn't the archbishop here?"

I said, "I am sure he was busy with something else." The looks on their faces indicated that they were not convinced. They understood, perhaps better than I did, that you were simply not interested.

This letter, which I never sent and sounds like a real griping session, summarizes how I felt that day: I could no longer stay loyal to an institution that promoted people who treated their hardest workers and colleagues so indifferently. The archbishop's way of relating toward me, and his overall arrogance toward the community I served and loved, had been a turnoff for years. Yet it wasn't until this very day that I had become truly aware of how disappointed I was in him as a spiritual leader and father.

This man had been entrusted to be the spiritual overseer of well over a million people in our community. Yet he often described South Florida as a "circus." Whatever community issues or controversies he couldn't comprehend, he simply dismissed. It was as if he never understood that when you are in charge of guiding a community, that community becomes *your* circus. You can't ignore it, or the tents will catch fire and the elephants will stampede.

A GROUP OF PRIEST FRIENDS who had been waiting for me at a nearby rectory expressed surprise by the brevity of my meeting with the archbishop that day. Since the news about the photos had already broken, as I arrived I found them channel surfing on the big television in the rectory living room. Every newscast, it seemed, had obtained those photographs of the priest on the beach with the "unidentified woman." For many, it ran as the top story.

To see myself with Ruhama on the news like that, with our private life so exposed, was very awkward at first. My family was always united and loving, but I never appreciated their support more than I did in those first hours and in the coming weeks and months. Even as one of my dear cousins was losing her battle with breast cancer, in the midst of this very emotional time, my entire family found the energy to rally around Ruhama and me with tremendous love and compassion. A number of good friends also demonstrated unconditional support and understanding, which was a real gift.

The flip side is that some of the people we considered our closest friends also disappointed us because of their harsh judgments, lack of compassion or inability to accept what was happening. I suppose there are always people whom you trust and think you can count on, only to see them turn away from you or hear of them talking behind your back instead.

Throughout the first week following the scandal, I received phone calls from a cardinal and other friends associated with the Vatican. Their main concern was that I not "abandon" the Roman Catholic Church.

"Albert," one cardinal suggested, "you can be laicized immediately. Just don't leave."

To be laicized means that you retain good standing within the Church, but you cannot continue serving as a priest. Thousands and thousands of men have gone through that process in order to be allowed to marry in the Church and continue within the Roman Catholic tradition, accepting the condition that they never work as priests again. In other words, they are priests who are taken out of the game and put on the bench—the pews—where they must act as if they were never ordained or had no call from God to minister. Some also waited years and years, dealing with the Vatican bureaucracy, for this to happen.

I considered that option to be truly hypocritical and absurd in my case. I was insulted that anyone would even suggest such a thing, especially after seeing the corrupt secrecy over the sexual abuse of minors, and the fact that so many of those priests were never laicized and would be buried as full-fledged priests one day. In other words, those men keep the privilege of being officially recognized as priests until the day they die.

I didn't even like the terminology: To be laicized means being reduced to a lay state. I do not believe that human beings can be "reduced"! Someone who is ordained is not above anyone else. We are all equally children of God. Why should a person get "reduced" to the lay state? I wasn't about to continue playing that Roman clerical game.

Still, the reactions of these Church officials didn't surprise me. They were in the box and I was no longer ideologically there. In addition, I got caught and admitted my love publicly. It wouldn't have mattered to them if I'd had a secret lover—many priests did, and even fathered children out of wedlock, yet the hierarchy overlooked those indiscretions and even promoted some of these men to positions of prestige. It was really the fact that I was now being open about it that they couldn't tolerate.

After the pictures of Ruhama and me were published, I received countless letters, e-mails, and notes from priests of all ages and in various parts of the world. "Albert," many of them wrote, "the only difference between you and me is that you got caught."

Even within my own community, there were a couple of priests who had been given the honorary title monsignor (a priest that dresses in a bishop's outfit, but is still just a priest) who were known to have girlfriends for years. In the Roman Catholic Church, a scandal is not really a scandal until it becomes public. Even if people in positions of authority know what's going on, it's only a real problem if the image of the Church is tarnished when it becomes public. The image of the institution must be guarded at all costs—not the integrity or dignity of the individuals involved.

I had a friend who worked in the Vatican for many years and told me of the day he was assisting an old cardinal from Africa during his visit to the pope. This happened in the latter years of Pope John Paul II's papacy, when he had many physical limitations, including difficulties speaking.

The pope was sitting in his chair in the middle of St. Peter's Square, giving a talk on the importance of celibacy in the life of a priest. The cardinal, who had only functional knowledge of Italian, asked my priest buddy, "Is the pope talking about celibacy?"

"Yes, Your Eminence," my friend replied.

"Is the pope saying that priests should observe celibacy?"

Again my friend replied, "Yes, Your Eminence."

The cardinal sighed then. "If only the Holy Father knew that my wish is only that my priests keep one woman and not five."

In my case, the international media attention was an embarrassment beyond what Church leaders could handle or learn to forgive. There was no sexual abuse, no minor involved, no illegal activity. There was no lawsuit that needed to be settled. It was simply a man and a woman who fell in love: two single, consenting adults. The only scandal was that I was supposed to be celibate.

One of my brother priests was grilled on a talk show a few days after my scandal hit the headlines. He said something that really summarizes how the institution deals with these problems: "The Church is the only army that shoots its own when they are down."

I can assure you that we have had plenty of fallen soldiers—priests and religious who have dedicated their lives to service with great dedication. Many of them never really recover from the treatment by those in powerful positions in the organization that is supposed to be an instrument of God's mercy.

LIFE IS FILLED WITH MISSED opportunities. The reaction by Church authorities in my particular case could have been a teaching moment regarding the real struggle that celibacy poses for most priests, rather than focusing on my "fall from grace" as an example of what *not* to do and playing it like the biggest scandal around. A statement by the Church following these tabloid photographs recognizing the humanity of priests, and emphasizing that we all sometimes fall short of our commitments, could have helped the Church come across as an organization committed to healing all who go astray, including its own priests who continue living double lives. But that's certainly not what happened.

Those whom I'd call hard-core Roman

Catholics expressed feelings of betrayal, confusion, and even a good dose of anger. I knew this would happen. I even knew most of the people who would react that way, including those who had often received the most flexibility from me in their desire to get close to a Church that did not always receive them well. Looking back now, I suppose I can understand their reaction, since to them this event was shocking and unexpected, whereas I had been struggling with my feelings internally for a long time.

At the same time, more progressive members of the community wondered why it was necessary for me to leave the Church. They had no problem with a priest having a hidden girlfriend and continuing his ministry. I was surprised when several people suggested that as a possibility: staying as I was and continuing to lead a double life.

But there was also great support from other quarters, some of it unexpected. Many celebrities and fellow television personalities went out of their way to express their friendship and to speak well of me and my work. A great number of pastors, rabbis, and people from other religious traditions showed me unconditional support, compassion, and understanding. For this, I was grateful.

My mother, too, found support. I was expected to attend the 2009 Mothers of the Year Award

Luncheon at Jungle Island, hosted by the Cuban-American National Council, to see my mother honored by that group. I was afraid to attend the event for fear that my new notoriety might mar this wonderful day for my mother, who truly showed me what it was like to love God, so I sent a letter for the news anchor serving as mistress of ceremonies to read, saying, "My mother is the most spectacular person in the world."

My mother was one of ten women being honored at that event, but she was the only one to receive a standing ovation—a sign of support for her, and for me as well.

Ultimately, I realized that everyone has an opinion about your life and how you should live it. Those opinions will bounce between one extreme and another, hitting every possible point in the middle. And when it comes to the lives of priests, everyone seems to have a variety of informed—and even more so, uninformed—opinions!

Clearly, it was time for me to get away, to retreat in near solitude so I could contemplate beginning a new way of life and a totally new way of serving God. This was a real turning point in my life as a man and as a priest. I needed to take advantage of it. In my heart it was clear that the time really had come for me to move on.

At my baptism surrounded by my parents, aunts, uncles, and cousins—a few weeks after my birth at San Luis Rey Roman Catholic Church in San Juan (Puerto Rico), summer 1969. I consider being baptized my greatest honor.

Alberto Ricardo Cutié Boyé at one year old. My wife loves this picture.

With my dad when I was almost two. My dad's 1969 VW Bug, which later became my first car when I was sixteen, is right behind me.

Albert as a Boy Scout when he was ten years old.

First Communion at the age of seven—in front of the altar at my home parish where I grew up, where I was confirmed, and where I celebrated my first Mass as a priest—St. Timothy's in Miami.

DJ Albert at fourteen, playing under the Florida sun at a school function.

My family, just before my dad was diagnosed with terminal cancer: (from left to right) Alberto, Albert, Alina, Yoly, and Yolanda—spring 1991.

Parochial Vicar (Assistant) at St. Clement's in Fort Lauderdale, my first assignment. May 1995.

Greeting the schoolkids just a few days after my ordination to the priesthood in May 1995 at the parish of my deacon internship—Saint Mary Star of the Sea in Key West, Florida.

Performing a baptism on my first year anniversary as a priest—May 1996.

A moment of prayer at the Spanish Mass: children gathered around the altar for the *Padre Nuestro* (Our Father) at St. Clement's Church in May 1998. This day we were welcoming the new priest, who is standing to my left. The community was mostly made up of new immigrant families from Mexico, Central America, and the Caribbean.

Conducting the talk show during *Padre Alberto*'s first season—consoling a suffering mother on the set.

On the front steps of the church, at the Mass for Celia Cruz's funeral in Miami, surrounded by clergy and wondering what we would do with the huge crowd of people gathered on the streets. *Courtesy of the Celia Cruz Estate.*

Preaching at St. Francis de Sales (Priest-in-charge from 2005 to 2009). This was a beautiful small parish in the middle of the noise and activity of South Beach, a popular tourist and party town.

Speaking to a missionary bishop in Latin America, during one of my final visits to the Vatican as a Roman Catholic priest—on the main street that leads to St. Peter's, the famous Via della Conciliazione right in front of an ancient papal residence.

(From left to right) Bishop Onell Soto (retired bishop of Venezuela), Diana Frade (my bishop's wife), Ruhama, me, and Bishop Leo Frade (Bishop of Southeast Florida).

At a yearly ecumenical service praying for the unity of Christians: (from left to right) Reverend Guillermo Revuelta (Presbyterian), Reverend Pablo Miret (Baptist), Reverend Alberto Cutié (Roman Catholic), and Reverend Rafael Garcia (Episcopal). Three of the four are now former Roman Catholics. At that service, I told the Episcopal priest on my left, "Pray for me, because I think I will be joining you soon." January 2009.

(From left to right) Christian, Ruhama, Albert, and my mother-in-law, Judith, on the day I officially asked for Ruhama's hand in marriage.

Ruhama and I after receiving Holy Communion as husband and wife.
Courtesy of Danilo J. Fajardo, Photography by Danilo, Inc.

With our mothers, brothers, and sisters on our wedding day—Ancient Spanish Monastery St. Bernard of Clairvaux, June 26, 2009. *Courtesy of Danilo J. Fajardo, Photography by Danilo, Inc.*

With my dear friends (from left to right) Javier Cruz, Willy Delgado, Alfred Meneses, who are surrounding Christian and me. These are the guys who were my DJ partners. They supported my desire to serve God when I told them as a teenager I wanted to be a priest, and they remained my dearest friends through it all. Our wedding would not have been possible without their generosity and support. *Courtesy of Danilo J. Fajardo, Photography by Danilo, Inc.*

Our wedding day: Ruhama and I before the altar of the Spanish Monastery—a place like us. That historic building started out Roman Catholic and became Episcopal (Anglican) when it was brought in pieces from Spain. *Courtesy of Danilo J. Fajardo, Photography by Danilo, Inc.*

Albert and Ruhama in Athens during our honeymoon.

Ruhama returns to the tomb of St. Nektarios to fulfill her "*promesa*" that she would come back with her husband. During our honeymoon in 2009.

Albert and Ruhama (honeymoon) on the island of Mykonos.

Albert and Ruhama (honeymoon) on the island of Santorini.

Ruhama visiting the orphanage and Episcopal home known as "Nuestras Pequeñas Rosas"—a truly inspirational place in San Pedro Sula, Honduras.

Looking like "the three amigos," Albert, Ruhama and Christian making the mandatory visit to get souvenirs at "*El Mercado*" in San Pedro Sula, Honduras.

Bishop Frade officially receives me as a priest of the Episcopal Church. Many news reports falsely stated it was my "ordination," but a person cannot be reordained. I had been ordained to the priesthood fifteen years before this day, and now I was being received as a priest in my new spiritual family.

Celebrating my first Eucharist as a priest of the Episcopal Church, surrounded by (from left to right) Deacon Ruby Cruz, Bishop Soto, Bishop Frade (my bishop), Bishop Holguin, and Deacon Miguel Baguer at the Church of the Resurrection.

(From left to right) Reverend Marco Antonio Ramos (Baptist), and Rev. Martin Añorga (Presbyterian) hand me a Bible as a sign of my new ministry as the Priest-in-Charge of my new parish.

Ministry continues: celebrating the Sacrament of Holy Baptism with twin boys, family, and friends in our parish community (June 2010).

Ruhama and I at the baby shower organized by members of our parish family at the Church of the Resurrection, September 2010.

CHAPTER NINE

◈

IF IT BLEEDS, IT LEADS: RUMORS, PAPARAZZI, AND TABLOIDS

Having worked for so many years in the media, I was well aware of the journalist and conservative Christian political commentator Armstrong Williams, who always said that the two most widely adhered-to rules in any newsroom are (1) Sex sells, and (2) If it bleeds, it leads.

In the view of most journalists, sensational news—especially if it's bad, and there's a bit of flesh involved—is a surefire audience grabber. I also knew firsthand that the way in which the media presents an event can have an incredible impact on what the public believes to be true.

In my own case, despite years of trying to make a difference in the world by serving my communities and spreading God's Good News on the radio and television, my scandal on the beach was the item that earned the most attention in the media. At first I was very hurt by this, because it made me wonder if nothing I had done before this one sunny day on the beach had really mattered to anyone after all. Where were all those people who had benefited from my years of dedication as the welcoming, nonjudgmental priest?

Among the media pundits, even the kindest and most professional journalists ended up saying, "I don't want to judge Padre Alberto," just before issuing a judgment anyway. In one article by a Republican female journalist, for instance, she wrote, "I will not judge him," and then just a few sentences later, she added, "He should have known better. He made a promise to be celibate." Easy for her to say!

I had never, in all of my years of listening to people talk about their struggles, used that phrase: "You should have known better." I had always left the judging up to God. I tried to help people pick up the pieces of a broken life or fix whatever situation was causing them pain, and I did so with compassion and flexibility. I wished that my colleagues in the media would have done the same, but for the most part, they did not.

Instead, several referred to me as a typical "judgmental priest," like the priests they'd grown up with, and showed very little regard for me as an individual. They positioned me as if I were an enforcer of typical Vatican rhetoric, which, if they had done their homework, they would have known I was not.

Much to my surprise, many journalists never asked the questions that I thought they should, such as: What was it about the institutional Church, the present situation, the sex scandals, or his own work that may have turned Padre Alberto away from the life he gave himself to years ago?

Or, more important: Are people allowed to

change, even when that change is not easy for the rest of the world to comprehend?

How the media treated my affair was hurtful to my family—and difficult to explain. Like many of us optimists, Ruhama and my mother and sisters, especially, still wanted television to be about the good things that go on in the world. They longed for stories of love, peace, and happiness. I found myself having to explain that controversy is what sells newspapers and makes ratings go up, and that people in the entertainment business—even those we had once considered true friends—weren't as interested in our personal well-being as they were in making their "product" more attractive.

One of my good friends, who happens to be a Hollywood producer, explained the media circus to me this way: "Most of us love to watch train wrecks."

I knew that was true; after all, I'd been stuck in traffic jams on the freeway and rubbernecked along with everyone else who might never know what really happened, or who was at fault, but who want to see the wreckage for themselves.

Now I was the traffic accident leading the news. And it was a spectacular wreck, because it combined the ingredients of religion and sex with a little fame flaming on top. Everyone seemed to want to view as many gory details and shards of broken glass as possible.

Or, to think about what happened another way, consider the Spanish proverb *Del árbol caído, todos hacen leña*, which means, Everyone makes firewood from the fallen tree. Everyone wanted a piece of me, including a number of people I thought incapable of such things.

Surviving the media feeding frenzy after the photos appeared in the Mexican tabloid proved to be a true test of courage for both Ruhama and me. As hard as it was to receive such harsh criticism and sensational coverage on the radio, on television, and in the tabloids, the worst was when my family would ask, "But aren't a lot of these people supposed to be your friends?"

That question really pierced my heart. In my work as a priest, and one who was close to the media, I had spent many sleepless nights and waking hours trying to respond to the needs of all, but I had especially reached out to those who were traditionally uncomfortable or felt excluded from the Church. Some of my colleagues and ultraconservative Roman Catholics gave me a hard time for being so open to everyone. I guess I was equally critical of those within my own Church who excluded those who were divorced and remarried, those who lived outside of the traditional box, and even a good number of media personalities who were rejected or mistreated simply because of their notoriety. Now that it was my turn to receive help and support, however, I discovered that it was rarely there.

What do you say when you see the very people in the media whom you once helped and tried to care for, spiritually and professionally, frivolously spreading false rumors about you without bothering to research the facts? What can you do when others attempt to discredit you when you are already down? And how do you explain to the people you love most in the world—your own family—that people are upset and willing to turn on you, simply because you did not grant them the "exclusive" interview they were expecting?

In those first days, I received hundreds of requests for interviews from local, national, and international outfits. Some in Europe even offered money. I never once accepted money for an interview—contrary to another horrible lie that was spread and repeated all over the place. I was not ready to grant another interview; I had limited myself to one in English and one in Spanish.

Even with that precaution, the authorities of the Roman Catholic Church were so upset about me speaking out publicly about my situation that I received a nasty letter with all of the canonical language informing me that I would no longer receive my salary or pension. I was out!

Indeed, my ouster was the fastest one in the history of the Church in Miami. I knew so many priests who continued to receive salaries and benefits for months, or even years, without doing a day's work. Meanwhile, all of my benefits were stripped away within hours—even my health insurance was suspended in a matter of days. There was never any personal concern for me or my family. Apparently, it was the institution and the leadership of the Church that was hurting and needed to be consoled.

None of this deterred the media from extending the story for months and months. Neither did it stop the paparazzi and reporters from some tabloid shows following us everywhere. No matter where we went, they were always there, sometimes hiding behind a car or a tree, but often popping up with cameras in our faces right in the open and waving a microphone in our noses.

Certain friends would call and say, "How can you take it?" They were worried and concerned, and they were right to feel that way. It was emotionally draining to become the center of so much false speculation and negative publicity. Pictures of us going in and out of my new rectory—the parish house for priests near my new church—often appeared with the caption "The expensive new home bought by Padre Alberto." Anyone who bothered to look at public records would know that the property had belonged to the Church since the 1940s and was home to dozens of Episcopal priests, their wives, and children before we lived in it.

Through it all, Ruhama and I spent time praying together. We prayed for ourselves, those who were hurt and confused, but we also prayed for our persecutors, who had to know they were making false allegations and deliberately creating lies to try to hurt us. Even with all of the faith in the world, it's not easy to pray for those who persecute you, but for us it was the best way to deal with the noise—both inside and outside.

The first few months were intense. Some stories we could laugh off, but many of them were evil and hurtful. It seemed to us that anyone, no matter who they were or what level of credibility they possessed, could make up any number of lies on any tabloid program or magazine, and their story would gladly be aired and repeated by more serious news sources, as if it were totally true.

What was most surprising to me was that a number of the journalists who reported many of the unsubstantiated stories were people who consider themselves professionals. I once called a dear friend who is a news anchor at a major network and asked if they were really going to report something that was totally false. "Father," he replied, "today's newscasts are unfortunately becoming entertainment magazines."

I was still stunned to see the number of made-up tabloid stories reprinted by the most respected news agencies with headlines that were totally false. The most absurd stories suggested that I had deliberately staged those photos with a woman to cover up the fact that I was a homosexual or involved in some other more "scandalous" situation. Others chipped away at Ruhama's character through interviews with people who falsely claimed to be former boyfriends. Naturally, the media had no interest in interviewing anyone who might pay us compliments or even speak the truth. Several friends and acquaintances tried to speak out and they were turned away by media, because they had nothing controversial or sensational to say.

Ruhama and I had to remind ourselves that only we knew the real truth. We were convinced that only God would be the real judge of our actions, and there was ultimately great peace in knowing that.

Previously, I had always been under the impression that there was a huge difference between tabloid shows and real news programs, between sensationalistic reporting and true journalism. Unfortunately, today it is very difficult to know the difference. And they all find ways to protect themselves legally, so there is very little one can do to stop it.

Ruhama, whom most people really knew nothing about, was a very private person. She was always shy and seemed like the last person in the world who would want to be in front of a camera. She was a devoted single mother who had been divorced for thirteen years before we got married, and she had dedicated all those years to hard work and bringing up her son properly. I could not understand why she was so viciously treated. The first rumor was that she had two children, one older and one younger, implying that the younger one was mine. It wasn't enough for the celibate priest to get caught on the beach with his girlfriend; they also wanted the train wreck to include a child out of wedlock. We don't know who started the rumor, but all of the news agencies repeated it during the first few days, until they actually did their research and got the truth.

Naively, I never expected some of my media colleagues to completely wipe the floor with my reputation, even if they felt under great pressure to criticize me because of the large number of Roman Catholics in their audiences. But that is exactly what many of them did. Ironically, most of the ones who carried on and appeared the most scandalized by my actions were only nominal Catholics, rarely interested in attending a Sunday Mass or even following the basic teachings of the Church.

As a priest in the media, I was the one who had often been accused of trying too hard to bring them closer to the faith of their upbringing and making that old Church—and many of its practices—more accessible to them. While I have no regrets for being an open-minded, welcoming, and nonjudgmental Roman Catholic priest, when it came to receiving some of that same compassion in the particular situation I was now facing, it was sorely lacking.

Oddly, those who were toughest on me were the liberal Catholics who were living with their partners out of wedlock or engaging in other activities that had nothing to do with traditional values. All of a sudden, these people acted more Catholic than the pope and came across as deeply offended and scandalized by my behavior.

I don't know if it was comic relief provided by God or just a funny coincidence, but almost exactly five months after I announced my decision to join the Episcopal Church, the Vatican announced that it was going to design a special program to make it easier for conservative Anglicans to join the Roman Catholic Church, including married priests.

The irony here is that my announcement about joining the Episcopal Church caused many conservative commentators—including members of the secular and Roman Catholic media—to highlight what they described as huge differences between our two churches. Some went so far as to say that "Padre Alberto has changed religions," which I always considered absurd, since we profess the same creed and possess the very same apostolic traditions and origins. The Episcopal Church is part of the Anglican Communion, which professes the Catholic faith and no other. We are also a reformed church, but we share the same apostolic faith and origins as Roman Catholics.

Once the Vatican made its announcement welcoming Anglicans, however, there was a total turnaround in media attention, including suggestions that I could go back to the Roman Catholic Church as a married man and be under the pope again. How absurd was that? Suddenly, because Rome had waved a magic wand, we were really not that "different"!

The announcement even went so far as to suggest that Anglicans who join Rome can preserve aspects of their "distinctive Anglican liturgy and spiritual traditions." One day, we were the bad guys, and the next, we were again part of the big, happy Church family. Hallelujah!

Most media outlets don't do their homework well when reporting on faith issues and tend to present religious news in a catchy, superficial way. Some are smart enough to have religious consultants who advise them or offer commentary on issues of faith and religion. But when ignorance about faith traditions is obvious in the media, religious folks get the blame. We deserve it: We *church folks* have gone out of our way to make theological topics and religion more complicated and less accessible. Instead of doing all that we can to make faith issues easy to understand, we alienate the public with sophisticated words and complicated practices. Faith is meant to be an experience that brings peace and joy to the human heart, building community by bringing people closer, not only to our Supreme Being but also to each other. Faith should bring people to the recognition that we all come from the same place and are headed toward the same place. We are not divided into different creeds and denominations by an act of God. We are separated because the human family always has a tendency to find more differences than commonalities, more tensions than harmony.

The media, if it ever became interested in this, could do a great deal to bridge many of these gaps and bring people of different faiths together, instead of highlighting what separates us. I have always tried to be an instrument of that type of unity by being open and welcoming in my ministry, by actively participating in dialogues and programs with people of diverse faith groups and denominations.

Ironically, a few days before the pictures were published, and without a clue as to how drastically my own life was about to change, I chatted with a reporter at a media event. The reporter asked me to comment on President Lugo in Paraguay, the former Roman Catholic bishop who left his ministry to become president. He had been accused of fathering children while supposedly serving as a celibate man of the cloth.

"The news surrounding that bishop is just one more indication that the Church needs to look at itself, and ask if celibacy could be revised or made optional," I told the reporter, adding that judging this man, or any other person, was not our role. "God is the only one who can judge what is in the hearts of human beings."

Apparently, the media didn't agree with me on that point.

CHAPTER TEN

RETREAT AND REFLECTION

The day after the pictures were published, I spoke to the auxiliary bishop for well over an hour and told him everything that was on my mind and in my heart. I was there because at our very short and tense meeting the archbishop had asked me to go see the auxiliary bishop to make arrangements for a "retreat." The auxiliary bishop was patient, kind, and understanding. I explained my situation in great detail and told him I had been struggling ideologically with many important issues in the Roman Catholic Church for some time, including celibacy. I also told him I was seriously contemplating getting married and having a family.

I specifically spoke of my plans to join the Episcopal Church and that I was already in conversations with Episcopal leaders. In response, the auxiliary bishop suggested that I needed to go away to "reprogram my ideas." Then he seemed to catch himself saying something that made me sound like a computer that needed the hard disk replaced. He abruptly changed the word "reprogram" to "rethink some of your ideas."

I knew exactly what he was suggesting. In the past, I had seen more than one colleague sent to those places where they try to "reprogram" you— institutions set up by the bishops themselves to help priests with addiction issues of every kind, or to tend to priests in need of psychological or psychiatric care. Sometimes they call them retreat houses, but that is not what they actually are. I didn't believe that falling in love and being at odds with the Church on a variety of pastoral, disciplinary, and deep ideological issues was something that justified being institutionalized or reprogrammed, and I told the auxiliary bishop this outright.

"These ideas and convictions have been rooted in my heart for a good while," I said.

In fact, I had been discussing them with friends, parishioners, and other clergy. I believed that it was probably my very open-mindedness on these topics that led people to my parish and allowed them to feel at least somewhat comfortable in the Roman Catholic Church of their upbringing— even if they didn't wholly practice or believe the Church's many outdated ideas.

The conversation with the auxiliary bishop ended peacefully. He was kind and gave me his blessing, but I realized that he was ultimately dissatisfied with my conclusions. He even seemed a bit flustered by our conversation. He handed me a handkerchief to wipe the tears from my eyes as I left, which I later realized were tears of relief: I had finally let it all out and told a Roman Catholic bishop what I actually felt about everything! I left there feeling great peace.

I told him that I would go away for a while to reflect, but did not think it would change my decision. Of course, when I left that meeting, I knew full well that the archbishop, who had seen me the day before, would be getting an update from him. At least, that is the way it usually worked.

EVEN BEFORE I COULD SEND the letter requesting my leave of absence, I received one from the archbishop marked "Personal and Confidential." I couldn't read the letter myself, since I wasn't yet in Miami and my mail was being delivered to a friend's parish. I asked that priest friend to open it and read it to me. From the sound of my friend's voice, I could tell he was uneasy reading it to me at first because of the harsh content, but I insisted he read it anyway.

The letter granted me a leave from the Church and listed a slew of restrictions, including the immediate suspension of my salary and benefits. I was stunned and heartbroken at how severe, impersonal, and legalistic it was. The archbishop had never in my memory issued this kind of punishment to any other priest, even when those priests were accused of abusing minors or manifesting other criminal behavior. I knew this as a fact, because I signed paychecks and paid archdiocesan benefits for some of these priests— for years.

For instance, a certain priest had been accused of picking up male prostitutes. He had also received international media attention for his misconduct because he, too, was a recognized public figure and former president of a local university. Yet, unlike in my case, Church authorities never said a word about it publicly. As a matter of fact, that particular priest went on to work alongside the archbishop for many years following his scandal—without repercussions.

We also had several priests accused of sexual abuse and other situations with minors. I had personally replaced priests in parishes devastated by those accusations, and it was I who had to read the letters from Church authorities before thousands of parishioners.

Not only that, I had made it a point to reach out a hand to the accused priests, when very few would. I tried to call them up on occasion and to listen to them when they needed to cry or talk about how deeply hurt they were by the Church. Regardless of what they were accused of, or of what they may or may not have actually done, I tried to make them feel less like lepers within their own Church. I took them to lunch or helped them out financially if I could.

What had I done to offend the Church so much that they would issue such a harsh punishment? I went public with my declaration of love and admitted that I'd had an inappropriate relationship with a woman. I wasn't the first priest to be involved in an issue like this, but I was the first prominent priest to ever discuss his dilemma with the international media while still in the Church. Now I had been cut off from my parish and my position at the radio station, as well as my salary and benefits.

I don't really know what the Church meant to accomplish by treating me this way. If I had been a man on a cliff, intending to jump, this would have felt more like a shove to get me off the ledge than a helping hand back to safety. I felt that all of the nastiness I was experiencing was a confirmation from God that it was indeed time to move on and serve as a priest in a much more humane church—at least in one that could publicly admit its humanity and debate it openly.

I tried to imagine what I would have done if I'd been in charge of the Church, and I think I would have said to this struggling priest, "Let me listen and help you get through this. I want you to make decisions that are good for your personal future, whether you stay or move on."

This experience with the Church hierarchy reinforced the lesson I'd been learning all along: When it came to facing the consequences of one's actions, priests were on their own. Now I was the one abandoned by the Church to sink or swim. I should have expected it, because I had seen it so many times before.

The other person I spoke to in confidence was the Episcopal bishop of the Diocese of Southeast Florida, Leo Frade. He, too, had seen the pictures, and when he saw me, he smiled and said, "I guess you've really moved on, Albert," referring to past conversations we'd had about my ideological differences with the Roman Catholic Church.

As we talked, I couldn't help but compare Bishop Frade's response to my own bishop's. Here was a man who was totally compassionate and concerned about my well-being as a person. He was as upset by the Church's treatment of me as I was, but the difference was that he had experienced it all before when he had received Roman priests into the Episcopal Church in the past. He was familiar with what I was going through.

I thanked him for his honesty and told him then what was in my heart: I was finally ready to be received and serve God as a priest in the Episcopal Church. He was very understanding, and opened the door to me serving God in this new way as a married man by helping me work out all the details of this transition, which is a process that takes at least one year.

A FEW DAYS AFTER THE scandal broke, I boarded a plane to take me to my retreat. I was seated on the aisle, with nobody occupying the middle seat. I felt an enormous sense of relief as the plane took off. Finally I didn't have to talk to anyone. I could read my newspapers and the book I chose for the trip and be totally left alone.

The young man seated next to the window was bopping his head, singing to himself and looking a bit nervous. I decided to start with the newspapers. These were full of articles and commentaries on my "scandalous pictures." I knew that I needed to read something more uplifting, but this was my get-it-out-of-the-way moment. Besides, I wasn't technically starting my spiritual retreat until I got off the plane, so I gave myself permission to spend time on the news.

After a while, the young man who had been singing to himself said, "This is my first time on a plane and I'm really scared."

He had a Spanish accent and I felt a jolt of paranoia. I didn't want him to recognize me, so I made sure to respond in English, assuring him everything would be all right.

"Yeah, but you remember 9/11, right?" he countered.

"Don't worry. That's not going to happen today," I said.

"I hope not, because I'm a singer and I am on my way to sing with Ricky Martin," he answered.

I was afraid that at any moment he might ask me what I did for a living. Sure enough, before I could finish that thought, he asked, "What do you do?"

"I'm a priest," I responded quickly.

He looked into my eyes. "Padre Alberto! I knew I recognized that voice!"

We shook hands and began talking. I tried to speak softly, but he congratulated me in a loud voice. "Father, we are with you!" he cried. "What you did is natural. You have nothing to be ashamed of."

I thanked him, thinking I could get back to my reading, but no such luck. He wanted to keep talking—and he wanted all of the details.

Once the seat belt lights went off, a woman from the back of the plane approached us and asked if she could sit between us in our row. She immediately struck up a conversation with the young singer.

I was relieved to be left alone. Then the singer said to the woman, "Do you know who he is?" He gestured at me.

She looked at me with a blank face. Again, I was relieved.

But the singer went on. "He is Padre Alberto, a famous father for us Latinos."

The woman looked at me and nodded. "Now I know why God sent me to sit here. I want you to know what I do: I give advice to pastors and their wives."

I was shocked! God had sent me an angel from heaven with a direct message. I listened closely to everything this woman had to tell me.

The woman looked into my eyes and said, "Listen, you should not be afraid, because you are an agent for change. You are on a mission from God and you should just let Him guide you."

I really couldn't believe it. This was too much. I had been through many sleepless nights; maybe I was going out of my mind. But this woman was real, and as she sat next to me, quietly offering me words of comfort, her message brought me peace and light in the midst of the pain and darkness I was experiencing.

As the plane landed, I thought, "God has always been good to me. Why wouldn't He be now? I need only to listen to hear Him."

I REMAINED IN SECLUSION FOR ten days. No phone, no e-mail, no newspapers, no visitors. I wanted only to reflect.

My cell phone was constantly bombarded with phone calls and text messages from international, national, and local media outfits all wanting me to talk. I spoke to none of them. It was particularly difficult for me to turn away acquaintances and a few friends who expected an exclusive interview because of our work relationship in the past. But I had promised myself, and my family, that I wouldn't speak to the press again until I was ready to announce my next step.

It was horrible to feel so much pressure from people who identified themselves as my friends but were so insensitive to my need to just get away. All of a sudden, their business was more important than our friendship.

I couldn't understand how, after so many years of making myself available to them in their times of need and struggle, they couldn't do this one thing I needed them to do: leave me in peace. Many took it personally that they didn't receive a call back. Some even used the opportunity to mention on the air that I was no longer behaving like a friend, or said that I was becoming antimedia. I was glad to be away.

I had also done what I could to hide Ruhama from the media. This was a real challenge. Certain media outfits reported that we had been flown on a celebrity's private jet to New York. Others claimed that she had fled the country to her native Guatemala. None of the tabloid versions were true. As a matter of fact, very little of what the media was reporting about us was true.

In fact, Ruhama was still in Florida. It was the start of Christian's summer vacation, so she took him to Orlando. What better place to hide than in a crowd of tourists at Disney World? She was determined, as I was, to escape the constant harassment and find a bit of peace for herself and, most important, for her teenage son.

Christian had no idea of the intimate nature of our relationship before those pictures were published. When we were forced to tell him, his reaction was surprisingly, overwhelmingly positive; he had come to think of me as a good friend in the years we had known each other.

"I'm happy for you both," he told us. "You love each other, and that's what matters most."

Wow. I had never expected a fifteen-year-old to respond with such maturity and assurance, but he did. I felt blessed once again.

Ruhama and I didn't see each other during those ten days. That was one of the hardest things, because it is very difficult to support and protect the people you love from a distance.

Thanks to Nely Galan (the creator and mastermind of my first television program) and her family, we were able to meet after my retreat in her home in Los Angeles—far from Miami and the paparazzi, who in those days never left us alone. Nely is a great friend, and she and her family offered Ruhama and me a great deal of support in those difficult days, just before I was getting ready to announce the decisions I had made regarding my future.

While all of this speculation about what I would do next raged in the public arena, I continued my private conversations with Bishop Frade. These were frank and open discussions about a decision I had been delaying for far too long.

We met confidentially, because some members of the media were constantly hounding me, and I didn't want another thing published before I was ready to make a formal announcement. My personal process of thinking about becoming an Anglican had already been going on for a few years, so I wasn't shocked when some in the press began to suggest it. Still, I wanted to have the opportunity to think and pray to confirm this was truly God's will for me.

It was also important for me to explore with Ruhama whether she was also equally interested in taking the step with me. While this was not a requirement, since people in many good marriages belong to different denominations and respect each other in their diverse spiritual traditions, I had a pretty strong feeling that she was equally interested in taking this step.

I had kept her informed about my conversations with Episcopal clergy and clergy from other denominations who had offered me their fellowship and sincere friendship. She and I both knew it would be difficult for people—especially Latinos—to understand that I wasn't "changing religions," as many reported. I had no wish to abandon my creed, the sacramental life, or many other aspects of my faith.

Ruhama and I were both familiar with the Book of Common Prayer, and we had discussed the major differences between Roman Catholicism and Anglicanism. From my point of view, it would be a natural transition. The Episcopal Church is part of the Anglican Communion—part of the

Church of England—which has a rich tradition dating back to the early centuries of Christianity. Anglicans and Romans share the same basic creed from early Christianity; we also share many common traditions and practices.

In fact, Anglicans are "catholic" in our beliefs and practices. Contrary to the popular misconception, Anglicanism did not start with Henry VIII's fight with the pope in the sixteenth century. We have a much richer heritage and tradition that is evident in the many centuries of Christian history in the Church of England. Anglicans are not, as I've heard some say, "Catholic lite" or "Catholics without a pope." We consider the Bible, tradition, and reason as pillars. We celebrate the Eucharist and we also honor Mary and the saints, though our devotions are optional and not imposed. Our liturgy is based on the same apostolic traditions, stemming from the early Church.

The issue of reason in the Episcopal Church is very important, because Anglicans are challenged to make their own decisions based on what is biblical and true, not on what an external authority decides at a given moment in history. My fundamental theological positions about God hadn't changed—and probably never will. However, my ways of understanding Him had.

The start of my ideological evolution dated back to several years before the media fiasco that resulted from those pictures of me with Ruhama on the beach. I had been pondering my own religious transformation for a good while. To change religions means that you change your fundamental belief system, but I wasn't interested in doing that. My priesthood and my dedication to my faith—the faith of my baptism—would remain intact as a member of the Episcopal Church.

From a lay perspective, one of the biggest differences between Episcopalians (Anglicans) and Roman Catholics has to do with authority and governance, since we do not have a centralized authority that governs and makes decisions for the entire Church. Decisions in the Episcopal Church are made collaboratively; both laity and clergy are involved in Church authority and in choosing leaders. This was the way it was done in early Christianity. I found many things in Anglicanism that were closer to the early church than what had become common practice in the Roman Church of my upbringing. Latinos, especially, have been indoctrinated to believe that there is only one true Church and that there is no salvation outside of it. I had come to believe that wasn't possibly true. God is simply too big for that!

MY NEW BISHOP UNDERSTOOD MY thinking and my situation as a priest—and as a man. He showed me the type of humanity one expects from a spiritual leader, an authentic

266

concern for the person and not only for the image of an institution.

At the same time, I recognized that Bishop Frade was about to take a risk if he announced his acceptance of me and allowed me to continue ministering in South Florida as part of the Episcopal Church. Conservative sectors within the Roman Catholic Church, and even more than a few in the Episcopal Church, would have been scandalized and would have worried about the impact of it all. I felt blessed that Bishop Frade knew me well and was willing to go out of his way to handle the situation with respect toward my dignity as a person and a priest, regardless of the feathers that would be ruffled in and out of both churches.

On May 28, 2009—after I became absolutely sure God wanted me to move on—Ruhama and I were accepted into the Episcopal Church, and I read this statement before the countless members of the media that were present:

Dear friends:

The Book of Psalms tells us, "Show me your ways, O Lord, and teach me your paths."
    These words have accompanied me for many years.
    The life of a man or woman of faith is a constant search for the will of God—we

are always seeking God's path for each of us. Today I come before this community that I have tried to serve and continue to love with all my heart, to announce that I am continuing the call to spread the message of God's love and the vocation God gave me to priestly service. More than ever, I am sure that God is love and that He is the source of all love.

I have searched my soul and sought God's guidance. I have also spoken to friends in the Episcopal Church and in other Christian denominations about their service to God, and I have been a witness to the ways that they serve God as married men, with the added blessing of forming a family.

I also must recognize that for a long time I began to have spiritual and deep ideological struggles. Those who know me understand that I would never want to hurt anyone—especially my family, friends, and the Church community. Furthermore, my personal struggle should in no way tarnish the commitment of so many brother priests who are celibate and faithful to their promise. I will always love and hold dear the Roman Catholic Church and all its members who are committed to their faith.

Today, I have decided to become part of a new spiritual family within the umbrella of Christianity, one that shares the same roots and is not too far from the traditions and worship that I am accustomed to. As I have been saying and writing for years through my work in communications, instead of focusing on our differences, let's work together, so that all may come to believe in a loving and good God, even in the midst of this changing world.

I ask everyone to please respect my privacy and the privacy of my loved ones. There have been lies, innuendo, rumors, and hurtful actions by those seeking to profit from my life and struggles. I respectfully ask that all these things stop now.

As we begin this new stage in our lives, I ask that you extend to me and my loved ones the same courtesy and respect that every human being deserves. I am humbled by the support of so many people throughout the world and in our own community; and especially friends and family, who have given us unconditional love and support.

Thank you and God bless you,
Father Albert

· · ·

THE ANGRY REACTION AND ELABORATE
response to this statement by my former boss, the
archbishop of Miami, made it seem to all the
world as if I had been dishonest in expressing my
concerns and future plans to him or his auxiliaries.
I was convinced that I had been as honest as I was
able to be with him, especially given that he
granted me such a brief and impersonal audience.
During that meeting on the afternoon of May 6,
2009, the archbishop had made it pretty clear that
he was not even remotely interested in knowing
any details about my personal situation. His main
concern was to protect and defend the image of
the institution he represented, and maybe even his
own image as the local leader of that institution.

It had been my understanding that the auxiliary
bishop I met with the following day, with whom I
had shared the details of all my ideological
differences with Roman Catholicism and my
intentions to enter the Episcopal Church, would
convey these details to his boss. I don't know
exactly what happened in those three weeks
between May 6 and May 28, but it appeared from
the archbishop's response that they had engaged
in no real communication about my situation at
all, even though it seemed to be on the mind of
everyone within and outside the Church
community. Given the notoriety of the situation,
that seemed almost impossible to me.

Even though my letter of resignation was hand-delivered to the bishop's office on the morning I made my announcement about joining the Episcopal Church, the archbishop publicly claimed that he did not receive it and knew nothing about it. But my letter *was* there, at least several hours before the press conference at Trinity Cathedral. He even had the nerve to use the example of the prodigal son in referring to me, yet when he'd had the opportunity to put that beautiful parable into practice on the day I most needed an understanding father figure, I received quite the opposite treatment. The father in the story of the prodigal son did not question, judge, or intimidate his son, but instead did everything he could to lift him up, showing mercy and understanding. When I was in trouble and went to see the person the Church identifies as a priest's spiritual father, I got questions about the image of the Church and very little concern for my own well-being—not to mention the total absence of concern for my family.

I found it hypocritical and unjust that someone like the archbishop, who had so consistently acted like an aloof CEO of a Fortune 500 company—uninterested in me as a person, even when I had spent quite a few years solving problems for him—was now publicly complaining that I didn't give him a detailed personal explanation of what was happening in my life. He may have had legitimate sacramental considerations, but never a personal one! And he was the one who made it perfectly clear by his actions and apathy that he wanted it that way. I have known priests, bishops, cardinals—even people who work very closely with the pope—all over the world, and no one in the hierarchy had ever seemed as disconnected and uninterested in my life and ministry as my own bishop. For instance, when I published *Real Life, Real Love* (my self-help book) in 2006, I sent him the first copy—even before I gave one to my own mother. I got thank-you notes and acknowledgments from four cardinals, several bishops (including one from the Vatican), and other church leaders who received their copies weeks later, before I received a note or any type of acknowledgment from my own bishop, which came four months later. Distance, separation, and indifference regarding my very public ministry were his modus operandi. I never really understood why he behaved in such a way.

We are taught that we are called to be instruments of God's mercy, but those of us who've dedicated a great deal of time trying to bring that mercy to so many are rarely treated with compassion or mercy when we need it most. If I fell short in keeping the promise of celibacy—and I know that I did—what about the rest of the Church, that international "moral authority"? I wondered how this institution intended to deal with the realities of the twenty-first century, especially with all the problems related to clergy and their conduct.

Could the Roman Catholic Church ever become more humane and less dogmatic? How did it cope when the less than ideal happened? How did the Church deal with humanity, especially human sexuality, in general?

The answer became clearer and clearer to me: unfortunately, not very well.

CHAPTER ELEVEN

❖

OUR SIMPLE GREEK WEDDING

The outrageous stories about us continued to appear in the media. Meanwhile, after I returned from my retreat, Ruhama and I tried to stay focused on what was most important to us: beginning our new life together.

Despite the huge media storm and the hurtful actions of many who took advantage of the moment to make a quick buck, we began to enjoy an inner tranquillity that came with knowing that we had no more reason to hide our love from the world. It was so enjoyable for me to walk with Ruhama down the street, holding her hand or putting my arm around her the way any man in love keeps his lover close to him, without having to hide. My own mother and sisters welcomed Ruhama with open arms, and her family was very happy for her as well.

Through the generosity of a good friend of the Episcopal Diocese, who loaned us a beautiful house in Key Biscayne, we managed to escape the paparazzi for a few weeks to be alone together and plan our future, especially the day we had dreamed of for so long: our wedding. But the relentless photographers even found us there. It was that way for months, with cameras aimed in our direction anywhere we went. Occasionally,

Ruhama would cry, and ask, "When are they going to leave us alone?"

"Soon," I promised.

I had bigger concerns: I had to officially ask Ruhama to marry me. Most men ask the father of the bride for her hand. I asked Christian. He grinned and said immediately, "You can have her!"

So, one beautiful June evening, I enticed Ruhama into the car with the promise of a surprise. She had no idea where we were headed. I drove first to the place where we had seen each other for the very first time and couldn't take our eyes off one another from that moment on: the front steps of St. Patrick's Church on Miami Beach. We kissed on the steps, she cried, and we talked a little bit of that difficult time and how happy we were to finally be together.

Then I told her that we had to make one more stop before heading home. This time, I drove her to the same beach where the paparazzi had taken those now infamous pictures. It was a spectacular moment for both of us, hearing the timeless, inimitable sound of crashing waves and watching the sky transform from one blush of pink into a series of deeper colors as the sun set.

Four months had passed since that cold morning when we'd been spotted by the photographer. It felt a bit strange to be out there, even for just a few minutes. For a moment, it still felt like everyone was watching us and judging what we were doing.

In spite of this awkward feeling, I knew that this was a good way to begin to heal the past, to erase the many hurtful stories and false suppositions surrounding that day.

As we walked together, I fingered the box I carried in my pocket. It contained an engagement ring, a simply cut diamond set in a white gold band. While we had already talked at length about wanting to marry, I'd wanted to give her a ring at a special place and at the right time. This was it. In a few minutes we'd be heading to an engagement party organized by a group of our friends at my younger sister's house. I had bought the ring secretly from the brother of one of my radio cohosts; he was my favorite psychologist on the show, and his family was in the jewelry business. I knew that I could trust him to keep my purchase confidential. I wanted Ruhama to be completely surprised.

We walked along the beach as the sun sank lower in the sky, trying to locate the exact spot not too far from the multicolored lifeguard hut where we had put down our towels on our day of discovery. When we reached it, I knelt down in the sand and took the ring out of my pocket, presenting it to Ruhama. It was the moment we had dreamed about for so long.

"My love, will you marry me?"

Ruhama's brown eyes filled with tears, but she

smiled. "Yes," she said, and we kissed as the last rays of sun turned the pale sand to gold.

PREPARING FOR A WEDDING UNDER any circumstances can be stressful. In our case, the ongoing soap opera that the tabloids were busy creating around our romance made this doubly so, but we tried to ignore as much of it as possible; especially since they appeared to have such very little interest in the truth. We only made it through this time with the power of prayer and by reading good books that let us escape the day-to-day encounters with reporters and all kinds of curious people almost everywhere we went.

Luckily, we had help from many good people along the way. For instance, Ruhama's sister-in-law took her to see Ms. Carmin, a friend who sold flowers and was a decorative genius. Ms. Carmin didn't recognize Ruhama at first; when she asked the names of the bride and groom and the location of the wedding, Ruhama told her and then began to cry.

Immediately, Ms. Carmin looked up and said, "I will help you. Don't worry. Just tell me what you need."

When Ruhama explained the type of flowers she wanted, Ms. Carmin said, "Everything you need will be free. I will take care of it."

Ruhama couldn't believe this good fortune and generosity; for the past months, she had been hounded by people who only wanted to take from us, not to give. But there was still more. Unbelievably, this angel on earth, Ms. Carmin, also said, "I will find the cake and a very good chef for the wedding, so that you can have your special Greek food. You will pay only for the chef."

In a daze, Ruhama thanked her and left to find her wedding dress. Here, again, she was lucky. In the very first bridal store she walked into, the clerk showed her about fifteen different dresses. She chose the first dress she tried on "because it was the most beautiful one," she told me that night.

"Besides," she added, "it was seventy-five percent off. I guess today really was my lucky day!"

OUR WEDDING TOOK PLACE ON June 26, 2009, at the historic St. Bernard de Clairvaux Church in North Miami Beach, an old Spanish monastery originally built in Seville by monks and then brought in pieces to the United States, where it was reassembled and donated to house the church. Ironically, this church was just like us: It had started out Roman Catholic and become Episcopal along its life journey.

I arrived at the church that evening about fifteen minutes before Ruhama did. There was every form of media everywhere—mostly right at the gates of the historic monastery—and it seemed like hundreds of people were all trying to take my picture and shout questions. As we approached the church, they ran toward the automobile I was riding in with two dear friends, who were my groomsmen, and my stepson, Christian, almost climbing onto the hood and shaking it from side to side.

We drove onto the church property as swiftly as possible. One of my best friends from childhood was in the front seat, and because he is a big guy, several in the tabloid media insisted that he was my bodyguard—but no, he was just my big friend who was taking care of me and actually helped us to pay for the wedding.

When the limo with Ruhama and her bridesmaids drove in, the cameras and reporters detained it and shook it from to side to side. Hundreds of flashes went off as they tried to get a glimpse of the bride through the tinted windows. There were actually more reporters and cameras outside the church than there were family and friends inside; we had invited only about sixty-five people, including the two bishops and several priests and their spouses. We were advised to keep our wedding as private as possible, and as we were exhausted from all of the noise and public attention dogging us the past few months, that was the best advice.

Regardless of what was going on outside, inside

the monastery it was peaceful and prayerful. We had a devout celebration of the sacramental rite of holy marriage with our good friends Bishop Leo Frade and Bishop Onell Soto officiating. Everything went by as if in a dream.

As Ruhama walked down the aisle with her brother, our eyes locked, and we were taken back to that first moment when we saw each other on the steps of St. Patrick's and knew it was love at first sight. This love and this wedding were truly miracles from God.

Otherwise, perhaps the most memorable part of our wedding ceremony was how we both prayed, listened to readings from sacred Scripture, and knelt down to take Holy Communion together—in peace before God—for the first time as husband and wife. It was a real blessing! I thought of how the apostles, some thirty-nine popes, and most priests for over a thousand years were also married. I imagined the thousands of priests who were married in the first twelve hundred years of Church history, when celibacy was optional; those too must have been joyful celebrations surrounded by other married clergy, members of the community, family and friends. This was not something new!

Our families and friends joined together to celebrate with great joy what was perhaps the most controversial wedding in Miami's recent history: the marriage of the celebrity priest and his secret girlfriend. For us, it was just the culmination of over a decade of loving one another.

Our first dance was magical. We had chosen "Always and Forever" by Heatwave because it expressed so well what we had felt for each other from the very start. After twenty-two years without dancing, I danced nearly four hours nonstop that night. I couldn't help but remember my first days after entering the seminary at the age of eighteen, when our dean of men (as the disciplinarian was known) told us, "Seminarians don't dance!" I had taken him at his word, so you could say that I was enthusiastic on the dance floor but more than a bit rusty!

The food at the reception was Greek, to honor that side of Ruhama's heritage. Greece was where we chose to spend our honeymoon, too, and where our dancing continued. God had blessed us with the possibility of being together, and we were determined to live this new life, with nothing to hide, as fully and joyfully as possible.

WE ONLY HAD FIVE DAYS in Greece for our honeymoon because we were on a tight budget, but we had one very special, nontourist site that we absolutely had to visit. Almost exactly one year before our wedding, Ruhama's father had been on his deathbed in Greece with terminal cancer. When she went to visit him, she had made a brief visit to a Greek Orthodox monastery on Aegina, an island about seventeen miles from Athens. Ruhama's father was Greek Orthodox and her son, Christian, had been baptized in that church.

People from around the world visit the monastery to see the tomb of St. Nektarios, because many claim that praying to God by his tomb results in great miracles. A year ago, Ruhama had come here to pray for her father. She had also lit a single candle for us in that prayerful place, promising God that by next year she would bring her husband to visit. Visiting *"el santito"*— the little saint, as Ruhama called him—was an essential moment at the start of our married life together.

It was a difficult journey that required maneuvering our tiny rental car around curvy, narrow roads on the island. Finally, we arrived at the cozy monastery at the highest point on Aegina, where we had a breathtaking view of the blue ocean surrounding the Greek isles.

Standing together there, Ruhama and I said a prayer of thanksgiving to God for finally bringing us together as husband and wife. Our mission was accomplished. In spite of all the opposition and criticism, we had finally joined our lives.

CHAPTER TWELVE

THE MYTH OF CELIBACY

I have always believed that God is love. But here's the mystery: For most of us, *finding* true love and *living* a life of true love doesn't come easily. It is a struggle, perhaps the most valuable and fundamental struggle of our human existence, simply because it is the one that we all share. Nonetheless, when a priest falls in love, it's still logical to ask what could possibly lead a man who already has such an abundance of love in his life— ministry, the Church, the priesthood, the people he serves, and the promises he made before God—to become involved in a "secret" love affair?

Some immediately conclude that it must be the result of that particular priest's loneliness and a desire for sexual intimacy. Others confine the priest's actions to that black-and-white Roman Catholic box of immorality and sin. Many are offended by the seeming indifference to the Church's official disciplines—especially to the celibacy requirement or promise.

Yet, having been through this experience, I know in my heart that these snap judgments can't possibly cover any individual's unique situation. It isn't as simple as a man or a woman committing his or her life to the Church, then feeling that there is a choice to make between the love of God and the very natural—and good—desire to love another human being. That is the dilemma I have tried to present in this book, in its fullest, most complex form, because this dilemma is a heavy burden carried by so many people—not just in the clergy—who fall in love but can't express it, and find that their own lives are destroyed as well as the lives of others who care about them.

As I've written elsewhere in these pages, this dilemma cannot, and must not, be reduced to the basic fight between good and evil. Falling in love with another person, when you are committed to the Church, is not just about breaking a promise or committing a sin. Those who give their lives to the service of God and neighbor are mostly loving, caring, responsible, and faithful people; they are truly dedicated to doing what is good.

Yet, like all human beings, we come to this special profession and unique way of life with our individual limitations and our particular interior struggles. We priests and nuns often fall short of the ideals set before us by the Church and the idealized versions of ourselves that other people hold. However, unlike most people, we have to deal with our human failings, our difficulties and our growth, in the public eye as we learn to reconcile what God expects, what the institutional Church expects, and what others expect—no matter how unrealistic those expectations are. It's a lot of pressure!

The situation is comparable to a person who falls in love and gets married with every intention to keep those sacred vows of matrimony, then discovers that the relationship doesn't go as planned. One person changes, or the other one does, and they change in ways that cause them to follow divergent life paths instead of working together as a team.

For a long time, I endured a tug-of-war between something that was good—my love for God—and another thing that was also good—my love for the woman I wanted, with all my heart, to love, honor, and cherish in marriage. It was an interior battle between a supernatural love and a natural love. I got caught in the trap of thinking that the only way to experience both loves as a priest was to hide one of them. Now I have come to believe that both of these loves were given to me by the same God, who is ultimately the source of *all* love and really does not need any of us to hide what is good.

WHEN YOU CHOOSE TO BECOME a priest within the confines of the Roman Catholic Church, the battle to live a celibate life begins early on. Celibacy is not a natural state of being for most mortals. Those of us who initially embrace it are taught to believe that celibacy is a necessary spiritual component for the priesthood, only to discover that it's a really difficult path to follow.

We try to comfort ourselves by looking around at our priest brothers and telling ourselves that they, too, are struggling as we are, and as committed to our Church as we are. And then, as we slowly discover that this is not the case, and realize that celibacy isn't something the Church itself takes that seriously, the struggle seems not only difficult but often pointless.

As a young man, I always found it difficult to stomach the common misconception that God calls only people who don't have a life, or who aren't interested in the same things as the rest of humanity. Of course, where celibacy is concerned, you can't really blame people, because they are only reacting according to the Church's skewed approach to sexual morality, and the fact that the Church perpetuates the idea that priests should somehow be above earthly desires.

As far as the Church is concerned, a young man who is interested in becoming a priest, or in staying in the priesthood, has no right to like girls. He should be asexual and not think about "those things." A vocation to serve God implies a lack of interest in what every other human is naturally interested in. It is as if the Church prefers its clergy to be spiritually and emotionally healthy, but sexually castrated. Today I am convinced that this simply does not work for most people.

I am sure that those expectations play a big role in the arrested emotional development of so many priests. The seminary system itself isolates people; when you are not allowed to grow and develop with your peers, both men and women, your ability to develop meaningful relationships becomes impaired at an early age.

Thinking about celibacy and my early priesthood makes me reflect back to that first menial job I had pulling weeds. As it turns out, that job was the logical first step on my journey, because ministry—and all of life in general—shares a lot of similarities with pulling weeds. I have spent a lifetime engaged in a constant struggle to make the world a better place by educating, encouraging, healing, and comforting those who are in pain or grieving over life's unexpected challenges and tragedies. To me, the call to serve God was a lot like pulling weeds: I always wanted to make good things grow and chase evil away.

As one of God's ministers, my top priority has always been to help people find God and His mercy by showing them how to acquire the tools they need to root out sin and evil from their lives. I teach people to weed their own spiritual gardens, as the weeds creep into their lives in a variety of ways: a physical or mental illness, a troubled past, a professional or financial crisis, relationship struggles, problems with their children, you name it.

We all struggle with things we'd like to root out

of our lives for good. However, the source of that struggle is often something we have been led to *believe* is good or bad, not necessarily *what truly is* good or bad for you.

As a very young man, I felt truly and passionately called to do something I knew would never be easy: to serve God. And, yes, as a Roman Catholic from birth, I was at one time convinced that the best, and most effective way, to serve God was as a parish priest. To fulfill that conviction, I made a promise to be celibate, with every intention of keeping that vow forever. Little did I know how very difficult the struggle to hold to that promise would become—or how my own ideology would change.

Imagine, if you can, that you find a passion as a young person that changes your outlook on life forever. You throw heart and soul into pursuing that passion, totally convinced that it is the only way to live, and you follow that path for twenty-two years. Then, one day, you begin to discover that your passion was in some ways misguided and led you to a place where you weren't meant to be, a place where you no longer felt at peace.

For twenty-two years, I was literally on a one-way road that led to my discerning, preparing for, and living the life of a Roman Catholic priest. Then, gradually, something happened: Life happened, and presented me with a radical change in direction. It's not as simple as it sounds, but change—and sometimes radical change—is a real part of the human experience, even though we often put all of our energy into resisting it. If you don't embrace that change, you will never learn from it.

As much as I personally struggled with the requirement of celibacy in my own life, I never wanted to become the anticelibacy poster boy. I still believe, even after all that has happened in my own life and the strong evidence presented by various experts on the subject, that a significant percentage of priests really do try to honor their promise to be celibate as an ideal, and I admire them for it.

Unfortunately, though, people tend to admire the sacrifices—like celibacy—that their priests make more than almost anything else. The fact that priests are viewed as leading different, and even holier, lives than ordinary people causes people to put their priests on pedestals, despite the fact that, in reality, men and women of flesh and blood do some of God's best work. That person up on the altar is just another mortal like the rest of us, other than the fact that he heard a personal call from God and dared to respond to it.

A good friend of mine, a married man in his late sixties, once told me, "I was wrong to put you up so high; one day I woke up and realized, 'Albert is just like me!' "

His remark made me laugh, but it also made me

think about how much healthier it would be for all of us if the people in the pews could somehow see through the smokescreen of the priesthood and find the flawed man dressed in robes before them. What better role model to follow than that of a man who constantly struggles to do his best to serve God and his community?

Long before my affair was made public, I had a long discussion over dinner with a group of celebrities and their spouses. Our jovial dinner party was attended by recording artists, producers, talk show hosts, and a number of news anchors.

At one point, a dinner guest asked me how I managed to keep my commitment to the priesthood in the midst of all of the temptations and allures of modern-day society. "It's not like you're living like a monk," she pointed out. "You're actually working out in the world like the rest of us."

I was very frank, and simply told her, "Listen, priests are people, too. We all have the same struggles that you do."

"Father," she replied, "I've never doubted that priests are people. I apologize for giving you a hard time."

In all honesty, her question wasn't all that unusual. She was simply raised with certain religious concepts and was led to believe, like too many others, that priests are *way up there* and the rest of us are *down here*—on earth!

The question is: Who on earth put priests way up there, anyway? Why *do* so many people have a tendency to put spiritual leaders up on an altar so high? How did we get to the point of exalting priests to the point where we dehumanize them? Was this a theological phenomenon created by the Church, or a simple psychological need that all humans have to create icons that we can revere and adore? If you pay attention to history, I think it's fair to say that it was a little bit of both.

That "attitude of altitude" so common among clergy has always been a real interior struggle for me, especially since I have never considered myself better than anyone else. I am convinced that one of the reasons we're suffering such a dire shortage of clergy and spiritual leaders in most major world religions today is because most young people don't want to be treated as some sort of "superhuman" creature, without the right to express the needs and wants of a normal human being. Most shy away, rightfully so, from a life committed to spiritual matters because the expectations are just too unrealistic—and most of them have nothing to do with spirituality, but with Church rules.

Most rabbis, priests, and ministers would agree that there are people in our congregations who are much holier or closer to God than we are. In fact, a committed layperson can often be a better and more authentic servant of God, simply through setting good examples and showing a deep commitment to the faith. In addition, these laypeople are freer than we are, seldom becoming as tainted by the politics of religious institutions and the often rigid attitudes that accompany "professional" religious folks.

I am convinced we all have equal access to God—even those who feel they have no clue or religious training of any sort. In Christian theology, we believe that all are baptized into a priestly, prophetic, and kingly people. But that concept has not really entered the minds and hearts of most people sitting in the pews. Having spoken to countless people through the years, I am left with the impression that most people think that priests have a more direct connection to God than they do.

I can assure you that no such thing exists. It is essential to remember that those who are called to serve as priests are chosen from among the people in the pews.

I have always admired the Nobel Prize winner Mother Teresa of Calcutta for her practical approach to the spiritual life, and particularly for her way of explaining her call and her very public recognition of her own humanity.

"We are like pencils in the hand of God," Mother Teresa said, and that's a great way of looking at any type of spiritual leadership role today. Many of the great saints throughout history illustrate Mother Teresa's concept of what any spiritual leader should be.

Not too long after her death, Mother Teresa's spiritual director wrote a book revealing that Mother Teresa, too, suffered through certain times of darkness, during which she almost lost her faith in God. Many people were scandalized by this, but even more were inspired by her honesty and ability to dissent from certain ingrained ideas.

At the end of it all, I believe that Mother Teresa's approach is certainly the healthier, more realistic, vision of the ministry. Too many people have been hurt or offended by the "fall" of those they have idealized—and I'm speaking explicitly of my own fall, because I am well aware that a good number of people were scandalized by my falling in love, and especially by the tabloid photos of my public displays of affection for a woman I loved despite my promise to live as a celibate man.

If we see those who feel called by God as superhuman or somehow different from us, we too often forget that our spiritual leaders are simply instruments of the *only one* who is ultimately perfect. Spiritual leaders—including priests and other members of the clergy—are called to be instruments of God, not the music. For only God can really be the music, the message and the end.

I often wonder about the apostles Jesus chose to be the leaders of his new organization, or movement, which today we call Christianity.

There is no doubt in my mind that these boys were real characters. I think they would have had a very difficult time entering a seminary or theological school today.

Would the original apostles have passed the exams, even the psychological exams? Probably not. Most would have been turned down if they were judged by present-day standards. It's plain to see that some were extremely rigid and hardheaded, insensitive to women and children, ambitious, inconsistent, unfaithful, and even emotionally imbalanced—you name it!

In a reflection on the apostles and their personalities, one anonymous author observed that of all of the apostles, the one most likely to have found his way into the priesthood today was Judas Iscariot—because he was manipulative, knew how to make connections, and was sneaky enough to find all of the loopholes. Sad, but comical, and true as well.

NOWHERE IN THE BIBLE, or even in two thousand years of Christian tradition, do we find evidence that Jesus ever intended his closest collaborators to be celibate. The wealth and power of Rome had more to do with the original practice of celibacy than spirituality. Clerics were mostly married until the Middle Ages, when concern over loss of Church lands to the heirs of those priests led to the imposition of the celibacy rule.

Jesus designated St. Peter, a married man, as the first pope, so He must have accepted the idea that a man could be married and serve God. Most of the apostles were married, as were thirty-nine "successors of Peter," or popes. In fact, for twelve hundred years, celibacy was not mandatory among priests.

St. Paul believed that spreading the Gospel would be easier if a man didn't have a family to provide for, yet he only decreed that elders, deacons, and bishops be "the husband of one wife" as a way of cutting down on polygamy among the clergy.

From the beginning (especially looking back to the prophets and kings of the Hebrew Scriptures), there were all kinds of characters, with every possible personality trait and deficiency, who were called by God to do great things. Any honest look at the Bible will give you a good sense of this reality. God calls all kinds of folks: saints and sinners, prophets and kings, poor and rich, faithful and unfaithful.

The problem has never really been in the calling, but in the answering of that call. As human beings we have certain ideas of what our lives will be like. The prophets, disciples, and other biblical characters found in the Hebrew and Christian Scriptures all had lives when they were called. They were fishermen, businesspeople, kings and farmers—people from every possible walk of life. One could say they just had a radical change of plans.

However, that change of plans never included a requirement to live without a spouse or family. In fact, there was never any requirement to disconnect from humanity. On the contrary: It was their very connection with the world and the rest of humanity that made those chosen ones desirable servants of God.

There are presently many Catholic priests who are, indeed, married and in good standing with Rome, specifically priests of the Eastern Rites, who never had mandatory celibacy, and those received into the Roman Catholic Church from other denominations, especially my new spiritual home. Still, to be celibate is considered one of the most important spiritual aspects of a Roman Catholic priest by many within the Church and by practicing Catholics. Many of them point out that Jesus was celibate and argue that priests should be "married" to the Church. In their view, the parish is the priest's spiritual family; if you had your own family as a priest, you would have less time and energy to devote to your parish. That is nonsense and simply one more justification for an imposition that has proven to be all too problematic.

One could say that the whole concept of celibacy was flawed from the very beginning. Some historians and Church defenders will say that the idea of celibate clergy came with the Council of Elvira in Spain in about 306, which prohibited members of the clergy from marrying. Soon after that, sex was stigmatized as sinful. St. Ambrose (340–397) wrote, "The ministerial office must be kept pure and unspoiled and must not be defiled by coitus." Yet a good number of scholarly works, including the unique and exhaustive work of a layman by the name of Edgar Davie, also works by the former monk Dr. A. W. Richard Sipe and several others have come to the conclusion that the insistence on celibacy was very foreign to early Christian thought. It was certainly never an issue in apostolic times.

As time passed, priests again began to marry, or kept concubines during the Dark Ages. During this time, the wealth of the Church was increasing, and priests left Church lands to their heirs. The Holy See once again imposed the celibacy rule to protect Church real estate, and by the eleventh century, Pope Benedict VIII was forbidding the children of priests to inherit property. Pope Gregory VII, who declared himself the supreme authority "over all souls," went one step further by prohibiting married priests from saying Mass.

The first written law forbidding clergy to marry was handed down at the Second Lateran Council in 1139. While some still tried to argue in favor of clerical marriage, the law requiring clergy to be celibate became official practice for priests of the

Latin Rite, though it was not always respected. In 1563 the Council of Trent—mostly in response to the Protestant Reformation, which challenged many of Rome's nonbiblical practices— reaffirmed the practice of mandatory celibacy for most priests.

Rome's position on the issue has remained essentially unchanged since then, so many priests have continued to feel forced to live secret lives. For instance, the world's most famous Christian monk in our times was Father Thomas Merton. He was a Trappist, the strictest kind of monk, and the bestselling author of over seventy books. Recent discoveries have confirmed that, even as a monk, Father Merton fell in love and had a relationship with a twenty-five-year-old nurse.

Many of Merton's followers deny the affair, but there is solid evidence demonstrating that he was indeed involved with the woman. In his own words, *"We hugged each other close for hours in long kisses and saying, 'Thank God this at least is real.'"*

Of course, this whole episode initiated a lot of soul-searching: "I am humbled and confused by my weakness, my vulnerability, my passion. After all these years, so little sense and so little discipline. Yet I know there was good in it somewhere, nevertheless," as Mark Shaw wrote in *Beneath the Mask of Holiness.*

The reaction of many of Merton's followers,

who are far more progressive than most and cannot be considered mainstream Catholics, has been mostly positive. The humanity of the monk, expressed in his desire to love and be loved, is not considered shocking or scandalous. Yet the official Church will not say a word about it. For many in the institution it would be considered tragic or a terrible scandal.

Merton was not alone. Other prominent figures in Roman Catholicism have also had forbidden romantic relationships, though most were supposedly undiscovered until after their deaths. Do you really think that nobody knew what was going on while these men were alive? I'm betting that the housekeepers and cooks in the rectories and religious houses knew, even if nobody else did.

Another great mind in recent history was the German Jesuit theologian Father Karl Rahner. About two decades after his death, love letters were discovered that revealed Rahner's apparently celibate relationship with a woman. While nobody questions that Rahner honored his commitment to celibacy and the vows he made as a religious in the Jesuit Order, the letters do express a kind of intimacy that is exclusive to a man and a woman who love each other and have romantic interactions.

In other words, while there seems to have been no sexual contact, there was certainly an intimate romantic relationship between this prominent priest-theologian and a woman. Could that be considered a violation of the commitment to celibacy? To some, yes; to others, no. Rahner even outwardly questioned mandatory celibacy on several occasions. He challenged the institution's inflexibility in not allowing married men to serve as priests, although it was typically in the context of the pastoral need for a greater number of priests in certain geographic areas.

Today, that shortage exists almost everywhere in the world, not just in a few remote places. In one interview, quoted in *The Right to the Eucharist*, Rahner said, "If the Church everywhere, or in certain areas, is unable to find enough clergy unless it abandons celibacy, then she must abandon it; for the obligation to provide enough pastors for the Christian people takes precedence."

THE CELIBACY DEBATE ISN'T PREVALENT only among progressive bishops and liberal Catholics. I recall once being at dinner in the Holy Land with a group of very conservative lay ministers, most of whom helped distribute Communion, acted as readers during Mass, volunteered in their choirs, or were otherwise active in their parishes. At age twenty-nine, I was by far the youngest man at the table. I was also the only celibate man and the only priest; the rest of my dinner companions were all married couples.

As happened so often, the debate on celibacy began over dinner and, despite the fact that I was there, a young priest who was so clearly enthusiastic about his calling, most of the people at that dinner table avowed that they neither understood nor valued the practice of celibacy among priests. Ironically, these were conservative churchgoers—the kind of people who rarely question anything the official Church proposes.

Imagine, if you can, how sad and confused I felt, rising from that table after dinner, and feeling like those closest to me—my closest collaborators in ministry, not outsiders or the so-called unchurched—did not seem to value the life I had chosen, or the sacrifices I had made that were motivated by my love of God and the institution we all served together. Sad, because I realized that even those who claimed to be ultra-Catholic saw very little relevance in the commitment to celibacy, and confused because, as a young man full of life and possibilities, I suddenly wondered that night why one couldn't serve God while having a wife and children.

I would immediately stifle those thoughts in my early years of the priesthood. As time went by, however, it became more difficult to do that, particularly as I had the same conversations over and over again with mature laypeople in the Church—the ones who are supposed to be the most interested in supporting and encouraging young priests.

When we are discussing celibacy, it is amazing how many married laypeople have passionate opinions about the subject without having a clue as to what the practice entails. Many are indifferent or opposed to it. Others go out of their way to defend celibacy because that is what the Church says, and the Church is always right, in their eyes. Although in my younger years I was also a defender of the practice, a good number of laypeople spoke openly about this and other controversial issues with me; they perceived that I was honest and didn't immediately go on the defensive, or try to prove how wrong they were.

I assure you, it can turn ugly when certain priests defend celibacy or other Church disciplines as if they were sacred dogmas. In the minds of many priests, if Rome says it—that's it! There is nothing to argue about and nothing to question. The possibility of even thinking *outside the box* or having an intelligent debate about such issues is in itself unthinkable. Today's Church is afraid of open dialogue about most issues, especially those that can keep someone who would dare to engage in such conversations from climbing the ecclesiastical ladder that leads to power or desirable appointments.

Fortunately, I came to understand that my call to the priesthood was really to bring the Good News and to serve all kinds of people, regardless of whether they happened to agree with me or not, and there is great freedom in that! It took me years to understand it, but I eventually found that level of inner freedom. Even as a Roman Catholic priest, I refused to use the offensive words and backward ideas that sprang all too often from the mouths of those who were supposedly religious leaders, like "living in sin," "illegitimate child," "your baby can't be baptized because you were not married in the church," and so many others.

In truth, I found it awkward and more than a bit contradictory for a growing number of young priests—men living in the twenty-first century—to adopt the practice of making people feel guilty in the confessional and denying absolution. Instead, I worked hard to bridge the gap between today's reality and an institution that continues to promote old ideas—and even a list of old terms—to categorize and judge people.

As you've seen by now, my ideological transformation did not happen overnight. I believe that my work in very diverse communities, and especially in the media, led me to truly understand that people need priests who can hear all kinds of opinions and controversial views without being scandalized. Often, people called into my radio programs, wrote to my advice columns, or visited my church from great distances because they were convinced that they could only tell *me* and no other priest about what was on their minds, because they knew that their own parish priests would judge them or treat them harshly, with very little regard for their particular situations.

Many of the people who turned to me in their time of need complimented me. However, as I listened to more and more of the suffering they had experienced—some of it suffering brought on by their own priests, who seemed to be trying to provoke guilt and shame in them instead of offering love and understanding—my heart broke a little more. It saddened me to discover that so many priests came across as self-righteous and petty and appeared rattled when faced with totally human issues and experiences.

As I developed my own ministry and inner freedom, I gradually realized that I could never again be the slave of the ideological dictatorship that I had allowed to run my life for so long. Through feeling the pain of the many people who felt rejected by the Church or mistreated by their priests, I came to understand that today, more than ever, we have a great need for spiritual leaders who can listen, share a dialogue, debate civilly, and not shove concepts down people's throats.

While this is not an easy balancing act in a church that seems to offer only absolute, black-and-white answers to so many of life's most complicated questions, I believe that leaders in the Church must learn to engage in this civil dialogue if they are to offer spiritual guidance and human solutions to so many of today's problems. Repeating a list of set rules or doctrinal explanations just won't cut it for most people. While the Roman Catholic Church certainly doesn't have the monopoly on truth and the Inquisition has been over for centuries, many of its members still speak and act as people living in times long gone. The fact is that we live in a pluralistic society in which there is no longer just one way or one church through which one can find or arrive at truth.

That is where I believe my ideological struggle truly began. Yes, I fell in love, but my struggle began long before I experienced sexual desire for the woman who would become my wife. However, my struggle, on its deepest level, was about trying to connect an old institution, with too many archaic ideas, with a world that is constantly changing. In that world I found many people— from various religious, political, and philosophical traditions—who inspired me to see beyond what I had been taught was the only way.

Once upon a time, I was truly in love with the mission of the priesthood and everything it represented in my mind. I embraced the idea that I would be with people at the happiest and saddest moments of human experience—maybe a wedding or a baptism and a funeral all on the same day—and accompany people through the ups and downs of life. All of that fascinated me.

As I look back now, I realize that I also did everything possible to fall in love with the Church and all it was *supposed* to represent without really knowing, on any deep level, what the Church was as an institution. Unfortunately, love often means suffering, and I did suffer, because I was so passionate in my convictions and convinced that the Church was one thing, when it really was something totally different.

At times, all of the good things I thought were at the heart of the Church were actually very far from it, and eventually that was too painful to bear. But, like almost anyone else who has ever fallen in love, I wanted to give the object of my love, my adoration, my passion, the benefit of the doubt. Like any lover, I was determined to see the good and ignore whatever ugliness might leave me feeling disenchanted.

At times, I would scratch my head, trying to understand how I could have possibly ended up in the middle of so much dysfunction, but then I'd find a way to live with it. I confess that I most often found it much easier to deal with the mysteries of heaven than to confront earthly realities like the ones I discovered in the Church: indifference, apathy, and a lack of real accountability. Nevertheless, despite everything negative swirling around me, I remained convinced that my mission was heavenly.

I continued to be in love with the Roman Catholic Church for many years. My dedication was so absolute that I never really thought about my own wants, needs, or desires. I trained myself to think a certain way, the Church's way, and lived accordingly.

It was like an intense love affair, and one that marked my soul.

IN THE ROMAN CATHOLIC CONCEPTION of reality, priesthood is often spiritually and theologically compared to a marriage between the priest and the Church. One could argue that there are a lot of theological and emotional problems with this arrangement, but it is indeed one of the many ideals that the Church still promotes today—and that many young people are led to believe.

I was raised in a family with great morals, where marriage was honored and my grandparents and parents all kept their vows to remain married to one another "until death do us part." I saw them love each other in good times and in bad, in sickness and in health, all the days of their lives. Consequently, I have always held the institution of marriage in high esteem, and I took seriously the idea that priestly promises are a sign of *marriage to the Church.* Living in a state of "infidelity" and breaking the promises made before God was certainly not something I could easily accept—even as I was doing it.

People who have no clue what it really entails will tell you with great conviction: *Nuns are married to God and priests are married to the Church*. It makes you wonder how this "marriage" worked for the apostles and their successors, including the thirty-nine popes who were married until the Church made celibacy mandatory in the twelfth century. Were they *also* married to the Church? Were they just as much priests as I was, even though they were married to an actual human being and ordained? Yes, they were—and I am sure they were probably much better priests for it.

There are also thousands of Eastern Rite priests who are married, because the Catholic Church in those regions of the world does not require celibacy of their priests. Ironically, today there are Anglicans (like me) and ministers of other Christian churches who are accepted into the Roman Catholic ministry with their wives and families as part of a special provision that began in the United States and is slowly becoming more universal.

All of this seemed like a contradiction to me: Why them and not me? Why is celibacy such a big deal for some and optional for others? Did the marriages of rabbis and ministers of different faiths, many of whom I got to know both professionally and as friends, make them in any way less committed or united to God than I was?

The answer was always the same: No way!

Thus, the breakdown of my own departure from the promise of celibacy began at an ideological level. For some within the institution, it is deemed impossible to change your mind or evolve, for that would be considered an infidelity or confusion about one's faith. But human beings must be allowed to change their minds about what they believe to be true and good. Otherwise, we are mere robots.

Those who were paying attention knew that I was no longer happy or fulfilled within the Roman Catholic structure, and that I really needed to move on even years before I fell in love. Making a clean break is not always so easy, though, and for me it turned out to be quite complicated.

Was I suffering a crisis of faith? No—my faith in God was growing stronger every day. It was a crisis of ideology and a profound change of mind and heart. I never expected that I would mentally, psychologically, and spiritually evolve and change my mind the way I did, but I finally came to realize that I no longer held many of the positions that appeared to be so dear to the institution in which I chose to serve God.

This has been a difficult and painful process. But I realized that the "Roman way" was no longer my way, even as I hesitated to admit that truth to myself. In addition to disagreeing with the institution's teachings about celibacy, contraception, divorce, attitudes toward homosexuality and women in ministry, for instance, I often had conflicts with canon law (Church law) and the way it was applied, because I always felt that it had very little to do with biblical principles and everything to do with mere human precepts—ways of legislating people's lives and excluding people. Canon law kept more people from being at peace with God than anything else in the Church.

Imagine what it's like to have to tell people who come looking for a priest, with a great deal of pain in their hearts, that you cannot hear their confessions or give them absolution because they were not married "in the Church." Canon law is often the excuse used to keep people from important things like receiving Communion, remarrying, or participating fully in any number of sacraments. The emphasis on that book of "laws" is what makes intelligent young priests develop a bunch of hang-ups or a false sense of superiority. Too often, those laws serve as an excuse for clergy to act standoffish and dogmatic.

Many of those canons promote standards that very few people can meet. I believe that if most Roman Catholics really understood what their Church considers a mortal sin, they'd have to walk around feeling disappointed in their own behavior nearly every day of the week. I would even venture to say that, by traditional Church standards, 90 percent of the people who receive Communion on Sundays are doing it against the laws and norms of their own Church, but—thank God—most don't know it.

For over half of my life, I also lived in that black-and-white canonical world that claims to have all the right answers. That world provided me with a clear sense of security for a good while, and I wanted to believe with all my heart it was the way to salvation. Whenever the pope or any outspoken Church leader showed some degree of openness to the twenty-first century or an interest in really listening to the realities of today, I would feel excited about the possibilities that kind of openness could create, but for two decades I was still very much committed to following the party line.

Why did I stay so long? Partly out of fear. I got into trouble whenever I gave the slightest impression that the institution I was committed to serving needed to progress, relax, or begin to change. Because I was so paralyzed by my dilemma, it took a crazy media frenzy for me to finally move on and admit to myself that what I really wanted, with all my heart, was to serve God as a married man and be part of a church that shared many of my ideological positions—at least, one that was open to debating almost anything without the fear of condemnation.

When I try to make sense of why events unfolded as they did, I see that I was held back by my desire to avoid disappointing so many people who had always counted on me to affirm the teachings of that black-and-white world they were so faithful to—an institution I had represented so publicly for such a long time. It is difficult to leave what was once your ideological comfort zone and move into new and unknown territory, even when you are convinced that it is the right thing for you to do.

THE DEBATE OVER WHETHER PRIESTS should be allowed to marry has a lot more to do with attitudes within the Church about how we deal with the very important issue of human sexuality, and control over people, than with Church discipline or practice. If you look at the early days of celibacy, and part of the ritualistic reasoning behind it, there was a perceived connection between the sexual act and the worthiness of the minister to celebrate the sacraments.

In the first centuries of Christianity, for example, the Council of Elvira created a provision stating that a priest would lose his job if he had sexual relations the night before celebrating Mass. Can you imagine God, who created sex and allowed it to be the ultimate expression of love, asking people not to engage in it because it is somehow incompatible with worship on the next day?

The Church promotes a culture of sexual

repression and negative attitudes about sexuality, and the hierarchy feels compelled to make decisions about the way people choose to love and serve their God. Ultimately, this is more about control than it is about sex.

In today's Church, those showing enough courage to express opposition to the requirement of celibacy are being motivated in large part by witnessing the many types of sexual dysfunction among celibate clergy. For some of these priests, I believe the dysfunction results directly from entering the religious life as teenagers, especially if they were forced to do so by parents who believed that the honor of having a priest in the family would grant them a secure place in heaven. That may seem archaic, but it is still the case in some cultures.

Others chose celibacy with the thought that accepting a life with no expression of physical intimacy was a demonstration of their faith, only to find that struggling with celibacy bled into their emotional lives. Many may have been victims of abuse or were raised in emotionally dysfunctional families, and due to a variety of life experiences, they may have acquired a negative vision of any type of sexual expression. These are the people who, even in marriage, are never able to have a healthy sexual life and often make their spouses victims of their own unresolved past.

The Roman Catholic Church has made some

strides in moving beyond the thought of sexuality as a faculty God gave us "just for procreation." For some time now, the Church has also taught that sex is an expression of love that unites a married couple. It was John Paul II who opened the way for the "Theology of the Body" promoted by many conservative Roman Catholics today.

Yet there are still too many people within the Church who act as if they are asexual and lack any urges at all. The asexual person finds a comfortable fit in the Church's hierarchy, especially in positions of authority, because the system expects them to be that way. A person who is too honest about his or her "sexual feelings"— or any other feelings, for that matter—doesn't go far up the Church ladder.

This is the crux of the Church's sexual problem: Whether a candidate for priesthood is straight, gay, or struggling to find his identity, how can he talk about it if the institution he is committing his life to gives him every indication that it really doesn't want to know the truth about him as a human being?

WHEN YOU LIMIT YOUR POOL of priestly candidates to celibate males, you are basically telling God whom to call and how to call them. That doesn't make sense. Why should Church authorities be the ones determining the pool of candidates qualified to serve God, especially if the

Church has no real plan to deal with the shortage of healthy, active men prepared to live the promise of celibacy—other than to accept their cheating as long as they appear celibate on the outside?

Yet the hypocrisy of the sex problem goes beyond that. Often, the most outspoken promoters of celibacy and the homophobic agenda in the Church don't live up to the practice they so vehemently defend in public. I remember one day when a young gay woman came to me in the confessional, devastated because her previous confessor had said, "You and your partner are endangering your eternal salvation."

She cried so much that I asked her, "Who said this to you?"

When she told me the name of the priest, I could hardly believe my ears. He was well known to be gay and secretly partnered! It turned out that he was among the toughest confessors on young gays and lesbians, often denying his penitents sacramental absolution. I often thought, "I wonder if that happens to him when he goes to confession."

In response to the Church's sex abuse crisis, the Vatican put out an official "instruction," basically stating that homosexuals would not be allowed in seminaries. This new rule will only serve to push people further into the closet. It certainly won't encourage anyone to deal with their sexuality in a healthy way.

What makes this rule even more impossibly hypocritical is that the very office in Rome that issued that document is staffed by some of the most flamboyantly homosexual clergy. One day, while filming a documentary on the Vatican, I visited several offices of the Curia in Rome. I'll never forget how I was taken off guard when some members of the crew asked me, "Father, who are these guys?" referring to the number of visibly effeminate men in Roman collars and long cassocks walking around.

I knew what they meant. They thought, Here is this institution that says homosexual acts are intrinsically disordered, that homosexuals are not normal people created and loved by God. Yet that exclusive and backward agenda didn't match what we were seeing with our own eyes. A few years later it would become public, in what seemed to be continual media reports, that there were indeed a significant number of promiscuous gay priests and laymen working in the Vatican offices, even within the papal household. While all this does not necessarily have to do directly with celibacy, it is certainly somehow connected to it, because of the sexual culture it creates beneath the surface.

The bestselling novelist and priest sociologist Andrew Greeley has proposed a unique solution to the clergy shortage and celibacy issue. He suggests that we create a type of "Priest Corps," in which men can give five to ten years of service and renew it if they feel inclined. If they later feel they want to be married, they can move on, serving as priests on an as-needed or emergency basis. Greeley believes that this policy would motivate men to give the best of themselves and not fall into the all-too-common mediocrity so prevalent among clergy who become bitter and tired with time.

As realistic as I consider Greeley to be, it surprises me that he still fails to identify celibacy and the sexual lives of priests as one of the biggest problems facing the priesthood. He claims, "In the worst case, the Catholic Church in the United States . . . may go down the drain, but not because of attacking infidels, not because of celibacy or homosexuality or sexual abuse, not because of secularism and materialism, but because of incompetence, stupidity, and clerical culture—all enemies from within."*

I agree regarding the negative impact of incompetence and a dysfunctional clerical culture, but I disagree with his dismissal of the huge negative consequences of celibacy and priest scandals (of whatever sort) within the Church, as well as the possible link between them. These scandals continue to undermine the Church's spiritual and moral authority. They also highlight

---

*Andrew M. Greeley, *Priests: A Calling in Crisis* (The University of Chicago Press, 2004).

the level of incompetence of leaders at every level, who cannot seem to muster the basic administrative actions required to respond to them.

Nobody ever talks about the amount of time and energy Church authorities spend in dealing with the dysfunctional lives of priests, therapy, rehabilitation programs, and a host of other things that are all related to the consequences of abject loneliness and isolation in the lives of many priests. A lot of that wasted energy could be focused on the Church's actual mission of love and service to humanity.

I have spent quite a bit of time listening to and corresponding with priests all over the United States, Latin America, and beyond, mostly because of the familiarity people feel toward someone who appears on TV and radio. I have also dealt with many priests face-to-face, some of whom I consider friends, who were accused of some form of sexual abuse or were forced to abandon their ministry due to an infraction against celibacy. In every one of those cases, I am sure that something as basic as a thirst for human contact played a major role in the good or bad decisions they made.

THE REACTION OF THE MEDIA to my situation reopened the heated debate about whether priests should be allowed to marry and fully live out the gift of their sexuality. This is a legitimate debate in most people's minds, including among those who are the most influential decision makers in the Church hierarchy. More than a year after I became an Anglican and chose to serve God as a married priest, I heard a local church leader speak of what I did as a "slap in the face of my brother priests." I never heard a bishop say that about the priests who had abused and sodomized children and continued serving in the Church for decades. It was once again clear that some Church leaders believe a priest who decides to leave, gets married, and continues to serve God in another church is committing an unforgivable sin.

At least two cardinals have recently made public comments about the possible end of mandatory celibacy, but they always do it at the end of their careers, once they're no longer interested in staying in Rome's good graces. Church authorities know it's a hot topic and not something they can continue to ignore. It's not a matter of *if* the celibacy requirement will change, but *when*.

The fateful day that the pictures showing me kissing and caressing Ruhama were published, I began receiving correspondence and calls from people around the world, including a few from the Vatican, pledging that they would pray for me. The most emotional ones were from certain Church leaders, who pleaded with me, saying,

"Whatever you do, Albert, don't leave the Church."

At that point, almost three weeks before I made the official announcement that I was leaving the Roman Catholic Church, 99 percent of the mail and calls were positive. I also received books, CDs, and personal notes from priests, women, and children who had been involved in situations where their lovers or fathers were also priests. They wrote to share their stories with me.

After our marriage, I appeared on the *Oprah Winfrey Show.* I was aware of her show, of course, and the media had even compared us, calling me "Padre Oprah." Still, I wasn't sure what to expect; I'd had many bad experiences with the press by then. As it turned out, Oprah was a very kind person and comfortable to be around, which makes her a wonderful interviewer.

Following my appearance on *Oprah*, I once again received thousands of e-mails and letters. Of course, there were mixed reactions, ranging from incredibly positive support to the typical hateful rhetoric from people who feel betrayed by anyone who chooses to live and minister outside of the Roman Catholic box. Again, though, most of the mail was supportive. It included correspondence from many Roman Catholics— including clergy and religious—who believe that the Church needs to review some of its practices and allow a wider group of people to embrace the call to ordained ministry, including women and married priests. The press who interviewed me also received a great deal of mail.

One of the most moving notes was this one:

My oldest brother was ordained at the age of twenty-seven. He struggled greatly in maintaining his celibacy promise. He was a brilliant priest, and served God with honor. He died of AIDS at forty-two.

I often think of his struggles, which were all private ones, unknown to his parents, his siblings, and his many admirers until his diagnosis. My brother walked the halls of his hospital, ministering to others with AIDS right up until the point he could walk no more.

He and I prayed for his forgiveness in his last days, and he had only enough strength to squeeze my hand to acknowledge that he had confessed his sins. I have no doubt that my brother was forgiven. I believe he is now in the embrace of our Divine Creator in heaven, along with my father, who, along with my mother, gave my brother unconditional love during his very painful last years of his life.

I gave the eulogy for my brother. I share this story with you, so that you can appreciate the deep meaning of your interview in many people's lives . . . I thought your interview with Father Cutié about his relationship with the woman he loves brought understanding and acceptance.

There are a good number of priests in every corner of the planet who have fallen in love and continue to exercise their priestly ministry while involved in loving relationships. Church authorities know this. One of the things that surprised me most was hearing from so many men and women who have accepted that living this type of double life is the only option, even with all the pain and inner turmoil that the lifestyle entails. While I have not met most of these people in person, they have become a very significant group for me. There are more priests and women in this situation than anyone can imagine. I once met a bishop in a Latin American diocese who confided in me that every priest in his diocese had a girlfriend; most of his priests had fathered children in those relationships. His was a small rural diocese and he had only a dozen priests for a large geographical area. This was his reality, and he couldn't do anything about it if he wanted to keep the few priests he had. Those priests are often on my mind and in my daily prayers.

In my first years of ministry, it was hard for me to understand how a situation like that could happen—or be permitted. But, with the passage of time, and as my ministry in the media took me all around the world, I began to understand how impossible celibacy is for most people. The phenomenon of Roman Catholic priests who are officially celibate but leading secret lives is present all over the world, particularly in parts of Latin America, Africa, and other places where priesthood is still considered a sort of status symbol.

In some of these areas, it's common to hear people openly speak about priests who have fathered children and have hidden partners, sometimes even in the guise of the church housekeeper. It is a reality that many bishops have to deal with, because they are often responsible for paying tuition at religious schools and sustaining those mothers and the children fathered by priests. Even to this day, a number of these men and their hidden partners write to me. I hear their daily struggles and I can relate; like most of them, I never expected to be in such a conflicted state.

Falling in love isn't something you plan; it simply *happens*. When priests confess the guilt associated with not fulfilling one of the promises they consciously made at ordination, I feel their pain. This is something that tears at your heart, because if you are called, you never stop having the desire to please God and, in some way, the institution that insists on that specific way of being a priest.

What continues to truly intrigue me is how diverse and radical people's reactions are to the dilemma of a priest falling in love and the discovery of a hidden relationship. Some prefer to look the other way and keep their opinions to themselves. That is what the institution teaches us: *Say nothing.* In the official Church, silence is too often mistaken for prudence. This is why, even when those in authority know something is going on in a priest's life, the tendency is to avoid confrontation.

Sadly, this then becomes the system. Because silence is the Church's fallback position over any sort of controversy, speaking out on issues can be very damaging to those seeking positions of leadership within the institution. I once heard a Vatican diplomat say, "It doesn't matter what you do, as long as nobody finds out."

Of course, if you take a wrong step and your situation becomes public, you're left to sink or swim on your own. Even the most compassionate and caring Church leaders don't know what to do with someone in that situation. Transparency when dealing with tough political, social, or sexual scandals is rarely found among Church leaders. The system just doesn't know how to handle it.

These days, extremist Roman Catholics are a new force to be reckoned with, since they are mostly young and have been steadily growing in number since the Church introduced changes to renew itself in the Second Vatican Council. A good number of people within the Church have been resisting any form of that renewal and the changes it implies, ever since the historic council introduced by Pope John XXIII. These are the folks who defend celibacy and every other Church discipline as if they were unchangeable truths, without knowing the history or reasoning behind the practices they defend.

Among them are those who appear to be convinced that Jesus spoke Latin at the Last Supper, and therefore think that everything should still be in Latin to keep tradition alive. Some of these "defenders of the faith" (as many perceive themselves) possess a certain degree of theological knowledge, but the vast majority are just people with uninformed opinions who are fearful of the future. If the pope says something, they believe him verbatim. Rome likes that.

These extremist Roman Catholics have created their own version of infallibility and it applies to everything, not just faith and morals. Many of them are still convinced there is no salvation outside of *their* church. I often think they will be very disappointed when they get to heaven and meet St. Peter at the gates—first, to find out he was a married apostle and pope, and then to have to sit at the same heavenly banquet with people of all faiths. Don't they realize that in heaven there is only going to be *one* table for all of us?

I once gave an interview for a newspaper in Guayaquil, Ecuador. I was asked all kinds of controversial questions about Church positions. The next morning, they decided to make the headline "Padre Alberto Says Celibacy Is Not a Dogma." For many people, including the very conservative volunteers of the television network I was associated with at the time, all hell broke loose! People wrote angry letters and e-mails, and filled the blogosphere with their backward-leaning opinions. They had very little regard for dialogue, debate, or honestly questioning the Church's nonbiblical positions on a variety of controversial subjects—mostly having some connection with sex, of course. Little did they know that the headline was actually correct according to Roman Catholic theology; celibacy *is not* a dogma and several recent popes have actually said it.

It's funny, but when these extremist types write to me directly, they always seem to forget that the person they are addressing is *still* a priest. (Sacramental theology clearly teaches that once someone becomes a priest, he is always a priest.) They go on tirades about how scandalized they are about my "forbidden affair with a woman," "living in sin," "fornicating," and, of course, how my actions have *damaged* the Church.

I always respond by simply stating something like: "I thank you for taking the time to write and

I wish God's blessings upon you and your family."

Do these folks realize how they contradict themselves? If they truly loved the priesthood and defended it so much, why would they take the time to attack or insult me, a priest? In your own biological family, when a person fails in some way, does he become any less a part of your family? Do we have to agree with all of the decisions of every member of our family, every time?

As people who believe in forgiveness and redemption, why can't we value the good in everyone, even when we are hurt by their errors or sins? I often wonder if the message of love in the Lord's Prayer has any bearing on their lives as they're repeating, "Forgive us our trespasses as we forgive those who trespass against us . . ." Perhaps even more important is the message of God's unconditional love reaching all these supposedly *devout* churchgoers?

It's sad to have to say this, but following so many sex abuse scandals, many of which involved minors, some people were so blinded by rage and disappointment that they're now unable to make distinctions between sin, criminal behavior, and ordinary human weakness.

Ironically, you do not see the outrage from conservative Roman Catholics when priests display unhealthy sexual behaviors, as long as the priests deny it and hide. In some ways, many choose to act like parents with a problem child: They'd rather look the other way when their child is acting out and deny the bad behavior that the rest of the world sees so clearly.

Roman Catholics are taught that the priest is married to the Church, and many feel possessive of their priests. They therefore act like they have a sort of divine right to give their opinions about every priest, whether they really know anything about that particular individual.

You will often hear Catholics say, "Father So-and-So is an excellent priest," when they really don't have a clue who the real person is behind the collar. Like many people everywhere, Roman Catholics base their opinions on mere assumptions or appearances.

When people would say to me, "Father Albert, you are a saint or an angel," I'd answer, "Pray for me, because I'm human just like you, and we're not in heaven yet!" On radio and television interviews, I have always spoken honestly about my own struggles to live a more spiritual life.

I once received a phone call from a traditional-minded Catholic who complained, "Father, you should never admit to having flaws. You should have all of the virtues."

He sounded convinced of that! He and other radically conservative Catholics are the most likely to feel hurt and disappointed at the fall of a priest, because they are taught to believe in an ideal world, far removed from reality or the consequences of living in this day and age. They have an almost romantic idea of priesthood, as I once did.

Several months after getting married, I received a Christmas card from a family I always had a great relationship with and had shared many ups and downs with, but who could not support my desire to marry and continue serving God in a new church. The one-line card summarized what they felt very eloquently: "We will always remember you with affection, even if you abandoned your flock."

In other words, there was not an ounce of interest or concern in me as a fellow human being. My actions were simply too hard for them to accept, or to even try to comprehend. They often made me feel as if I had committed the worst crime. I thought to myself, If they only knew the things many of the priests they look up to and go to now are doing. . . .

EVEN MONTHS AFTER THE PICTURES were published, no matter what kind of priestly scandal hit the news, there always seemed to be a reference to my own affair—even in cases where no comparison could come close. One of the hardest to stomach was the story of a stripper who accused a priest of seeking her out at strip clubs and getting her pregnant. DNA testing proved that the priest was indeed the father of her child. A little research showed that, several years earlier, Church authorities had settled a lawsuit with the woman for $100,000. The stripper also claimed that she had been married and that the priest had paid for her divorce. The story went on and on, but Church leaders *did not say a word*—total silence.

It was sad to see a priest I knew to be a very good human being caught up in a situation like that. The only way I could make sense of it was to have compassion and try to understand the deep level of loneliness this priest was probably experiencing. In his supposedly celibate life, he must have been so lonely and depressed that his only relief came from the "intimacy" of his relationship with a stripper—someone he had to pay in order to fulfill his desire for companionship.

This is one of the real scandals nobody wants to see in the Church: good people, mostly good men, who are so lonely on the inside that they are often driven to satisfy basic human emotional and physical needs in all the wrong ways. How is it possible that we have an institution in the twenty-first century with rules that forbid those called by God to love and make love with another human being, when those rules drive so many people toward destructive behaviors?

In the best of these cases, priests have an adult consenting partner. Other times, priests replace that type of intimacy with alcohol, pets, food, pornography, sex abuse of minors, or even an exaggerated desire for material things. It is common to see clergy—men I consider good priests—buy endless gadgets to avoid dealing with the emptiness they feel on the inside.

I remember one priest who could never be transferred from one parish to another, because he had a room filled with VHS movies he'd bought and no other place to put them. Some even spend to the point of sinking deeply into debt and never climb out again, since most priests are really not earning much.

Ultimately, the system of celibacy promotes fear, not freedom. It forces everyone who feels an authentic call to serve God as a Roman Catholic priest to think that they're wrong to also have the desire to love another human being.

What is truly amazing is that, even with all of the scandals about priests in the news, a significant number of idealistic young people are still inspired enough to follow the path to the priesthood or the religious life as sisters. They firmly believe God has set this path before them. I know exactly how they feel, because the same thing happened to me. I, too, was a romantic idealist who dreamed about belonging to a Church and a fraternity that I eventually discovered did not really exist.

I have to confess that I am concerned about

these young people. What will happen to them when they realize that the system of celibacy is so dysfunctional and has so very little real emotional support for anyone within it? What will they do if they find themselves in the very situation I found myself in? What destructive behaviors might they accept for themselves in order to cope with the system they are accepting?

And what happens if they discover, as I did, that one love does not necessarily exclude the other?

CHAPTER THIRTEEN

DISPOSABLE PRIESTS

I often think back to that exact moment during my ordination when the bishop called us into a special conference room with our families and said, "We will take very good care of them."

I have never forgotten that phrase, or even the expression on the archbishop's face, as he uttered what I took to be a sincere desire on his part—and on the Church's part—to care for his priests. Perhaps in his own mind, he thinks that he did. If that's true, then he and I have a very different understanding of what it means to take very good care of someone.

To me, those very significant words represent a promise that you will demonstrate personal concern for the people who serve under you, especially when you throw them into difficult situations that you, yourself, have ultimately created and are responsible for resolving. But the truth is that many, many priests I have come to know through my lifetime sincerely believed that the Church would take care of them, that the institution they had given their entire lives to, in some cases, would at least demonstrate basic compassion and offer a helping hand when they were in need. These men were sadly disappointed.

Instead, the functionaries of the Church often

threw them under a bus when faced with bumps in the road, and there was little evidence that the highest among the hierarchy cared about them in the least. Yes, there have been a few exceptions, but the norm seems to be that the higher priests move up in the institution of the Roman Catholic Church, the more interested they become in fashioning and maintaining their own careers and images. Very few at the top will sacrifice their desire to climb for anyone or anything.

One of the most destructive priestly habits is indulging in the culture of ambition, which leads to a disregard for other human beings in the competition for power. Some priests even pay the Vatican for honorary titles and positions of prestige; I see this as ultimately the same drive to fill their intimacy needs with another unhealthy pursuit.

These frustrated people use the Church as a way to climb higher and higher in status, pushing everyone out of their way to get there. This path gives them control over others. It has little to do with service, ministry, vocation, or the Gospel of Jesus Christ; it has everything to do with what "being successful" in the Church is all about. This culture of ambition is partly responsible for destroying the lives of many good and dedicated priests.

Probably the example of this that hit closest to home for me was the case of my own pastor from

Key West, Florida, where I served as a deacon-intern. This pastor was a selfless, hardworking man whose sexuality I never thought much about, truthfully, because to me he seemed asexual. I never knew whether he was attracted to men or women, because of course I had been raised not to ask questions like that of a priest. Meanwhile, I had better things to attend to, particularly since my pastor encouraged me to get involved in the crisis of Cuban refugees arriving on Florida's shores in such dire poverty.

Several years later, when the Church's sex abuse scandals erupted in Boston and rapidly began traveling around the nation, the media began putting pressure on Church authorities to examine their personnel files and clean up their messes. Bishops were scared, and the direct result was that many priests were called and asked to step down, resign, or retire—mostly against their will, and often in a matter of hours. During that initial three-year period of the shocking pedophilia scandal, more than seven hundred priests were dismissed in the United States.

Priests who had been accused of even "vague situations" decades ago were disappearing all over the country. My Key West pastor was one of them: He was removed from his parish largely because of accusations regarding an inappropriate situation with a minor some thirty years before. Nobody knew the details of this accusation, despite the fact that Key West is such a small town and the kind of place where it's always difficult to keep a secret. All I ever knew was that my pastor was "asked to retire," a nice way to say that he was being removed. Situations like his caused a deep hurt in my soul. It's not easy to see the people you admired and respected most disappear from ministry due to skeletons in their closets. And he was not my only priest mentor to leave active ministry that way.

Years later, I attended this man's fiftieth anniversary as a priest. We celebrated his golden anniversary in the tiny chapel of a nursing home, because priests who were removed for situations regarding sexual abuse were mostly hidden and never permitted to celebrate Masses in parishes ever again. Many couldn't do it publicly at all, in fact, but the archbishop happened to like this particular pastor and made an exception.

It was heartbreaking to see how the institutional Church treated this man and many of its other longest-serving soldiers. If there is any truth behind the concept of red flags and how they serve to alert us in life, this anniversary was a huge one for me: Here was a priest I respected, a man who had served his Church for half a century, and now he couldn't even say a special Mass in a normal parish church or chapel. That was really the worst kind of punishment for a priest, I thought.

Throughout that guarded Mass, I couldn't help but remember all of the good work I had witnessed this man doing with my own eyes, and all of the lessons about parish life I had learned from him as a deacon-intern. I recalled how this pastor had done everything in his power to create a parish that was a warm, welcoming place for all. He had raised the money to renovate St. Mary Star of the Sea, restoring the dilapidated church to its former glory. He had reopened a convent that was closed, so that nuns could return to Key West and teach children in the little parochial school.

I kept thinking about all of the programs, projects, and energy that this man—who was well into his seventies at that time—put into a parish that his predecessors had allowed to go to ruin due to their mismanagement. Now, just a few years later, here he was, celebrating his fiftieth anniversary in a tiny, uncomfortable nursing home chapel with seats for no more than twenty people. About thirty of us crowded in anyway. Because there was no choir, I led the singing that day, trying to create a Mass that was as joyful and reverent as possible; we also chanted a few traditional hymns and the main parts of the Eucharist.

Right after that anniversary Mass, one of this priest's friends introduced himself to me and said, "I'm another one of those chartered priests."

"A chartered priest?" I responded in confusion, for I had no idea what he meant.

"Yes," the priest said. "I was among those removed from ministry with the Dallas Charter."

Now I understood. With the Dallas Charter of 2002, the U.S. bishops made a move that the public applauded as a zero-tolerance policy for child sexual abuse. While the motive for this might have been a good one, the problem with the Dallas Charter is that it also included the almost complete elimination of due process and other canon law procedures originally put into place to protect priests and the people from injustices that can often occur in the Church—and in our society.

The anniversary of my former pastor was a good day, but a somewhat sad one for me, because it was just one of many instances where a priest who had done so much good work for the Church was made to feel ostracized. It was further incriminating evidence that the institutional Church is more concerned with its image than with the ministry of mercy and compassion.

Many priests live in totally ambiguous situations after being removed from their parishes, because their bishops prefer not to be tarnished by having any association with the fallen priests. This is true all over the world. Whatever happened to the concept of a shepherd not abandoning his sheep?

Today, we are living in an era of CEO bishops. There is too little regard for the individual and too much concern for the institution; raising money is often the priority. I detested this lack of personal concern on the part of the Church for its own clergy. I'm not even talking about providing anything material for these fallen priests. A simple phone call or letter would demonstrate some degree of gratitude for the service rendered and the years of dedication.

Who knows what my pastor and other accused priests were accused of, or how true the allegations were? There was no way to find out, despite the fact that we live in a country where everyone is supposedly innocent until proven guilty in a court of law.

In the end, it didn't really matter. My pastor was banned from ministry and his life's work forever. The legal system can take years to clarify the truth despite settlements involving millions of dollars. Many priests who believe they are innocent feel betrayed by these settlements, because they see the money of the Church being wasted to clear false accusations. Laypeople also feel betrayed by their bishops, because while they are closing churches and eliminating essential services due to lack of funds, they are also paying huge amounts of money to settle cases of abuse that may or may not have credibility.

On top of that, at a personal level, very few in the Church, both clergy and lay, ever make any attempt to reach out to these men, who may have been priests for decades, doing good work. I was particularly bothered when one of the priests I replaced after he had been accused of a sexual abuse incident never even heard from the young priests he had mentored and even financially supported. These were guys who had nice chalices and expensive vestments for their first Masses, thanks to this now "fallen" priest. Weren't we taught that the Gospel mandate is to reach out to those in greatest need? Why was this kind of reaching out so difficult for my brother priests?

Unfortunately, this is common behavior among priests, who imitate the institution of the Church and march to the beat of its drum. I personally called every one of those priests and asked them to please contact their fallen mentor, but only about half of them actually did it. It was sad.

The lesson here is clear: When the Church gets rid of you—that's it!

OLDER ROMAN CATHOLIC PRIESTS seem to be better at dealing with the Church as an institution. They are more tolerant of priests with all kinds of habits, double lives, and dysfunctions and seem altogether better able to live with the dictatorial style that is so prevalent in the Church hierarchy.

I admire today's elderly priests, because many of these men possess a freedom not felt by those trapped in the ambition of climbing the institutional ladder. The older priests are no longer competing for positions of power or for a hat. Maybe that's why they seem to possess a tendency to be open to everyone. Their experiences make them more flexible in their approaches to life and to human weakness. They are not so trapped in the box. Even when they remain publicly very respectful of it, many of them know that they must do this for survival.

The reason why some older priests never retire is because their lives would have little meaning without their work. For others, the thought of not "being the boss" and "in charge" would be too much to handle. Another real factor is that, in many countries, there are no adequate pension plans or health insurance for retired priests, so they stay on and on.

A lot of what I have just mentioned about older priests also applies to a great number of nuns and religious sisters who are in the same age category. There truly are heroic women within the Church today; their credibility continues to be very high in spite of all the scandals. Perhaps this is because they're often not part of the bureaucratic institution and mostly keep close to the people they serve. These women are generous, self-sacrificing, and very dedicated—yet receive little recognition.

In fact, women in religious orders and congregations that value education are often better prepared to preach and teach theology than the majority of priests and bishops. Yet recently the Vatican commissioned an "investigation" of women religious in the United States, simply because any group within the institution that the hierarchy perceives as going beyond the prescribed box is suspect under the current leadership.

This is embarrassing. Imagine the level of insecurity that must exist within the Vatican if they have to actually investigate one of the most dedicated groups within their own organization, especially at a time when countless bishops and other Church officials (even within the Roman Curia) apparently need much more investigating, if you consider the many problems caused by their mismanagement and lack of apparent accountability to anyone. Someone should tell the Vatican that nuns do not need to be investigated; they need to be congratulated for their lifelong dedication and for putting up with an often misogynistic organization that has often treated them as cheap labor. I have always considered that nuns and religious sisters are one of the Church's greatest strengths and treasures!

A hardworking and dedicated nun who has served the Church for decades was recently notified she was excommunicated by a U.S. bishop (actually someone I met when he was a priest and I was a young seminarian) because she allowed a young woman to terminate her pregnancy at a Roman Catholic hospital in order to save her life. Did anyone in the institution bother to learn the details or understand the terrible dilemma that nun was faced with? These are the facts: A twenty-seven-year-old woman, already the mother of four children, suffered from pulmonary hypertension and agreed to her doctors' recommendation that she terminate the pregnancy only after it became clear that she would die otherwise. The religious sister, as head of the hospital's ethics committee and a hospital administrator for years, participated in the discussion with the doctors, the patient, and the patient's family. Obviously, this nun was "pro-life" and was not an "abortionist." But in today's Roman Catholic Church, there are never any grays; it is either the institution's way or the highway. Using your God-given reason is not at all necessary; just follow the rules and you'll be fine. It seems that nobody in the official Church sees the way this nun has been treated as a scandal, but it is the worst kind of scandal. Many dedicated people—clergy and laity alike—are too often sidelined and disrespected by the official Church.

As a matter of fact, one of the internal scandals that the Church never deals with publicly is the way it treats its own priests and longtime dedicated workers. While not all priests are removed or retired the same way and not all bishops function like CEOs, there are canonical (official Church law and protocol) games they can play to move people around when they feel like it, or to oust them whenever they please.

The greatest crime is what is often done with many elderly priests—and even some bishops—at the end of their journey. The universal norm is that everyone is supposed to retire with a written resignation by age seventy-five, including bishops. However, Rome makes exceptions to this rule all the time, especially with those who have been good to the Church financially.

Here is what I have observed: If a bishop reaches age seventy-five and he has not been a "party-line" person, he is immediately replaced—or even sent a coadjutor (one who shares his responsibilities) before he retires. On the other hand, bishops who have made it clear that they are loyal to Rome stay around until they are almost eighty, or even older.

That model is also replicated by local bishops with their elderly pastors. Some are like kings in their own kingdoms—for life. Others are moved and transferred using norms that are certainly not applied to everyone equally.

To the people in the pews, the treatment of pastors is sometimes confusing and sad, even frustrating. But the people who pay the bills and sustain their church have no say in who their parish priest is, or on how long he can stay. As a matter of fact, laypeople are rarely consulted for any decision making, even when they are the most affected by the decisions that are made regarding their own local parish communities.

In countries where democracy is not valued, this probably comes as no surprise. However, in a democratic country like ours, it makes a huge difference. In many cases, people just leave; they leave their spiritual home and shop around for a new church if they're upset by a pastor's inexplicable removal (or if that pastor is allowed to stay despite being totally ineffectual and incapable of continuing to lead a parish). They may even make a complete getaway from the faith and be turned off from organized religion forever.

My point is that so many of the older priests—and these days, there are many, with the median age of priests hovering around sixty in the developed world—are treated poorly and unjustly. While the Church talks about protecting the "dignity of human beings," it rarely does that for its own. Never mind the loneliness of being alone and usually not having much to live on. I have witnessed how older priests endure humiliations because of a lack of basic competence and sensitivity displayed by those in charge. Even for priests who remain free of scandal all of their lives, a lifetime of service might go without remark, and their active ministries can be terminated abruptly, often with little appreciation.

I recall the story of one priest who discovered that he was being removed from his parish only when his replacement stopped by "just to see the place." That older priest had been in his parish for over thirty years. It was his home. He was beloved and admired by his entire congregation, who had no clue what was about to happen.

After the younger priest walked in and announced to everyone that he was the new pastor, nobody from the institutional Church ever called the deposed priest to tell him he was officially retiring, or to inform him that someone else was being assigned to take his place. Imagine what that does to the morale of a man who is in his midseventies, after serving as a priest for half a century, to be treated as a lowly employee without respect.

This happens too often and most people have no clue that it is happening within their own parishes—a place where we expect to hear about justice and loving one another. Unfortunately, for me, the Church is an institution that too often seems to lack basic humanity.

The laypeople in the pews also have some responsibility for the mistreatment of priests. Most priests who are transferred rarely see or hear from people in their parishes again, no matter how dedicated a particular priest was to their needs and to serving their families. The institution encourages that type of disconnect so as not to get in the way of the new pastor, giving a whole new twist to the saying "out of sight, out of mind." This way of dealing with transitions within the Church makes most priests feel like sacramental ATMs being replaced with new models at the whim of the institution. The majority of these good men die after retirement, once they have left the places where they served for decades.

Parishioners will say, "I wonder if Father So-and-So is still alive?" but few ever find out what happened to their priest after he leaves. I believe it is just as devastating to the people as it is to the priests.

Seeing the utter lack of humanity and concern displayed by so many within the Church—even among priests for one another—often made me feel tired and disillusioned. How is it possible that we are supposed to be preaching about compassion and social justice, and promoting the dignity of every human being, yet not practicing those same tenets in-house toward one another?

Many priests will tell you plainly, "If I weren't a priest, I don't know what I would do." That may sound romantic or dramatic to some, but it sounds sad and dysfunctional to me. As one elderly traditional priest who was disappointed with the state of the clergy once told me, "A man who doesn't have the choice of becoming a good family man and a hard worker in the first place should never become a priest."

His point was a good one: The priesthood

should not be a place to hide dysfunctions or avoid reality; it should be a freely chosen vocation for a group of people who are spiritually and intellectually motivated for a great mission.

As with any other professional group, the quality and authenticity of the lives of your colleagues directly affect your job and your personal commitment to everything it entails. Today, I fear that there is an abundance of people becoming priests simply to wear vestments, say Mass, and do as little as possible. A real sense of mission and passion for priestly work is simply not there in a great number of clergy.

ANOTHER PROBLEM THAT I HESITATED to acknowledge for a very long time is the jealousy, envy, and negative male competition among the clergy. Gossip—much of it hateful—is abundant among priests.

When I was a very young priest, a bishop organized a dinner with the purpose of creating fraternity among some priests of a certain geographical area. As he left the dinner, he announced, "Well, I'm going now, so you can all talk and gossip about me."

He was speaking the truth. What many priests like to do more than anything is gossip about their bishops. Priests are rarely happy with the bishops they have; they're always hoping that the next one will be better.

There are some basic expectations that every priest has of his bishop. Mostly, priests want bishops to leave them alone and let them work. Both the clergy and laity expect their bishop to be more than a CEO sort of functionary who perceives his first obligation as protecting and defending the image of an institution. Bishops are called upon to act as shepherds and spiritual fathers—that is their specific role in the Church—especially to the parish priests who act as foot soldiers, doing the day-to-day work.

Like all organizations and businesses, the Church has a structure and a system of checks and balances. The bishop is the shepherd of a geographical area, and in that area there are many parishes, run by individual pastors. Just as the pastor is the shepherd of his people, so should the bishop be the real shepherd of his pastors. Unfortunately, that rarely happens in today's Church, where the support systems seem almost nonexistent.

As an older priest once told me, "Celibate men spend too much time navel-gazing." At the time, I dismissed him as being negative, and his comment as a sign of his own personal bitterness with his colleagues.

Later, I realized the truth in his words. Rather than helping them focus on others and the service of God, celibacy makes a lot of men egotistical and self-absorbed. And that navel-gazing is being done by the entire institution, as the Church spends too much time focusing on itself and not enough time trying to understand the world around it. This causes a variety of problems for priests, but especially the absence of any real sense of fraternity among priests.

Occasionally, I wished that I had someone I could really talk to openly, especially as the sex abuse scandals drew more and more media attention and I was called upon to respond to them publicly and at the parish level. Priests are often too isolated even from one another because of our schedules and the demanding work we do. I was always fortunate to have two or three very good priest friends, and others who were truly supportive of me, especially among older priests. Yet I was becoming aware of a deep emotional void within myself.

As a young man entering a Roman Catholic seminary, I had always been under the impression that I was joining a special type of lifelong fraternity, one that would help to sustain me throughout my life and ministry. While I certainly met some priests who became my friends, far more seemed to give up on fraternity a few years into ministry and spent more time with their dogs, cats, or computers than they did with other priests. I knew too many priests who had no friends at all. They seemed to use the clerical state and celibacy as tools for isolation and never quite developed normal people skills.

For instance, I had one classmate whom I always called or e-mailed on his birthday and on the anniversary of our ordination. It was all I could do, since he never found the time to get together, no matter how many times I asked. I remember when we were just out of the seminary, whenever he needed someone to talk to I would go, no matter what time it was or how far the distance. All of a sudden, he totally drifted away. After a few years of sending e-mails and messages with no responses, one day I decided to print out all of my messages and mail them to him in a large envelope with this short note: "I am really concerned for you and interested in your well-being. Did you ever get any of these?"

His response—the first word I'd heard from him after several years with no communication at all—was brief: "My real friends have my correct e-mail address and phone number. They know not to bother me with useless messages."

I was unbelievably hurt by his reaction. This was, after all, someone I was ordained with. I considered him not only a classmate and friend but a brother priest. I never heard from him ever again.

As time went by, however, and I met more and more priests through my travels, I realized that his off-putting, isolating behavior was common. I've heard from young priests who got the cold shoulder from pastors they served with as assistants for years. One young priest told me how he went into the office of his priest boss on his last day of an assignment to thank him for all the good things he had learned from him and how he really appreciated his guidance; the priest responded, "Okay," and continued his work as if he had said nothing at all. To this day, they have not been in contact. They worked together for two years, but that did not seem to matter. Isn't that totally strange? My point is that too many priests appear to be almost emotionally dead; at the very least, they are unable to receive and communicate affection in a healthy way. No matter how much I tried to value it and offer it, priestly fraternity was not easy for me to come by, and I wasn't sure what existed in that world of priests to replace it.

To this day, there are many brother priests and seminarians I helped and supported with what I considered my sincere fraternity, who have been unable to pick up the phone, send a note, or demonstrate the slightest bit of concern about my very public situation. Whether they approved of my decisions or not, it would be the humane thing to do—especially toward someone who offered you unconditional support when you needed it in the past. It really comes down to this: If bishops don't behave like spiritual fathers and priests don't behave like brothers, can the Church really claim that priestly fraternity exists?

• • •

COMMUNICATIONS, AND ALL THINGS related to the media, is another area where the Church has a real problem. I was a priest who was convinced that my mission was to spread God's word, and it was extremely frustrating for me to observe how today's Church exhausts more resources trying to clean up its public image with legal settlements than it ever spent on spreading God's message.

My frustration hit its peak while spending time on the communications committee for the United States Catholic Conference of Bishops. This was a disheartening experience, not because of the bishops involved—they were mostly gentlemen and hard workers—but because we spent hours talking about how to spread a message of faith to the people of our country with a paltry budget of about $4 million a year. Meanwhile, the entire body of bishops easily spent $400 million that year on settling sexual abuse lawsuits.

The little radio station I ran in Miami had a larger operating budget than the entire media department of the Catholic Church in the United States. Is it any wonder, then, that the official Roman Catholic Church seems to have no real audible voice in North American society?

Any number of small fundamentalist churches—located anywhere in America—have a larger budget for radio and television than the entire

Roman Catholic Church, and a lot more enthusiasm to do something, too. It never made sense to me that the largest Christian denomination in America cannot do what it needs to do to communicate in a world of communications.

To try to understand this, you just have to look at how the Church is organized, with authority and centralized power so intermingled with the way the mission is carried out. It would seem ideal to have someone—or even several people—in the Roman Catholic Church offering a spiritual perspective on issues that truly affect people's lives, but that is not where the institution's interests lie.

Anytime the Vatican or the national Church refers to the media, it is to accuse the media of attacking the Church. What they don't seem to realize is that the Church is not really being attacked, but challenged to be what it claims to be.

The Roman Catholic Church has spent many millions of dollars to do other things, but never to get its message out into the world. Beyond those who actually step into a church—only a fraction of whom claim to be baptized Catholics—nobody ever hears what the Church has to say.

As a bishop quite familiar with communications within the institutional Church once said to me, "Most of the work done by a committee on the subject of Church media is in a file cabinet at the main office in Washington, D.C."

Many poor countries in Latin America have their own Catholic television channels, but unfortunately they have very few quality programs. You have to applaud the bishops in those developing countries for speaking directly to their people and not running from the media, as they do so often in the United States. In those countries, there are few comforts and even fewer resources, but at least faith doesn't seem to take a backseat to budgets.

Some say that the Church does poorly with the media because those in media are not usually under the control of a central authority. I have even heard bishops complain about "who controls the message the people in my diocese are getting."

The message implied in those words is that only the bishop can ultimately teach in the name of the Church, and that people who are not under his authority and jurisdiction could be a problem. Charismatic figures are almost always seen as a threat to an organization that feels it must be in total control of everything and everyone. How can such an institution survive in this globalized media world?

The bottom line here is that the Church spends money on all kinds of investments, but very few have to do with its fundamental mission to get the message of salvation out there. It's no longer a secret that the investment made in the settlement of lawsuits involving the sexual abuse of minors—and the number of dioceses that have had to file for bankruptcy as a result of it—is just one example of the *institutional sickness* suffered by the Roman Catholic Church.

This suffering will continue unless real reform comes its way. The Church has done a poor job of presenting a good image to the world and an even worse job of covering up its mistakes, despite the investment of so many resources to do just that. The return on most of the Church's investments to keep people quiet has been zero. Even many who were paid large sums of money to say nothing came out years later and shared their horrific stories. Too many bishops have even flat-out lied to their people, saying that "insurance covers the costs of these settlements," when everyone knows that insurance never covers everything.

AFTER SEVERAL YEARS IN THE ministry, I came to the understanding that most of my priest acquaintances—with very few exceptions—fell into three basic categories, with some falling into two or even three of them:

1. Those removed from the Church
2. Those accused of sexual or other crimes
3. Those who felt disgruntled and/or isolated

During the sex abuse scandals of 2001 and 2002, the Catholic community in the United States began to see a number of its most talented and dynamic priests thrown out rather quickly—with almost no due process. There was a lot of pressure from the media, and the Boston press was particularly responsible for spearheading the eventual resignation of Cardinal Bernard Law, although he was certainly the scapegoat for the hundreds of bishops who were more directly involved in the crisis.

In those days, it was common to see a different priest in the newspaper every day, with the horror stories surrounding their particular abuse case (or cases) from years ago. The cases typically involved underage males in their teens. Very few bishops suffered any direct repercussions, which simply confirms that there is special protection for those at the top.

Many of the priests removed—for whatever reason—were notified over the telephone. Some never heard directly from their bishops, but were informed through other Church officials who did the dirty work. Others disappeared in the middle of the night, simply leaving ambiguous good-bye notes for parishioners, rarely explaining the reasons for their sudden departures. In some cases, parishioners to this day have no clue why their spiritual leaders disappeared.

The way most priests were treated said a lot to me about the type of institution I had given my life to—and it was scary. This is the other side of the story that we will never hear from anyone in the media: the shoddy way that priests are treated—even when the accusations made against them lack credibility.

As all of the craziness was going on on the outside, I began to see the real modus operandi of the Church, especially with regard to how the institution treated its priests. I had no choice but to examine the Church's methods, since I was directly affected; again and again, I was asked to replace a few of these discarded priests. I also knew, and respected, several priests who were removed from their parishes. What's more, my work with the media led me to be the spokesperson about the scandals on both Latin and mainstream television.

Ultimately, I realized that the Church is an institution that speaks often about the importance of human rights and respecting the dignity of every human being, but doesn't follow its own teachings. Of course, the most notorious behaviors among the clergy are real crimes against children, but those are not the only things the Church deals with when it comes to priests. Even when the accusations against a priest are of a serious nature, there must still be a legal process to discover the truth. Whatever happened to my archbishop's message of the Church being your family, and "We will take very good care of them"?

Treating people who work and minister for decades as cheap labor is a terrible injustice. Yet that is what the Church does with its own. In my own case, despite the fact that Ruhama and I were two single, consenting adults and there was no crime involved, the Church immediately suspended me from all duties and removed me from the payroll. What's more, my medical insurance was canceled within two weeks, and I found this out only when I was at the doctor's office and the secretary said, "Father, you are not in the system anymore—you have no insurance."

Sadder still are the funerals of priests. Certainly all funerals are sad, but the grief that I associate with a priest's funeral has little to do with death and a lot to do with life. In the case of a deceased priest, the man being laid to rest is one who has devoted his entire life to baptizing babies, celebrating weddings, preaching, giving comfort to the sick, and attending to countless other important community events. Yet when it's time to say good-bye, few people attend his funeral. This is especially true after priests retire and are no longer active or in charge of a parish. Most of them sail off into the sunset totally on their own.

Obviously, a priest may have a biological family of his own, but where is the spiritual family he has known throughout his life?

CHAPTER FOURTEEN

THE CHURCH
THAT TIME FORGOT

Like most kids of my generation, I was a great fan of the television show *Sesame Street*. The impact of this entertaining, educational television program on early child development is well documented. Recently, I came across a reference to the show while reading an interesting article highlighting new trends in children's television.

In that article, the author, Lisa Guernsey, states, "*Sesame Street* is no longer changing the world as much as trying to keep up with the world's changes."

I couldn't help but make the connection between *Sesame Street* and the Roman Catholic Church. The Church is also an important institution in our society, and it, too, is no longer trying to change the world—at least not the way that Jesus expected it to—because it is failing to keep up with how fast the world is changing.

Often, in speaking with priests around the world or while listening to sermons, I sense a great divide between what the Church tries to teach and the reality of most people's lives. Few Church leaders own up to the fact that clergy who remain stuck in the sacristy or behind the altar can't possibly make a difference in society. Any organization that fails to embrace contemporary society and speak to the world as we know it, and in a language it understands, is an organization in the process of extinction. It's not enough for the Church to create YouTube videos and have a Vatican Web site. Today's Church has to be ready to deal with speaking to the world with the same transparency and prophetic voice that we see in the Gospel.

Look at the parables and teachings of Jesus, and you will find basic things: seeds, trees, mountains, sheep, and the most basic human expressions. Why can't religious leaders communicate and connect with that same effectiveness today? I believe it is the only way that today's religious establishment can begin to bridge that great divide between the Church and the people.

Today, the institution is trying to perpetuate itself by importing priests from developing countries. These priests mostly can't be understood when they stand up to preach on Sundays, not only because English might not be their first language, but because they come from other cultures and are clueless about life in the United States. This makes the Church ineffectual in spreading the Good News of God. People put up with it—mostly the elderly—because they are emotionally tied to their churches. But young people get up and go elsewhere. The sad thing is that they are moving on in great numbers, even to the point of being totally turned off by the religion of their upbringing.

Church authorities seem to be more concerned with presenting their truths, even if it means disconnecting from the world as it is and from the real-life issues affecting our times. One of the chief examples of this is human sexuality. Everybody knows this—at every level of the Church—but nobody wants to open that Pandora's box, because dealing with sexual morality in its deepest dimensions is not politically correct. Some people in the pews, especially the most educated, talk about it, but their opinions mean next to nothing to the hierarchy.

When it comes to sexuality and other doctrines of the Church, there is an unwritten rule that "those who wear the hats" always know what's best, regardless of their personal or professional training. Today's Roman Catholic Church no longer listens to the people, and that's in sharp contrast with the early Church, which was much more democratic and took great interest in the opinions of both men and women.

Many of the Church's rigid positions were a struggle for me to accept and convey to the people I served as a priest. As I slowly developed my own way of ministry, I began to realize that the Church spent a great deal of energy on defending its positions and condemning modern-day practices, and very little time examining strategies for becoming more effective in its real mission. The Church hierarchy always saw the enemy as "out there" rather than analyze its own flaws.

One classic example of this type of behavior was displayed by the priest who celebrated the Eucharist at my niece's first Holy Communion. This was the church I had grown up in, received all the sacraments in, and where I celebrated my first Mass. The parishioners were very welcoming and loving, and made no big deal about my presence, because they knew Ruhama and I were there with my family on a special day. Nevertheless, the priest standing in the pulpit in front of fifty seven-year-olds making first Communion spent almost twenty-five minutes preaching about the evil present in the world and "those terrible people who leave our Church"; making a pretty clear reference to me and my wife. I couldn't believe what I was hearing, but all I could do was sit there patiently with my mother, my wife, and my family. He never said anything to the children, but spoke over their heads to give the adults a piece of his mind. I was not surprised. Just another missed opportunity—and I had lived through so many of those throughout the years.

The level of institutional arrogance within the Roman Catholic Church is so high that there are many issues the hierarchy consider nondebatable, or even unmentionable. Anything that seems to challenge the present system is considered a form of dissent, even in matters that have little or nothing to do with basic doctrines.

The debate over celibacy in the clergy is just one example of a much deeper problem: the inability on the part of the institution to examine the validity of its positions in the modern world. If celibacy is truly a gift that comes from God, how can it be a requirement for everyone who feels called by God to be a priest in the Western Church? Can a gift be imposed by an institution that acknowledges celibacy as a human law, and not a divine one? Does anyone within the institution dare to question or begin to think that maybe this imposition and/or requirement has a lot to do with why celibacy is a problem for so many priests and not quite the gift it is supposed to be? Is there any real consideration given to the numbers of young people who would be motivated to serve God if they were also allowed to have a marriage and a family?

The answer to all of the above is no.

I APOLOGIZED PUBLICLY ON SEVERAL occasions for breaking my promise of celibacy in both written statements and interviews. Still, many people proclaimed that I was not sorrowful enough, or even insisted that I hadn't really apologized. I wondered how many times they needed me to say, "I'm sorry."

I can understand the pain involved in

discovering that a priest has broken his promise. Yet the extreme hostility made me wonder what their reactions would have been if I had been involved in a different type of scandal. I hadn't ever heard such adamant criticism of priests accused of being child abusers, paying prostitutes, or soliciting sex in parks.

As the comedian David Letterman joked one night, "They found Father Cutié in Miami on the beach with a lady, and they're giving him a hard time. If he'd been with an altar boy, they would have simply transferred him to another parish."

It was a crude joke based on too many true stories. The sex abuse cases that earn the most airplay are disproportionately homosexual in nature and caused great damage to the image and credibility of the Church, due to the countless lawsuits and almost constant negative media attention about pedophiles within the institution.

A number of Church leaders and other experts in society began to wonder if the sex abuse scandals correlated with homosexual activity among priests, but that has been proven false. Homosexuals are no more likely to be child abusers than are heterosexuals.

Moreover, the study that was commissioned almost twenty years later by the United States Conference of Catholic Bishops—known as the John Jay Study—clearly concluded that 81 percent of the victims of child abuse were indeed male, but most of the boys victimized were over age fifteen. In April 2010, the Vatican secretary of state blamed gay priests for a pedophilia problem during a press conference in Santiago, Chile, but the Vatican quickly backpedaled, admitting that 90 percent of sex abuse cases involve priests with adolescent boys. Within the Roman Catholic Church, classic pedophilia hasn't been the predominant problem; instead, the majority of abusers have been homosexual men attracted to teenagers.

Even after all the money spent on scientific studies and advice from experts in the areas of human sexual development and the real dysfunctions among clergy, homophobia and ignorance still reign. In 2005, when Cardinal Joseph Ratzinger was named pope, he issued a document focusing on gay priests that once again called homosexuality "objectively disordered," then added that gay men would be allowed into the seminary only after a period of abstinence and if they did not display "deep-seated homosexual tendencies." How objective does that sound? I can't imagine a real test or evaluation that can determine if someone has "deep-seated" tendencies toward anything.

There is, of course, no way to know exactly how many gay priests are working worldwide or how many of them actually observe celibacy. In his book *The Changing Face of the Priesthood*,

Father Donald Cozzens suggests that at least 60 percent of all American Catholic priests are gay. Whatever the exact numbers, a significant number of active homosexual priests continue to be ordained, but they are forced to be cautious, repressed, and mostly closeted homosexuals— unless, of course, those priests are in Rome. One recent article in the Italian weekly magazine *Panorama* points out that the sight of courting priests is hardly an anomaly; for that particular investigative piece, a reporter posed as the boyfriend of a man running in gay clerical circles, and caught the sexual escapades of priests on tape. He also discovered that male escorts and transsexual prostitutes in Rome regularly rely on priests as regular customers.

Those Roman Catholics who do not want to accept homosexuals among their clergy are way too late. There are so many homosexuals, both active and celibate, at all levels of the clergy and Church hierarchy that the Church would never be able to function if they were really to exclude all of them from ministry. As one of the most prominent pastors in a parish near where I grew up used to say in jest, "If they get rid of us queens, they won't have too many people left to do the work!"

The oldest seminary in the country, St. Mary's in Baltimore, was at one time called "the Pink Palace" by a number of priests, seminarians, and laypeople associated with it. In the 1980s, promiscuous homosexual activity was actually very commonplace in seminaries, a setting that was supposed to be for celibate men (or men preparing to be celibate).

At my own seminary, at least one of the rectors and a number of priests on staff had been involved with seminarians in totally inappropriate relationships, but many of those men went on to big, wealthy parishes, positions in the Curia, or professorships. They all continued in ministry with few repercussions for their well-known promiscuous behavior. A group of laypeople once wrote a novel to try to expose their pastor and others in the hierarchy, but he was well protected by the powers that be.

The question remains: How can the Church condemn homosexuality so forcefully in public, yet continue to cover it up in a number of its own leaders? How could the Church make so many of the faithful sitting in the pews feel unwelcome to receive Holy Communion simply because they are homosexual, yet give them religious leaders who hide their orientation (and often promiscuous activities)?

Ironically, with the number of homosexuals in the Church, it is fair to say that in many cases it has been the heterosexual seminarians, priests, and religious who have felt left out in many Roman Catholic seminaries, religious houses, and dioceses. A young Franciscan friar I once worked with (who wasn't the least bit homophobic, or antianything, for that matter) used to tell me, "I live with a bunch of gay guys who don't really understand me."

I'm not saying that the Church shouldn't welcome homosexuals. Far from it. I'm just pointing out that the Church speaks out of both sides of its mouth. The institution that calls homosexual activity intrinsically disordered and often promotes a homophobic agenda publicly is the same one that ordains, promotes, and places closeted homosexuals in positions of power. That's no secret to those of us who have dealt with the institution at every level, from the local parishes to the Vatican.

However, when a seminarian or a priest gets involved *with an adult woman* in a consensual relationship, it is often cause for immediate dismissal and grave scandal, as in my own case. I knew one young seminarian in Latin America who was called into the cardinal's office because he was "spending too much time" talking to a young novice (a religious sister in training); his behavior was viewed by some of his classmates and priests in the area as suspicious.

When the young man explained that he and the young sister were just friends, the cardinal said, "If you were to have that type of relationship with a man, it would be easier to hide and we could avoid criticism, but we cannot protect you if you are involved with a girl."

A priest recently called me and told me his bishop removed him from his parish when he discovered his relationship with an adult woman. The bishop came to his parish, got up on the pulpit, and announced that the priest was being removed, but not for any wrongdoing with a child. The priest kind of laughed when he told me how he would have loved to get up at that same pulpit and say, "And my bishop is an active homosexual and we all know it."

The John Jay Study report, as well as my own anecdotal evidence, leads me to believe that many of the priests accused of being child abusers are in fact closeted gay men. A great majority of their "abuses" were homosexually oriented, with boys in their late teens. What if these men had been allowed to be in loving partnerships? Would these sex abuse cases still have happened?

There is no way to know. But my belief is that, gay or straight, people who are allowed to live in monogamous, committed sexual relationships regardless of their orientation are more apt to be well adjusted socially. Certainly asking all priests—whether straight or gay—to be celibate and 100 percent sexually continent isn't working for most.

In the 1990s, President Bill Clinton came up with the "Don't ask, don't tell" policy for soldiers in the armed forces. It led to a big public debate at that time and its repeal is the subject of an equally passionate debate today.

What most people don't realize is that the "Don't ask, don't tell" policy has been in place in the Roman Catholic clergy for a very long time. I'm convinced that the controversial policy wasn't invented by the United States military, but by the Vatican! You will find bishops who claim they will ordain homosexuals as long as they're committed to celibacy, and others who say they "never" ordain homosexuals. Many state one policy publicly, while doing something else in practice.

CNN once aired an interview with two cardinals, one from the West Coast of the United States and the other from the East Coast. These men gave opposite points of view on who the Church considers a "good candidate" for ministry. One said that he ordains homosexuals who are celibate. The other claimed that he could not ordain homosexuals at all. The fact is that *both* of them were ordaining homosexuals, but most of those candidates were never free to talk about their sexual orientation or even the way they planned to live a celibate life in their particular situations.

Priests will tell you that there is a sort of Pink Mafia in the Roman Catholic Church; this is the term describing the significant number of closeted homosexuals who live within the Church and occupy the hierarchy at every level of the institution. Those in the Pink Mafia actively promote their own, regardless of ability or credentials, though many prove to be very resourceful and know how to work the system. Ironically, these are often the same people who display homophobic tendencies when speaking in public and even in the confessional.

How is that possible? Because nobody within the Church talks about these things in public—and these priests are keenly aware that they must hide their truth from the laity, if not from their fellow clergy.

When the Pink Mafia is in control, their priest friends are given the best parishes, even named monsignors and put in certain positions not because of their particular qualifications or hard work, but because of their affiliation and fidelity to the Mafia. It is a kind of protective club and they are very good to one another.

I know of a particular diocese where the bishop was known by his own colleagues as "the Queen of the South." Mismanagement by the Pink Mafia was grand in that diocese, but it was rarely talked about or covered by the media. Novels, blogs, and countless commentaries were written about it, but nobody in Rome seemed to pay attention—and if they did, nothing was done about it for almost twenty years. It was even so talked about among the local clergy that Bill O'Reilly of FOX News began conducting an investigation into the corruption of certain individuals in leadership positions in that area. He was very familiar with some of the people involved, because he had been a teacher at a Roman Catholic school in that community. For some mysterious reason, that well-documented story never came out. Imagine having enough power to silence O'Reilly! That's serious.

Dealing with sexuality in an open and honest way is not a choice in a system that prefers to ignore sex. The Church simply doesn't allow for that type of openness. The result is detrimental to both gay and straight men, who need a lot more guidance regarding the decision to embrace the celibate state. People who are pushed deeper and deeper into the closet never have the opportunity to develop as sexually integrated people.

Whether the institution wants to acknowledge it or not, a good number of its most talented and gifted priests are homosexuals—and they are not all that quiet about it anymore. At the same time, there are countless priests who have hidden relationships with women, many fathering children. In most Latin American countries, the people in rural areas are accustomed to knowing the priest who has a hidden wife and has fathered children who call him "*tío*" (uncle).

The Church would be better off admitting who

its priests and bishops really are, and the reality of the presence of a significant number of sexually active people at every level of the Church, instead of putting up the false front that the clergy is composed of celibate males who made a choice between marriage and the celibate state "for the Kingdom of God."

The traditional saying that "silence is golden" should be "silence is expensive" when it comes to the Roman Catholic Church, which has spent billions of dollars trying to silence both accusers and the accused. Silence is expensive for another reason, too: How can the Church retain any credibility when it does not speak out and condemn what is condemnable, and people continue to get hurt?

THERE ARE PLENTY OF CONSPIRACY theories regarding the institutional Church— hence the popularity of Dan Brown's novels and others like them. Then there is the stuff that actually happens and seems so outrageous that you don't want to believe it.

For example, several authors have written extensively about how John Paul I did not die of natural causes, but was intentionally silenced. The Church would have us believe that anyone who suggests the pope was murdered is a Church hater. However, those who hold this belief don't necessarily hate the Church at all—some actually live and work within it; among them is a Spanish priest who has written several well-documented books on the subject. During a visit to Rome, I also heard this theory from a Jesuit who worked in the Vatican and was convinced that John Paul I was eliminated by those who were opposed to real reform in the Church.

I have to confess that I was among the people who believed that this murder idea was far-fetched. As I read the well-documented opinions of so many, however, I began to consider the possibility. After all, Pope John Paul I was a reformer; perhaps he was too far ahead of a Church that wasn't ready for change. He might not really have been murdered by Vatican operatives or members of the hierarchy related to the Italian Mafia, but it's pretty clear that many of his honest and spontaneously expressed positions were a nuisance for an institution that resists change at almost every level.

Progressive popes aren't the only ones who disturb the institution. Almost anyone who freely expresses himself in opposition to a variety of official theological, pastoral, moral, scientific, or even socioeconomic positions are silenced, dismissed, or excluded. Nobody has a monopoly on the truth. Yet the list of those silenced is longer every day. A number of honest intellectuals have been silenced because their opinions threaten Church positions, including Teilhard de Chardin,

Anthony de Mello, Hans Kung, and countless others. Perhaps one day these great minds will be called prophetic. They might one day even be canonized. Who knows? Meanwhile, the Church condemns their theology because it is in disagreement with the hierarchy.

Then there are the men and women who aren't precisely dissenters in matters of theology or at doctrinal odds with the Church, but cause trouble by daring to express outrage at the magnitude of the organizational corruption and dysfunction that exists within the institution. Such is the case of Father Thomas Doyle, a priest of the Dominican order. He is a canon lawyer who worked in the Vatican embassy in Washington, D.C., later becoming an air force chaplain and was among the first to raise awareness of the sex abuse of minors in the 1980s. Doyle coauthored a lengthy report about the abuses and spoke to those at the highest level of the hierarchy about what was happening.

Did the Church listen? Unfortunately, for so many victims and their families, no, they did not. He was mostly ignored and told to keep quiet. While working at the highest levels of the institution, Doyle predicted that the Church would suffer greatly, including financially, from the coming scandals.

While he is a hero to victims and laypeople who understand the depth of the problem, Father Doyle continues to be considered persona non grata by many in the Vatican. They have tried everything possible to isolate him from the mainstream Roman Catholic community.

ONE OF THE CHURCH'S BEST-KEPT secrets is the work of nuns and religious women, and the contributions of women in general. Women in the Church are often the most dedicated workers; they also make up the majority of most church congregations.

One such outstanding woman is a world-renowned Poor Clare Nun,* who is familiar to most Catholics as Mother Angelica. She founded EWTN (Eternal Word Television Network), the world's only international Catholic cable and satellite channel, and is a force to be reckoned with in all quarters, transmitting programs in several languages around the world. Besides the pope, Mother Angelica is probably the most recognizable living Catholic religious leader in the world.

Her work has incredible merit, even though many people reject the extremely conservative views she espoused later in her life. Mother Angelica was originally a leader in the early days of the Charismatic renewal, back at a time when

---

* The Poor Clares, founded by St. Clare of Assisi, are cloistered and dedicated to prayer.

many in the official Church considered Charismatic spirituality "suspicious." In a matter of twenty years or so she and her nuns went from the Pentecostal practices of speaking in tongues and waving their arms in the air to an almost opposite spirituality of Latin hymns and nothing that could be closely associated with Vatican II or church renewal of any kind. She started her entire mega-operation in the garage of her convent with a small donation, a tireless spirit, and a determination not to be intimidated by the institution she serves. Despite her accomplishments, many members of the Catholic hierarchy throughout the world dislike or even despise her. They won't always come out and say it, but many Church leaders would prefer it if Mother Angelica and her entire media operation would disappear off the face of the earth. Some of the most prestigious leaders in the hierarchy have tried to do everything possible to get her off the air in their geographical areas, but she has persevered. To this day, the network she founded continues to grow.

Shortly after I began working in secular television, I had a private audience with Mother Angelica for almost two hours. What an experience! I came out of that meeting convinced she was a woman of deep faith who had suffered a great deal in her life. Yet she was radiantly happy and at peace. If there was any bitterness in her, you really couldn't perceive it.

What was the source of that suffering? Mostly the bishops and others in authority who felt threatened by her incredible influence; even some powerful people in the Vatican, who felt she was a rebellious nun that they could not keep under control. She had an extraordinary capacity to raise funds and reach out to people through no-nonsense discourse. She was also a lot more independent in the operation of her international television network than the Church ever imagined—or wanted—a nun to be. What really irked officials is that Mother Angelica always spoke her mind, whether she was in agreement with the Church hierarchy or not.

I was very fortunate to be able to broadcast on her network. I never charged a dime for my work there, no matter how many hours or days it took. I considered it part of a special mission and a grassroots effort to bring a message of faith to the world. I knew what I was doing was not popular to the hierarchy, but the people in the pews greatly appreciated it, especially in the poorest countries in Latin America and the Caribbean.

One afternoon, I was in the Vatican Gardens taping a series about the roots of Christianity and the history of the early Church. The show was a coproduction of EWTN and a documentary filmmaker from Peru. The production crew was mostly made up of young laypeople who had never seen the Vatican and its private gardens so closely. We spent several hours there, being carefully escorted by a Vatican policeman, of course.

Late in the afternoon, the cardinal secretary of state came by. We were in the Vatican Gardens, but to him it was really his backyard. As he strolled closer, he said, "What are you doing?"

We explained that we were taping a documentary to be shown on Mother Angelica's channel. His face went almost pale at the mention of the controversial nun's name, and he said, "Father, I'm glad we have young people that can do these things now. . . ."

He then turned away and continued his stroll. It turns out that the cardinal was familiar with my work in Spanish television, because he had served as the papal nuncio in Chile and was very familiar with Latin America. But, at that moment, all I could think of was the expression on his face at the mere mention of the name of the most popular nun in America. Before that moment, I never would have believed that Mother Angelica was actually persona non grata to so many in the Vatican; yet now the second in command had confirmed it.

Another time, I was at a gathering of priests; there must have been three hundred or more. A bishop was giving—or reading—a long, boring talk. Worse yet, it was three thirty in the afternoon, when every decent soul should have been taking a power nap, especially when you are supposed to be in the midst of a few relaxing days. Nearly half of the priests were sound asleep, with more than a few audibly snoring, as if to prove my point.

At the end of the lecture everyone applauded, really thanking God that it was over, and the bishop opened the floor for questions and answers. I promised myself that I would be politically correct for once and not say a word. But then the questions got around to the media. I felt compelled to break my promise when the bishop made a nasty comment about Mother Angelica's influence on "our people," saying something to the effect that "We don't want our people to get their theology from Mother Angelica," in a derogatory tone.

At that, I respectfully greeted His Excellency, then asked, "Why do you bishops criticize Mother Angelica, who has done so much with so little, when our bishops have done so little with so much?"

I was referring to the exorbitant amount of money bishops spent on poorly executed media projects and so many other things, while showing little interest in being truly present through the media.

I was pleasantly surprised when the bishop apologized for criticizing Mother Angelica. He then acknowledged that he himself had been in charge of the communications committee in the Conference of Bishops and that they indeed had accomplished very little.

I use the example of Mother Angelica because she sacrificed herself and the protective nature of her cloistered life to be a real "marketer of the faith." Her ambition was to enter people's homes with God's word. While many within her own Church didn't agree with her theological slant, no one could deny that she was doing what she felt in her heart was right. Yet she was often a victim of the institution she promoted and defended so fiercely, due to the constant jockeying for power within the Church.

It's no exaggeration to say that Mother Angelica is persecuted by her own institution. Perhaps her most public confrontation was with Cardinal Roger Mahony of Los Angeles, which initiated a wild media frenzy at the time it happened. Mother Angelica claimed that one of the cardinal's pastoral letters left out a basic element of the Roman Catholic faith—the real presence of Christ in the Eucharist—and she challenged him head-on. He wasn't happy with that; nor were officials in Rome.

I will always admire Mother Angelica for her great courage and no-nonsense attitude. But I fear that in my former Church—and in our world— there are very few people like her who are willing to do what they feel their heart is asking them to do, no matter what consequences those actions may bring.

Knowing her and so many other courageous and well-prepared women as I did, I began to question why women should be excluded from the ministry. The argument against women in the clergy from most in the Church hierarchy is that Jesus chose male apostles, and priests are supposed to model Jesus on the altar. The official Church has also insisted that it is not authorized to change a custom created by Jesus; yet it has adapted and changed so many other things throughout the centuries. The fact remains that God created males and females in his own image and likeness; therefore, both men and women are made in the image of God—and can "image" God. Why, then, shouldn't we see a woman at the altar? What about the deaconess in the New Testament (see Romans 16:1)? Shouldn't biblical evidence have some weight?

ANOTHER GREAT MARKETER OF FAITH in our time was the late Archbishop Fulton J. Sheen, the first priest to ever host a program on national secular television. Even though he was a real institution man, he, too, was put through the mill. When his popularity soared, reaching an audience as large as his competitor's, Milton Berle, he was the victim of great jealousy on the part of Church leaders, not just for his talent and name recognition but for his fund-raising capabilities. The cardinal and other Church officials in New York did everything possible to remove him from the center of the Big Apple—even from his famous presentation of the *Seven Last Words* on Good Friday, which was originally at St. Patrick's Cathedral and then continued at the smaller St. Agnes Church.

Like Mother Angelica, Bishop Sheen also suffered greatly—mostly in silence and only speaking with a few trusted allies in the Vatican—just for being an extraordinary marketer of the faith. After he died, no one was lined up to take his place and nobody ever did. The bishops of the United States lost their best communicator ever, but his was a gift that the institution did not value. Because of that lack of vision, to this day the Church can't figure out how they are going to get their message out to the world.

BY NOW, MOST OF HUMANITY is aware of the shameful silence of Vatican officials, especially Pope Pius XII, during the Holocaust. This is an issue that the institution wishes would go away, but it will not, as long as the Church remains silent. Six million Jews were exterminated by the Nazis, and now, decades later, the Vatican is still searching for ways to make the institutional Church appear to have condemned this horrible human tragedy.

The evidence for a real condemnation of this atrocity by the Church is almost nonexistent; whatever statements were made were vague and weak. Diplomatic language can sound elegant when it comes from political functionaries, but when it comes from an institution that is supposed to speak for the voiceless, it sounds ineffective and even irresponsible.

In my own experience, I can honestly say that Vatican diplomacy is one of the hardest things to try to figure out; at times it's tough to tell if they are with the good guys or the bad guys. The people of Catholic Poland know this all too well; their pope, bishops, and Vatican diplomats were silent when almost three thousand priests were killed by the Nazis, who invaded their homeland in 1939.

Twenty years later, in 1959, another totalitarian regime took over my parents' homeland. As a Cuban-American, I experienced a similar level of frustration when it came to the way Vatican diplomats and local Church authorities dealt publicly with human rights violations and the many evils committed by the Communist dictatorship in Cuba. Too many times, I had to see Vatican dignitaries and other Church leaders visit and smile with the dictator at the same time that Castro was committing horrific human rights violations.

Working as a radio and TV host, I often had to

spend hours on the air, listening to the pain of the exile community calling to ask, "Why doesn't the Church say or do something?"

There always seemed to be an excuse on the part of the Church not to condemn what was clearly condemnable. (Most of the time, that excuse was the fear of losing some concession they were begging the government for.) Here I was, trying to convince my callers that being a true Christian meant defending the dignity of every human being, speaking for the voiceless, and working to build a better world. How could I defend the leadership of a Church that appeared to be so removed from that fundamental mission?

Personally, I did what I could, and so did many others within the Church on a grassroots level. For example, an older priest who spent years sending medicines to Cuba by getting people to smuggle them into the country in their luggage came to see me after he was diagnosed with terminal cancer, because he wanted his work to continue after his death. He was grief-stricken because, after years and years of providing that service, his archbishop showed no interest in his ministry. It broke my heart to see his eyes fill with tears as he spoke to me of the indifference he encountered from his own bishop.

Many people don't know that it is almost impossible to find the most basic medicines in Cuba, especially without American dollars. Later, after his death, a group of laypeople continued his work, which we were able to support with funds by raising awareness for this cause through my radio station.

In 2006, Fidel Castro was in poor health and needed an operation. The Cuban people were beginning to wonder what would happen, and in a regime with no freedom of expression and no free press, the rumor mill on the street was the best source of news. People in Cuba and elsewhere in the world began to hope for the possibility of change, perhaps even the end of a dictatorship responsible for the separation of so many families, the deaths of political dissidents by firing squad, the arrests of countless political prisoners, and so many other injustices.

In the midst of this, the Conference of Cuban Bishops put out a press release asking Cubans to pray for Castro's well-being. The actual text read: *Los Obispos de Cuba pedimos a todas nuestras comunidades que ofrezcan oraciones para que Dios acompañe en su enfermedad al presidente Fidel Castro (The Bishops of Cuba ask all of our communities to offer prayers so that God will accompany President Fidel Castro in his illness).*

People of faith are always asked to pray for their enemies and try to do good even to those who cause us harm. Asking people to pray for a sick man, even a dictator, was not in itself a bad thing. But the Church had ignored the hundreds of people who'd died in search of freedom, the thousands of political prisoners, and the millions of political exiles. Those same bishops never once put out a press release asking us to pray for the victims of that same dictator they were now praying for.

I'll never forget how upsetting that was to me and to countless others who longed for Cuba's freedom from tyranny. Deliberate or not, that press release made the Church appear to take the side of power, not the side of those who suffered.

Through an e-mail I sent to a few friends, I openly complained about the press release of the Cuban bishops. I said that the Vatican had plenty of diplomats, but that I was under the impression that bishops were shepherds who should be on the side of their people. That e-mail was quickly forwarded all over the place. As you can imagine, my position was considered a horrible insult to some bishops in and out of Cuba.

Almost immediately, I received several letters from bishops and one archbishop in Cuba who were deeply offended by my words. It was unheard of that a priest would speak his mind about what he saw lacking in a statement from a group of bishops. My own local archbishop recorded a message to be played every day on the radio station that I directed for his diocese— several times a day and for about two weeks— defending the statement at great length and offering "clarifications" to those who didn't agree with it. Every time I heard that message, it made my stomach turn, because it sounded even more insensitive to our community than the original statement from Havana.

To this day, the world is *still* waiting for the bishops of Cuba—and all other religious leaders within the island—to publicly and clearly condemn the horrors being committed against the Cuban people, especially those who are fighting for the freedom of expression and other basic human rights. Whenever the religious leaders of Cuba speak, they seem to be doing a song and dance to avoid any clear condemnation of the dictatorship. This applies to the religious leaders of almost every denomination—including my new church. Vatican diplomats may very well be talking behind closed doors, but the world needs them and others to give a voice to the voiceless and to say what needs to be said—without so much fear and diplomacy. In 2010, the Castro regime would once again find a way to involve the Church in the diplomatic work of being a type of "intermediary" for releasing political prisoners. Yet there are still no clear condemnations of the totalitarian regime with all of its injustices.

At least, that is what most people of goodwill expect from the Church. However, after a good deal of reflection, I have come to the conclusion that it must be very difficult for one dictatorship to condemn another. When the Vatican stops silencing, condemning, and eliminating those who dissent from certain archaic pastoral practices and even some of their theological impositions, only then will it begin to possess the moral authority necessary to challenge dictatorships to a profound change. Imagine one totalitarian regime telling another, "Hey, you got to listen to your people!" It just does not work.

IN MY OWN WORK AS a Roman Catholic priest, I always welcomed everyone. I tried to reach out to everyone and be a brother to all priests. I believed in the bond of priesthood and the fact that we were all in this ministry together, way beyond what each man was dealing with in his personal journey of life.

Everyone knows that there are saints and sinners in every organization, people who are open and those who are cagey and secretive. To all of them, I tried to be a brother and a friend, but the institution and the level of repression that exists within the Church create a certain kind of strange distancing that never allows people to really be themselves, and ultimately dehumanizes people. That's why so many clergy have secrets and maintain their silence instead of having the courage to act as change agents in the world.

After I moved on and joined the Episcopal Church, it was disturbing how a number of Roman

Catholic leaders, both in the United States and linked to the Vatican, tried to keep me from serving in organizations that are not even under their jurisdiction. I had been on the boards of a variety of Roman Catholic and nonprofit organizations that were ecumenical and nonsectarian by nature. Obviously, I was forced to resign from those directly affiliated with the Church, but I was surprised to receive a phone call one day suggesting that I resign from the American Bible Society, one of the oldest organizations in the United States of America that is not affiliated with any church and one that is self-governing. There was no doubt in my mind that certain Roman Catholic leaders, both lay and clergy, were putting pressure on them to remove me from the board of trustees—even though it's not an organization that is run or operated by Roman Catholic standards.

Something strange seems to happen to people who work, live, and breathe the Church twenty-four hours a day: Numbness sets in. No matter what level of corruption, dysfunction, or political garbage one experiences within the institutional system, we all still want to believe things are really not so bad. We prefer to think of the Church as something that is sacred, divinely instituted, and unaffected by the corruption of mortals. This is why it's not easy to come to terms with the inconsistencies.

Many people dismiss the Church's flaws as "the humanity of the Church." But the problem isn't the Church's humanity; it is the Church's inhumane practices and those who are more faithful to the institution than they are to the Gospel message of love. It is those practices that are causing the institution, beloved by so many, to become less and less credible as a spiritual authority in the world.

Most of us can deal with human error and sin. What we can't deal with is an institution that presents itself as holier than thou and ends up having a lot more skeletons in the closet than it is willing to admit.

CHAPTER FIFTEEN

COMPLETING MY JOURNEY FROM ROME TO CANTERBURY

The Anglican spirit . . .
one which refused to separate

- the sacred from the secular,
- the head from the heart,
- the individual from the community,
- the Protestant from the Catholic,
- the word from the sacrament.

Bishop Gordon Mursell in
The Story of Christian Spirituality

There they were: about fifty clean-cut, mostly young, married couples sitting in front of me. It was a Saturday morning and I was giving a conference on my self-help book, *Real Life, Real Love.* In that book I dealt with relationship struggles of every kind, but especially marriage.

The group I was addressing that day is what I call the typical "churchy" crowd, mostly devout Roman Catholics who *pay, pray, and obey.* On the outside, at least, they all seemed stable and happy. I was sure they all had at least two kids and a dog.

I dealt with the material in the book. Then, as I closed our discussion, I had to admit what I had been holding in for a long time: that I wasn't really the right priest for them.

407

What I meant is that this crowd didn't particularly need me. I have always felt like God was calling me to be the priest for those whom many in society think are lost sheep, the ones beyond the typical churchgoing crowd. We all have a little of the lost sheep inside us, but I think we all understand that some of us feel more lost than others—less religious and less able to understand the value of practicing any form of religious faith. That is the crowd God always led me to reach out to.

In this particular crowd, I was sure that every one of these churchgoing couples had a nice priest to take care of them in their parishes. They probably heard traditional sermons each Sunday and felt fine with that. They were spiritually fed and more or less happy with their food.

They didn't need me. The people who needed me most were the tough crowd, the not-so-churchy folks who needed a little more convincing to come to church in the first place. The ones who didn't go by the book and felt like the Church was out of touch with their lives (and it's sad to say they were often right).

That's why I always felt like my mission territory was, and continues to be, the media. There, you find all kinds of folks who really are looking for help, whether they share your religious convictions or not. That's always been okay with me. Learning to help bring peace to the hearts and minds of all kinds of people is what I always perceived as my particular task in media.

I think we are all lifetime students; at least, that is what I consider myself. And there are countless ways to learn to go where you need to go; everyone may not be going down the same exact path. Very few things instruct and shape the human mind as much as everyday contact with real people and their individual dilemmas. This is where the religious establishment has failed today: We don't pay enough attention to what people are really going through; nor do we value what they're experiencing. There is a serious disconnect between people and organized religion in general.

When you make a serious commitment to learn from people and to pay attention to their deepest longings and heartfelt struggles, the learning that takes place is unparalleled. You find yourself connecting theory with reality, and creating a bridge between an ancient institution with its traditional ideas and a fast-paced, uncertain, ever-changing world.

Most contemporary Christians—both Roman Catholics and people of other traditional mainstream denominations—are much more open-minded than the religious institutions they belong to, but they stick around mostly because of a cultural attachment to traditions, family ties, and even a certain amount of guilt associated with the question "What will people think?"

Ideological compatibility often has very little to do with people sitting in the pews of a particular church. Most people just want to feel welcomed and good on the inside. They want good preaching and good music; they ultimately want to feel inspired. Deep in their hearts, I am sure most people want their church to evolve and begin to embrace the contemporary world, even if the changes are bound to rock the boat (and they always do).

Because I am a longtime student of philosophy and theology, one of my favorite things has always been to read different theological perspectives and examine different concepts of God and faith. At some point, I became convinced that true religion is not something that can easily be learned from books or official declarations. It is mostly the experience of real people dealing with God—and struggling with their own spiritual lives.

If you pay attention to the Bible, that is what it is mostly about: the story of the people of Israel developing their identity as they grow and struggle in their relationship with God. Later, the followers of Jesus do the same thing again. Once you become a good enough student of the human condition, you become a better student of the things of God. If you think about it, God is easy to figure out: constant and full of love, compassion, and understanding. It is human beings who are not so easy to comprehend sometimes.

We all fall short. I know I did. But we all have that deep longing to live in peace and to reach ultimate fulfillment that most of us call heaven. Ultimately, the question in most people's minds is: Will I get in? And who will be left out—and for what?

I FIRST BEGAN TO READ a number of Anglican authors and contemplate issues surrounding the Episcopal Church in 2006, about three years before I officially joined. As a Roman Catholic from birth, I was interested in knowing more about a church that enjoys the treasure of both the reformed (Protestant) and Catholic traditions. I quickly discovered that Anglicans profess the same creeds and faith I grew up with, but with slightly less rigid interpretations. I also found that the way the Church is governed and authority exercised (what is known as our *polity*) is radically different. I realized quickly that the Episcopal (Anglican) way of *being church* was closer to the Gospel way and to my own thinking than the church I had been brought up in, in which authority is totally centralized.

In the Anglican Communion—as is the case in the Roman Catholic Church—there are also great controversies and issues that are considered explosive and divisive, mostly in the area of human sexuality. These issues caused me to struggle. However, my interest in the Episcopal/

Anglican tradition had much more to do with Church governance, pastoral practice, and even some interpretations of contemporary theology. I was very much attracted to things like intellectual freedom and the way that all people participate in the appointment of Church leadership, especially their local clergy and bishops. That is how it had been for centuries in early Christian times.

I began to perceive the Anglican way as my way. It is truly a church for the twenty-first century, a church that does not only talk about love and acceptance of all but actually puts it into practice. It was refreshing for me to see that controversy in the Episcopal Church was much more about whom to *include* and less about whom to *exclude*.

This became very important to me after decades of dealing with what seemed like an ideological dictatorship in the Roman Catholic Church, where the system is so controlling that I often felt punished for carrying out what I considered to be effective outreach and good pastoral work. I lived through so many instances of that type of oppression that I began to feel like a slave of a religious system and not a servant of God.

The day I was officially received into the Episcopal Church was one of the happiest days of my life, but it was by no means an easy transition to make. I was born and raised Roman Catholic and had a great love for the only thing I knew as "church." Yet I evolved ideologically and became very unhappy with many of those Church teachings later in my life.

For at least two or three years before being received as an Episcopalian, I had been doing extensive reading, not only about Anglican traditions and theological perspectives but also about the many controversies involving Episcopal congregations and problems in various regions of the Anglican Communion, including the United States. It wasn't easy to join something that many considered a sinking ship. I was well aware that it was a time of great debate and controversy within this Church.

However, within the Episcopal Church I also discovered a deep sense of ideological freedom and sincerity that was totally absent in Roman Catholicism. I spent quite a bit of time speaking with priests (a good number of them former Roman priests like myself) and bishops within the Episcopal Church, who offered me their sincere friendship. Through them, I was able to really begin the process of making the transition to my new spiritual family. E-mails, letters, exchanging books and notes—you name it, I did it! I wanted to make sure before I took that crucial step.

I heard many hurtful and untruthful things about the Episcopal Church in those days, even coming from Roman Catholic television personalities. For instance, one put forth that "Episcopalians don't really believe in the Eucharist," and another said, "Their sacraments are not valid." It was almost like the Inquisition all over again, only this time it was the twenty-first century. Nonetheless, I knew that I had found the right Church for me—and for my ministry work.

While it was not necessary that Ruhama be received on that day, she chose to take the step with me. She and I were both at peace with the decision, and we were humbled to be surrounded by such an incredible amount of love and support from the members of our new Church.

THE CEREMONY TOOK PLACE IN Trinity Cathedral, one of the most beautiful churches in the Southeastern United States and the oldest church in Miami. It's one of those truly regal churches—the kind you look up at from the ground, like some sort of holy skyscraper, and say "wow." It stands just feet from Biscayne Bay, yet its grand rose windows and columns give you the impression that you are in an ancient European cathedral, despite being in the heart of trendy Miami.

During the ceremony, a number of priests sitting right behind us—three of them former Roman Catholics—whispered, "We went through this years ago. Now you'll know who your real friends are."

I had no idea how much those words would

mean to me in the coming months, but I was glad to hear them.

The bishop spoke of the importance of change in all of our lives, and then said, "The road between Rome and Canterbury gets a lot of traffic." He also quoted a famous theologian who began his journey in Canterbury, ended up in Rome and later became a cardinal, John Henry Newman, who said, *"To live is to change, and to be perfect is to have changed often."*

The bishop was specifically referring to the numbers of Roman Catholic priests who have become Episcopal (Anglican) and the number of Episcopal (Anglican) priests who have become Roman Catholics in recent years. In both cases, to speak of a "conversion" would be inaccurate, for both churches profess the same Nicene Creed, which contains the fundamental tenets of Christianity, and our worship styles are almost identical.

While the Episcopal Church isn't under the pope, it does profess and teach the faith that comes from the apostles. It is a reformed Church that possesses elements of both the *Catholic* and *Reformed* branches of Christianity. But that message is not always easy to get out to the media, especially in a heavily Hispanic area, where so many Roman Catholics are convinced that theirs is the only "true" Church and the only "Catholic" one.

Besides that, many Roman Catholics think of their Church as a lifetime club: You become a sort of card-carrying member at baptism and you really don't have to do much else the rest of your life. Many take that so seriously that they never really do come back unless it's Christmas, Easter, or a family wedding.

When I made the decision to join the Episcopal Church and, what's more, to continue my ministry within this new spiritual family, what surprised me most was how scandalized people in the media professed to be. These were people who had often engaged in huge public disagreements with the institutional Church they claim to be belong to, so hearing them defend traditional Roman Catholicism—while knowing their particular backgrounds and bitterness with the Church—seemed both ironic and amusing. My jaw actually dropped as I heard some of them!

No matter how much Catholic schooling, religious education, and instruction a Roman Catholic receives during his or her lifetime, most adult members of the Church have no real clue about the basics of the Bible, Church doctrine, and fundamental practices. They feel at home with something they know very little about, yet they often seem at peace with their ignorance of those basics.

Does that sound strange? It's not, really. For many people, their faith is part of their family culture more than an ideology. Don't get me wrong; among the people who actually go to church most Sundays (usually about a fourth of those who say they are Catholic), many try to understand the Church and make some attempt at following its long list of rules. However, the overwhelming majority does not and isn't even interested in really adapting their everyday lives to those norms.

Too many of the problematic and most controversial issues within the Church have no real biblical foundation and are not even "religious" by nature. What aggravates and frustrates people the most are the man-made rules and practices that are defined and insisted upon by the institution, such as:

- Laypeople have no real say in the selection of Church leadership, even in the selection of their own parish priests;
- artificial contraception in family planning is prohibited;
- remarrying after a first marriage simply does not work and is forbidden;
- the option to marry for priests and bishops does not exist;
- homosexual persons face overall discrimination;
- women are prohibited from serving in ordained ministry.

・ ・ ・

DESPITE MY IDEOLOGICAL DIFFERENCES with the Roman Catholic Church, the overwhelming reason I took the step to become an Episcopal priest after giving my life to God as a Roman Catholic priest wasn't a huge difference in philosophy, but the experience of really listening to other people. Through my pastoral and media work, I hear regularly from people of all denominations—and even atheists—about their issues with the Church and organized religion. Even though I am a priest, the great majority of people do not ask about the things of heaven; they talk about their earthly everyday problems.

I REMEMBER LOOKING OUT INTO my Catholic congregation one of the last Sundays that I conducted Mass as a Roman Catholic priest and thinking, "I wonder how many of these people really fit into the description of what the official Church—not God—expects of them."

I knew I no longer did, either, but I wondered how many of those hundreds and hundreds of people who walked in and out of my church every Sunday understood that they were really not totally welcome by the official Church they belonged to. For example, I saw the man and woman who were married civilly for more than twenty-five years, yet never came up to receive Communion because they were both previously married in the Church and were told they were "living in sin." Each time I thought about it, it broke my heart. They did not pursue an annulment (or a declaration of nullity) because they were convinced this would make their children illegitimate.

Sitting close to them was a woman in her midforties who, like most married couples, used contraception to avoid pregnancy after already having four children. She was told by a priest at a nearby parish that she was committing a mortal sin and could not receive Communion until she "was open to life" and stopped taking the pill. She came to church without her spouse—with the exception of Christmas and Easter—because her husband couldn't stomach most of the Church's positions.

In addition, I had heard confessions in my parish from countless people—both men and women—who struggled with abusive marriages, extramarital affairs, and a lack of overall satisfaction and compatibility in their relationships. Many people stayed in these marriages that were never good to begin with, having been taught by the Church that marriage must be permanent, no matter how much two people change over time. The guilt they experienced was horrendous. Many people are convinced they must endure a miserable life, because that is what the Church says they must do.

I also saw homosexuals in those Catholic pews, both partnered and unpartnered, who desired to grow spiritually but had to deal with the stigma placed on their sexual orientation. This group of people included the most generous and giving church workers, collaborators, and community builders in most parishes. They were often discriminated against by religious folks, who are sure the Bible (which they really know so little about) condemns the homosexuals and their way of being.

More than once, as I was preaching, I would wonder why I was there.

It's very hard to defend things that make very little sense in today's culture and society. It's even more difficult to feel like you are the doctrinal police, having to enforce teachings and practices that you no longer believe to be relevant or true, especially when you have to do it in the public eye.

Most priests struggle with these things. They often talk about their ongoing struggles with a few trusted colleagues and mature laypeople, but they rarely confront Church leaders on these issues, because there is no vehicle in Roman Catholicism that allows for any type of debate or discussion on theological matters. People just live their lives and think, "Someday, maybe things will change." The problem, of course, is that here we are in the twenty-first century, and the Roman Catholic Church still isn't changing; in fact, in some cases, it seems headed backward.

My journey to becoming an Anglican was neither easy nor quick. I, too, was taught that there was only one true Church, and I was also a card-carrying member of that cultural group for a great part of my life. Yet the more I prayed and thought about the message of Jesus, the more I realized that His is a message of inclusion, not exclusion; a message of love, not rejection; a message of salvation, not condemnation. As society evolves, I believe our minds and hearts also need to evolve and open themselves to the message of a truly loving God.

My dilemma was resolved only when I began to understand that God made me to be free to love. I chose to remove myself from the many limitations I had placed upon my own life by refusing to live any longer within a kind of spiritual dictatorship. That was a box I no longer felt comfortable in.

At the end of the day, we all eventually come to realize that God *is* love. When we discover that, and really begin to live accordingly, the power of love guides our lives. There is great freedom in knowing that God put us on this earth in order to love and be loved. Fulfilling that divine plan, regardless of what your particular religious tradition might be, is about discovering the power of love in your life.

"Now we have faith, hope and love; but the greatest of these is love."

1 Corinthians 13:13

The Church I dream of . . .

I dream of a church that walks closely with humanity, while leading it to God.

I dream of a church with arms open to the world, not hidden in the sacristy and defensive.

I dream of a church that has love as its ultimate rule, goal, and motivation.

I dream of a church that is not afraid to work for justice and be prophetic when it has to.

I dream of a church that preaches heaven, without disconnecting from the earth.

I dream of a church where all human beings are welcomed as God's children—with no exceptions.

I dream of a church that is more concerned with compassion than adherence to human laws.

I dream of a church that listens more, and makes fewer official declarations.

I dream of a church that is not motivated by fear, but led by trust in God.

I dream of a church less concerned with its own image and more concerned with Truth.

I dream of a church that understands that human beings do not all fit into the same box and that there is a very good reason why variety is part of God's own creation.

I dream of a church that was already dreamed of two thousand years ago, when Jesus first brought it together as a community of love.

EPILOGUE

Time really does heal all wounds—or most of them, anyway, if you throw in a little prayer to help you along the way.

As the days, weeks, and months passed, people on the street continued to stop Ruhama and me to say, "We are with you!" and "God bless you!"

Just yesterday, in fact, we walked into a local drugstore, and when the clerk spotted us, she began jumping up and down behind the counter, saying, "My dream has come true! I've always wanted to meet you, Father Albert! And you're so beautiful, Ruhama! You'll have a beautiful baby! Father Albert, oh, my God, I've always admired you and now I admire you more!"

Despite the ridiculous tabloid stories, negative press, and some friends who turned away from us, we are happy in our lives. We have a new church family, a home together, and a second child on the way. We are blessed with an overwhelming amount of support and affection, sometimes from unexpected quarters.

At times my wife, who is still shy despite being a seasoned celebrity now, would be overwhelmed by the number of people who wanted to get to know her or even touch her. I'll never forget the time we were in a grocery store together, and a woman looked over at me and said, "Hi, Padre Alberto," in passing.

However, when she saw my wife next to me, the woman screamed, "Ruhaaaaaaaama! I just want to touch you and make sure that you're real!"

Ruhama didn't know how to take this kind of enthusiasm at first, but she soon realized the people just wanted to meet us as real people. The congratulatory remarks from ordinary people made an enormous difference to us; we felt buoyed on a cloud of goodwill by these real-life angels that God sent our way to reassure us that everything was going to be fine. It was, and it is.

Although I had been ordained as a Roman Catholic priest and completed the necessary training for ministry, I was required to serve for a year as a lay pastor and leader within the Episcopal Church before becoming accepted as a full-functioning priest, after passing all the necessary exams and interviews the Church requires. We received a lot of love and support from the laity, bishops, and clergy of the Episcopal Church in this very special period of change in our lives. We have been blessed to know pastors and their wives from every denomination possible and people from various faith traditions who have given us their unconditional love and support. They have offered us support and friendship, like I never experienced before in my life.

Just one year and one day after becoming an official member of the Episcopal Church, I was received (not re-ordained, because ordination is like baptism—you only need to go through it once in your life) as a priest of my new church family during a joyful ceremony. Bishop Leo Frade officiated, and my friends Bishop Julio Holguin of the Dominican Republic and Bishop Onell Soto, who is the retired bishop of Venezuela, assisted at the altar. The men and women of our clergy were also there in great number. I was thrilled to see several hundred people in the congregation supporting me during this important moment as well, many of them lifelong friends and members of the parishes I had served at for fifteen years as a deacon and priest of the Roman Church. Bishop Frade said, "Albert, you may not be a Roman anymore, but you are still a priest in Christ's one, holy, catholic and apostolic church." It was a joyful day!

We marked the event with a bilingual Mass at the Church of the Resurrection, the church that my bishop assigned me to when I asked him to give me the smallest, most challenging assignment he had. In the past year we have worked hard, building the congregation of just thirty people to one that has over 250, while at the same time raising money and doing repairs to the building and grounds. To draw people into this new parish, I started by listening to the people's wishes at an open "town meeting." After identifying the most pressing needs, I first tried to strengthen the English service with music and offer weekly activities, then added a Spanish Mass and Sunday school for children.

I am deeply satisfied with this mission of building up, especially since my congregation here is culturally diverse and the interest of so many spiritually disenfranchised people is making it grow quickly. Ruhama and I visit those in our parish who are alone, elderly, or sick; just last night, we went to a hospital to pray with a family whose son has a horrible infection. We're working on getting a new outreach program up and running soon, too, a feeding program for the needy. That's a crucial program for this area, where so many families are having a hard time getting basics on the table. Our program will, I hope, let them pick up at least a weekly grocery bag.

Our community outreach is active and ongoing. In addition to faith education for children, our church provides a place for senior citizens to gather every week for a sing-along by the piano, and a place where adults can come to take classes taught in Spanish and English, offered by our local college.

I also teach an adult class at our church once a week called Keep the Faith Night, where I try to encourage people to deepen the faith they learned as children so that they can carry it into adulthood.

We talk about basic theological concepts and apply them to our lives, because I see my mission as one of getting people to reflect on what's really important as they read and study the Bible. You have a choice in this life: Either you deepen what you believe and achieve a deeper sense of what it means to you, or you end up religiously ignorant or simply crawling forever.

I have made decisions based on what is good and true in my heart, although I realize that the way these decisions were made public caused great controversy. Thankfully, after the storm, I am still able to continue doing the work I have always loved best: I am a parish priest who is trying to make the world a better place.

For me, the joys, richness, and experiences of married life far outweigh the benefits of the celibate life. I am sure being married has helped me to become a better priest, as well, for I feel more connected to humanity, and the most effective priests are those closest to the flock.

God is love, and I have love in abundance to share.

ACKNOWLEDGMENTS

I want to thank God, who has blessed my life in countless ways with unconditional love and has always been my guiding light in all that I have undertaken, even in the many twists and turns one never expects. There is great peace in knowing my life has always been in God's loving hands—at every moment.

My beautiful wife, Ruhama, our son, Christian (aka CINO) and our new baby, Camila, have been a great source of joy and support in all I do in and out of church. Their love and their presence in my life is just one more sign and confirmation from God that life is definitely more complete when a man of God is also a family man. I love you and I thank you!

Among the most treasured blessings I have received throughout my entire journey of life is the love of my mother and father, my grandparents, my sisters and my entire family. I have always had their loving support in my life and I am truly grateful for that.

To my church family: those in the parishes and communities I served for so many years as a Roman Catholic seminarian, deacon and priest and the ones I have the privilege of serving now as an Episcopal priest of the Diocese of Southeast Florida, especially the Church of the Resurrection in Biscayne Park. Your words of encouragement, your support and your faith have been an inspiration to me throughout the years. You are always present in my prayers, especially at the altar of God.

To my very enthusiastic and devoted agent, Eric Rovner, your insights and guidance are appreciated. To Raymond Garcia and his entire team at Penguin, I express my gratitude for your great dedication and interest in this project.

Finally, to the countless people whom I have met and those I have not had the pleasure of meeting in person, who regardless of religious tradition, culture or denomination, have offered me and my family their prayers, support and understanding. I want to thank you for your great humanity. Your compassion and ability to look beyond the typical boundaries and prejudices that too often separate people has inspired me. It's good to remember the promise that one day we will all sit at the same banquet for all eternity.

Father Albert

Center Point Publishing

600 Brooks Road ● PO Box 1
Thorndike ME 04986-0001 USA

(207) 568-3717

US & Canada:
1 800 929-9108
www.centerpointlargeprint.com